The Seduction of Brazil

LLILAS TRANSLATIONS FROM LATIN AMERICA SERIES

The Seduction *of* Brazil

THE AMERICANIZATION OF BRAZIL DURING WORLD WAR II

Antonio Pedro Tota

Translated by LORENA B. ELLIS
Foreword and commentary by DANIEL J. GREENBERG

UNIVERSITY OF TEXAS PRESS, AUSTIN
Teresa Lozano Long Institute of Latin American Studies

The assistance of Margaret Bald in the translation of this work is gratefully acknowledged.

COVER ILLUSTRATION: *Second Visit of Roosevelt to Brazil* by Raymond Neilson, courtesy of the Franklin D. Roosevelt Library, Hyde Park, New York.

Originally published in 2000 as *O imperialismo sedutor: A americanização do Brasil na época da Segunda Guerra*. São Paulo: Companhia Das Letras / Editora Schwarz Ltd. Copyright © 2000 Antonio Pedro Tota

LIBRARY OF CONGRESS CATALOGING-IN-PUBLICATION DATA

Tota, Antonio Pedro.
   The Seduction of Brazil : the Americanization of Brazil during World War II / Antonio Pedro Tota ; translated from the Portuguese by Lorena B. Ellis ; foreword by Daniel J. Greenberg.
      p.   cm. — (LLILAS Translations from Latin America series)
   "Not an exact translation of the first edition of O imperialismo sedutor, published in Brazil in 2000; it is based on a text revised by the author. It also includes historical notes by Daniel J. Greenberg"—T.p. verso.
   Includes bibliographical references and index.
   ISBN 978-0-292-71993-4 (cloth : alk. paper)
   1. Brazil—Civilization—American influences. 2. Brazil—History—1930–1945. 3. United States—Relations—Brazil. 4. Brazil—Relations—United States. 5. Brazil—In mass media. 6. Popular culture—Brazil. 7. Popular culture—United States. I. Ellis, Lorena B. II. Greenberg, Daniel Joseph, 1948– III. Tota, Antonio Pedro. Imperialismo sedutor. IV. Teresa Lozano Long Institute of Latin American Studies. V. Title.
   F2510.T69 2009
   303.48'28107309044—dc22   2009006875

TRANSLATOR'S NOTE: This book is not an exact translation of the first edition of *O imperialismo sedutor*, published in Brazil in 2000; it is based on a text revised by the author. It also includes historical notes by Daniel J. Greenberg, who wrote the Foreword. These notes explain certain aspects of Brazilian culture and history that might be unfamiliar to readers. They are identified by roman numerals and appear in the Notes section at the end of the book.

This translation was made possible only with the support of Daniel J. Greenberg, the dedication of Margaret Bald and her tireless review, the suggestions of Richard Brandes, as well as challenging discussions with Felix, Roberto, and Fernando Ellis.

This book is dedicated to
Jordan Young
and to the memory of
Richard Morse
and
Mauricio Alvim.

Contents

FOREWORD   xi

ACKNOWLEDGMENTS   xix

LIST OF ABBREVIATIONS   xxi

INTRODUCTION   I

1. A True "Factory of Ideologies": The Office of the Coordinator of Inter-American Affairs   23

2. Brazil for the Americans: The United States of Brazil in the United States of America   59

3. The Boogie-Woogie in the Favela, or the Brazilian Attraction to the American Standard of Living   81

CONCLUSION: Americanization Was Not Imitation   III

NOTES   I2I

BIBLIOGRAPHY   139

ILLUSTRATION CREDITS   153

NAME INDEX   155

Photo sections follow pages 58 and 80.

Foreword

IN OCTOBER 1930, Getúlio Dorneles Vargas was inaugurated president of Brazil. Two years later, Franklin D. Roosevelt was elected president of the United States. Vargas and Roosevelt were both reform-minded politicians; both were masters of the craft of politics; both were populists. Both accumulated vast power and used it to effect major social, economic, and institutional changes that resulted in the social enfranchisement of the urban working class. And as chief executive, both mobilized their nations to intervene in World War II. For both the United States and Brazil, belligerency had far-reaching social, cultural, and economic consequences. Roosevelt died in office in April 1945; Vargas was removed by military coup six months later.

But while FDR and "Getúlio" shared many achievements, their political styles could not have been more different. Vargas ruled from 1930 to 1934 and 1937 to 1945 as an authoritarian dictator. FDR, while aggressive in the use of executive power, never violated democratic norms. Yet for purposes of Roosevelt's policy toward Latin America, termed the "policy of the good neighbor," Vargas was a staunch ally, "good friend," and fellow "democrat."

In 1933, Latin Americans had hailed "Good Neighborism" as a positive if overdue change in policy. Promising never again to employ armed intervention and to provide much-needed economic aid, FDR's policy seemed an abandonment of Washington's traditional pursuit of hegemony in favor of liberal internationalism.[i] If taken at face value, the Good Neighbor would have created a fair and egalitarian relationship, one based on the paired principles of self-determination and coequality of sovereign states. The Good Neighbor Policy promised a new era in which the United States, known south of the Rio Grande as the "Colossus of the North," would become a true partner in hemispheric relations.

The policy represented a radical change in U.S. treatment of its "sister republics." Since the administration of Theodore Roosevelt and his Big Stick Policy (1901–1909), Washington had used armed force to maintain military, political, and economic dominance in the Caribbean Basin.

Woodrow Wilson claimed to found the policies of his New Freedom (1913–1919) on democratic ideals, the best example of which was the famous Fourteen Points. But in 1914, U.S. troops occupied the Mexican ports of Veracruz and Tampico in an ill-fated attempt to force the dictator Huerta from power.[ii] While Wilson's "affair of honor" typified the "world policeman" views of that liberal internationalist, Mexicans of all political ideologies joined to oppose it. That outcome demonstrated that, regardless of pretext, U.S. intervention remained a hated symbol of "Yankee imperialism."

During the Harding and Coolidge administrations (1921–1929), so-called Dollar Diplomacy represented a shift from the use of armed force to financial and diplomatic intervention, especially in the U.S. backyard of Mexico, Central America, and the Caribbean. On several occasions, when Caribbean or Central American states verged on political or financial chaos, Washington persuaded client elites to place their nations' treasuries or customshouses under Yankee trusteeship. While Dollar Diplomacy was less bloody, more discreet, and "politer" than the Big Stick, the outcome remained equally offensive.

The maintenance of U.S. hegemony through armed force or banker's fiat fueled a surging Latin American nationalism between 1898 and 1930. From around the region, writers, political leaders, and even some military officers expressed outrage and a determination to resist domination. The fiery poetry of Nicaraguan Rubén Darío and the fiction of Uruguayan José Enrique Rodó responded to a surging American capitalism and its political and military projection south of the border. During the 1920s, the anti-imperialist and *indigenista* thought of Peruvians José Carlos Mariátegui and Víctor Raúl Haya de la Torre (both of whom had been jailed by the repressive, pro-U.S. Leguía regime) added an important Pan-Latin dimension to this movement. And the peripatetic crusading of Gen. Enrique Mosconi, Argentina's oil czar, evidenced the military's emergence as a nationalist force. Mosconi's promotion of economic nationalism revealed that a surging postwar Yankee capitalism was contesting British dominance in this southernmost part of the region.

Herbert Hoover claimed to abjure the use of armed intervention during his administration (1929–1933), and some scholars claim that he, not FDR, created the Good Neighbor Policy.[iii] But Hoover's use of armed intervention in the Nicaraguan civil war (1929–1933), depriving Liberal Party nationalist Augusto César Sandino of victory, seemed a wave of the past.[iv] Franklin Roosevelt followed by training the Nicaraguan National Guard and supporting the installation of the pro-U.S. Somoza dictatorship. The implication was that Washington would support Latin American dictators as long as they maintained order and protected Yankee economic and strategic interests.

Roosevelt announced his Policy of the Good Neighbor in his 1933 inaugural address, along with several other brilliant reform initiatives intended to arrest financial panic, lift the country out of the depression, and restore faith in the liberal capitalist state. But underneath, the policy was a shrewd defensive response to the social, economic, and political turbulence unleashed by the Great Depression, from the Rio Grande to Tierra del Fuego. Between 1930 and 1933, revolutions or coups d'état had erupted or were already in progress in Brazil, Argentina, Chile, El Salvador, Peru, and Nicaragua. And hardly had FDR entered office when Cuban dictator Gerardo Machado was forced from office by a bloody revolt.

Cuba's 1933 coup d'état brought leftist nationalist Ramón Grau San Martín to power, an event that tested Roosevelt's sincerity. Grau denounced the Platt Amendment, which had given the United States the right to intervene in Cuba's internal affairs. He threatened to nationalize foreign-owned utility and natural-resource companies, most of which were U.S.-owned. In a move reminiscent of Teddy Roosevelt's Big Stick, Washington sent a warship to Havana and withheld diplomatic recognition.

Meanwhile, special ambassador Sumner Welles lobbied the military and other influential groups to undermine the Cuban leader's viability. At the same time, the diplomat declared his support for the charismatic and unscrupulous Sgt. Fulgencio Batista, who had already begun plotting a coup d'état. In return, Batista promised that he would restore order and safeguard U.S. investments. The three decades that followed were dominated by Batista, an era that Cubans sometimes term "fraudulent democracy."[v]

The Cuban episode left Washington with a political black eye south of the border. But in other instances (in particular, Mexican president Lázaro Cárdenas's 1938 nationalization of Standard Oil), FDR avoided intervention. Washington generally kept its word, winning Latin American praise and warmer relations. Moreover, with the emergence of Nazi Fascism, the Good Neighbor became a vehicle for forging a continental alliance against the Axis's conquest of this hemisphere.

It is this aspect of Good Neighborism that Antonio Pedro Tota studies in his fascinating and innovative *The Seduction of Brazil*. An examination of U.S.-Brazilian diplomatic and cultural relations in the era of Roosevelt and Vargas (1930–1945), Tota's history breaks new ground in its focus on the role of government in the creation of popular culture. Prior to Vargas's arrival, Brazil and the United States had enjoyed a unique political and military friendship, dating from the First Republic (1889–1930). Brazil's foreign minister (1895–1912), the Baron of Rio Branco (José Maria da Silva Paranhos, Jr.) , used an amalgam of erudite negotiation and saber rattling to substantially extend his nation's borders. Consequently, every one of Brazil's neighbors (with the exception of Paraguay and Uruguay) grew smaller at its expense. Already the largest country in Latin America, Brazil became larger than the United States' forty-eight states.

During these years, the United States also emerged as a world power through economic growth and territorial and military expansion in the Caribbean, Central America, and the Pacific. Rio Branco negotiated an informal agreement with Washington based on a concept of mutual interest. In this "special relationship," Washington winked at Brazilian dominance in South America in return for Brazil's tacit acceptance of (and occasional assistance with) the maintenance of U.S. hegemony in its sphere of influence.[vi]

But Brazil's 1920s produced a contrary tendency in the rise of a powerful economic nationalism that rejected the precepts of the First Republic. That nationalism was a primary motive for several military rebellions known as *tenentismo*. Led by junior army officers such as Miguel Costa, Antônio de Siqueira Campos, and Luís Carlos Prestes, the *tenentes* bitterly criticized the Republic's political corruption and failure to promote the nation's economic development.[vii] Moreover, tenentismo opposed foreign domination of Brazil's economy, particularly by the United States and Western Europe. Along with other nationalists, most of the tenentes backed Vargas's October 1930 overthrow of the Washington Luiz government. After establishing his provisional government, the *gaúcho* (Rio Grande do Sul native) appointed several of the former rebels to strategic posts.[viii] Thus, Brazil's decision to join the U.S.-sponsored anti-Fascist alliance was not a foregone conclusion.

As Tota shows, the 1920s and 1930s saw the rise of pro-German sentiment in Brazil. Intellectuals who admired Germany as a national model vied with pro-American authors. Germany rapidly increased its trade and investment and exercised strong influence over German-Brazilian press and cultural organizations. After war erupted in 1939, Berlin actively sought a Brazilian alliance. While the United States was officially neutral, Washington also offered blandishments in return for a military pact.

Rather than showing support for either side, Vargas astutely adopted a wait-and-see attitude. Only after a protracted period of parallel negotiations did the *caudilho* (strongman) choose to hitch his fortunes to Washington.[ix] Thus, the Brazilian-American alliance was not anchored in shared democratic values or abhorrence of totalitarianism: Vargas was a shrewd and pragmatic student of Realpolitik. Only after the United States proffered a superior package, including an integrated steel plant, the provision of military aid, and good terms of exchange for its manufactures in return for Brazil's strategic commodities, did Vargas accept the alliance. This set the stage for the United States' "seduction" of Brazil.

After the January 1942 Rio Pan-American conference, Brazil became one of the first Latin American nations to break off relations with the European

Axis. Subsequently, German submarines torpedoed several Brazilian merchant ships, killing or injuring hundreds. In August, Vargas responded by declaring war on Rome and Berlin. More important, the president decreed that Brazil would send an expeditionary force to join the invasion of Europe. Arriving in July 1944, the Força Expedicionária Brasileira (FEB) played a significant role in the liberation of Italy, one of the first steps toward Allied victory.[x]

Significantly, Brazil was the sole Latin American ally to commit combat troops to the war effort. The FEB sustained heavy casualties in brutal mountain fighting against fortified, dug-in German positions. A true baptism of fire, the FEB's experience both bolstered the military's confidence and set the stage for a national political transformation. Thus, Vargas wrought a decisive shift in U.S.-Brazilian relations. While Getúlio's Brazilian-U.S. alliance was never ratified by formal treaty, it made his nation Washington's most trusted Latin American ally.

The novelty of *The Seduction of Brazil* springs not from retelling this story but from revealing the growth of cultural relations between the American and Brazilian peoples. In spite of their long diplomatic friendship, few people in Brazil or the United States knew much about each other. Long distances and the high cost of intercontinental travel made Brazil a rare destination for North Americans and vice versa. Few Americans spoke Portuguese, or Brazilians, English. But between 1920 and 1945, an aggressively entrepreneurial American film and music industry partly succeeded in breaching this cultural divide. Between 1930 and 1945, Hollywood produced many films that it effectively promoted in Brazil, dubbed into Portuguese. These motion pictures popularized a view of stateside life, culture, and style that dominated Brazilians' image of the United States.

Moreover, as Bryan McCann demonstrates, between 1920 and 1945, U.S. recording majors such as RCA-Victor, Columbia, and Odeon set up studios in Brazil and produced Brazilian popular music recordings for the domestic market. The studios encouraged Brazilian musicians to combine native genres such as samba and the *marcha* with American big band and jazz orchestration. The result was a musical syncretism that fused cultures and proved a hit with the consuming public.[xi] The studios, moreover, encouraged Brazilian performers to "cover" U.S. hit tunes, creating the *versão* genre (the Brazilian version of American songs). In similar manner, Hollywood motion picture studios worked with local producers and performers to create musical comedies for the local market. While imitating North American models, these productions utilized Brazilian themes, music, and dance and employed local talent.

But in spite of the commercial media's success in attaining some aspects of cultural exchange, by the late 1930s, neither country's public had a clear conception of the other; this was particularly true of Brazil. Consequently, in a program managed by the young Nelson Rockefeller, the State Department mounted a media/public relations campaign to acquaint the peoples with each other and to burnish their images. Vargas's Departamento de Imprensa e Propaganda (Department of Press and Propaganda, DIP) played a similar role in Brazil.

As Tota shows, Rockefeller's Office of the Coordinator of Inter-American Affairs (OCIAA) created a program of media and cultural activities to improve Brazil's image in the United States and vice-versa. Working with major players in the national newspaper, radio, and motion picture industries, the OCIAA financed programs using music, film, news writing, and book publishing to persuade the peoples to accept each other as friends and allies. Rockefeller's office played an active role partnering with U.S. radio broadcasters to promote Brazilian music and produce sympathetic "news" programs. The OCIAA also contracted with Hollywood studios to produce films presenting a favorable image of Brazil. And Rockefeller's agency urged newspaper and book-publishing companies to promote the new partnership by publishing accounts supporting the notion that Washington and Rio shared democratic ideals. As Tota shows, Brazilian singer/actress Carmen Miranda was a key figure in this process of cultural persuasion. Through the media of music, cinema, theater, and dance, Miranda became an international star while serving the purposes of the emerging alliance.

In a similar manner, Rockefeller and the Brazilian government financed visits by Brazilian artists, photographers, musicians, poets, and other culture creators, beginning with the New York World's Fair of 1939. Tota argues that, as North Americans experienced Brazil in this and other venues, their view of the country changed. They began to glimpse Brazilians as having more in common with them and Brazil as a sister republic in more than name. In some cases (e.g., the Brazilians' relative lack of racially discriminatory attitudes or practices), Jim Crow–bound Americans could learn from their neighbor's example. In the same way, Rockefeller's productions—films, performances of classical and jazz music, and radio programs produced for the Brazilian audience and broadcast by shortwave transmission—helped to shape Brazilian sympathies favorable to the United States. Significantly, Tota notes that the program's depiction of Brazil's political system—an authoritarian dictatorship from 1937 to 1945—was airbrushed or simply ignored. In the view of OCIAA propaganda, Brazil became a sister democracy in the fight against fascism. In a subtle subtext, Tota argues that the hearts and minds of both peoples had to be conquered before they could become true allies.

But Tota's suggestive use of the term "seductive" hints that the process of persuasion was not entirely voluntary. Rather, it contained exploitive and paternalistic elements that made the relationship more filial than fraternal. *The Seduction of Brazil* is highly critical of another aspect of this process: the mass media's manipulation of public opinion. Significantly, Tota focuses on the depiction of Carmen Miranda to demonstrate that the image presented of Brazil was not accurate. Instead, Miranda was stereotyped as a Latin female: of mixed race, sweet, sexually available, and compliant. The propagandists' use of symbolism was emblematic of the new relation between the United States and Brazil—one pregnant with exploitation and with little real benefit for Brazil.

In similar manner, the use of Brazilian music in U.S. radio broadcasts tended to adulterate and misrepresent the country's artistic contributions. Brazil's original and unique styles—chief among them, the samba—were mixed indiscriminately with Latin and Afro-Caribbean genres more familiar to the American public. Clearly, the goal was to coax sympathy from the South Americans. Argentina's tango was once even represented as Brazilian!

Tota argues that the resulting cultural relationship was consequently artificial—not a true encounter between peoples and cultures. Rather, in venues such as the Disney animated feature film *The Three Caballeros*, Brazil is symbolized by sanitized characters like Zé Carioca. Zé was a parrot whose friendliness, elegance, and cultural idiosyncrasies created a positive image of the country. Significantly, hemispheric "black sheep" Argentina (which had refused to go along with Washington's game plan) does not appear in the film. Instead, Donald Duck's visit to the Río de la Plata consists of an encounter with a friendly, yerba mate–sipping Uruguayan gaucho (Montevideo had signed on to the Rio Declaration). Produced in English for the stateside market, the plotline for *The Three Caballeros* differed somewhat from its Spanish-language counterpart, *Saludos Amigos*. In the latter film, Goofy's itinerary included Argentina. This may be explained as a bow to diplomatic reality: Washington's ostracism of Argentina was opposed by most Latin Americans.

Stateside-generated radio "news" programs such as *Ripley's Believe It or Not!* or *News of the World* discussed U.S.-Brazilian cooperation with overlaid aerial battle soundtracks. The subtext was clear: in both countries, Good Neighborism was synonymous with national defense. Rather than a real exchange of culture and ideas, the Good Neighbor Policy employed the mass media as part of the United States' "psywar." Brazilians and North Americans did "know" each other through the creative media's promotion of film and music. But the State Department's public relations campaign failed to produce a true exchange of culture or ideas. Instead, it attempted to seduce both peoples with the formulas, slogans, and stereotypes of propaganda.

In contrast, Cuba and the United States (two countries whose relationship was also characterized by pronounced economic exploitation and political dominance) *did* get to know one another. Due to physical proximity and mutual exposure to each other's music, films, sports, and dance, a true cultural cross-pollination developed.[xii] Ironically, and in spite of the protests of Cuban nationalists opposed to their country's domination, Cubans "knew" their neighbors better than perhaps any other Latin Americans did.

But the State Department's "factory of ideologies" could not create true friendship. Ironically, it was Washington, not Rio, which created most of the propaganda. Vargas's DIP, created as the propaganda ministry of a repressive, authoritarian Estado Novo (New State), simply acted as transmitter of U.S. material to Brazilians.

During the post–World War II era, Brazil's alliance with the United States became a near-permanent feature of its foreign policy. The Brazilian military had been trained by U.S. officers in the European theater. They were aware that their country's authoritarianism created a glaring divergence within the alliance, and thus emerged from the war as opponents of Vargas's continuation in office. When several of the top brass learned that the gaúcho was maneuvering to cancel the elections of December 1945 and thus prolong the Estado Novo, they forced his resignation. Before year's end, the same officers oversaw the country's first democratic presidential elections.

In 1947, moreover, Brazil signed the Rio Pact (Inter-American Treaty of Reciprocal Assistance). The United States thus succeeded in binding Brazil and every other Latin American nation to a collective security treaty aimed at the Soviet Union and its allies. The pact reflected a shift of U.S. policy from antifascism to containment of communism. But for Brazil, it signified closer alignment with Washington, especially with respect to the military establishment.[xiii] In the decades that followed, U.S. capital investment and trade expanded rapidly. During the 1950s, other countries—notably, Argentina, Mexico, Jacobo Arbenz's Guatemala, and socialist Cuba—would follow a different path, maintaining their independence in foreign policy.

In *The Seduction of Brazil*, Antonio Pedro Tota shows that the campaign to shape public opinion through the dissemination of popular culture was an effective tool of national mobilization. Especially for Brazilians, it was important to see North Americans as friends. However, the book also shows that the mass media could be used as a lever for political domination. Under the Good Neighbor Policy, the United States avoided the use of armed intervention but employed other means to secure the same end: continued hegemony in a period of weakened American capitalism and expanding European fascism. Widening the ties of popular culture served those ends well. Brazil and the United States were allies, but their peoples were not such good friends after all.   —DANIEL J. GREENBERG

Acknowledgments

THIS BOOK is being published in English thanks to many people, in both Brazil and the United States. I thank in advance those of you whom I forgot to mention. I am especially thankful to: Dain Borges of the University of Chicago, who said that *The Seduction of Brazil* is a "quiet book"; Mauricio Tenorio, also of Chicago but formerly of the University of Texas at Austin, who supported my book from the beginning; Seth Garfield of the University of Texas, who supported the idea that a translation of my book would help American students and other English-speaking readers understand how the Americanization of Brazil started; Barbara Weinstein of New York University; James P. Woodard of Montclair State University; Ralph Della Cava of Columbia University; Martin J. Manning, research librarian at the Bureau of Public Diplomacy, U.S. Department of State; Carlos Bakota and Matthew Shirts, old friends; Lorena Ellis, who aside from translating the text into English helped me find many "missing" details of this book; Daniel J. Greenberg of Pace University, for providing historical and cultural commentary for the English edition; Virginia Hagerty, Managing Editor at the Teresa Lozano Long Institute of Latin American Studies at the University of Texas; Kathy Bork, copy editor, who showed a lot of patience trying to understand strange meanings from the Portuguese/Brazilian/American cultural world; and Paulo Sotero, Director of the Brazil Institute of the Woodrow Wilson Center, who also encouraged me to translate my book.

List of Abbreviations

AIB   Ação Integralista Brasileira

AN   Arquivo Nacional/Agência Nacional, Rio de Janeiro

CPDOC/Fundação Getulio Vargas   Centro de Pesquisa e Documentação de
             História Contemporânea do Brasil

DEIP-SP   Departamento Estadual de Imprensa e Propaganda de São
             Paulo

DIP   Departamento de Imprensa e Propaganda

DNI   Departamento Nacional de Imprensa

FDR Library Franklin Delano Roosevelt Library, Hyde Park, New York

IBOPE   Instituto Brasileiro de Opinião Pública e Estatística

IPHAN   Instituto de Patrimônio Histórico e Artístico Nacional,
             Cinemateca Brasileira

LATR   *Latin American Theater Review* 27.2, Spring 1994, Univer-
             sity of Kansas

LSP   Library of Special Projects, CBS News, Latin American Sec-
             tion, New York

MPBRSD   Motion Picture, Broadcasting, and Recorded Sound Divi-
             sion, Library of Congress, Washington, D.C.

MPD/NAUS   Motion Picture Division, National Archives of the United
             States, Washington, D.C.

RAC   Rockefeller Archive Center, Tarrytown, New York

Introduction

*American things are not making us deaf, but they are making us blind,
and as in the classical image, we are like moths that the light attracts to
their death.*

LIMA BARRETO, "O NOSSO 'IANQUISMO'"

IN MID-1942, the construction of Parnamirim Field, the well-known
American base in Natal, Brazil, was completed. Airplanes began to arrive
in Brazil, bringing soldiers and technicians from the United States. They
departed from the Northeast of Brazil to North Africa to help British soldiers trapped there by the Germans under the leadership of Rommel, the
commander of the Africa Korps.[i]

Americans were living among Brazilians from the Northeast. In order to
communicate with the mechanics, before starting their airplane engines the
American pilots made a sign: a fist with the thumb straight up. It was the
"positive," the "thumbs-up."[1]

When the ordinary people of the Brazilian Northeast, observing the
American pilots for the first time, imitated the positive sign with the thumb
up, Brazil was already Americanized. Luís da Câmara Cascudo, the remarkable researcher of Brazilian popular culture and folklore, noticed the phenomenon of our gestures but did not foresee the extent of the thumbs-up.
Like the traditional touching of the earlobe with the fingers to indicate that
something was good or positive, the thumbs-up became synonymous with
agreement, friendship, beauty, questions, good morning, good afternoon,
and good night. It would be used, at least in Brazil, for almost everything.
It was much more internationalized than the earlobe touch, which had been
used until then. Thus, in the 1940s, the gesture, which symbolizes our Americanization, spread from Parnamirim Field throughout Brazil.

It was very difficult for many to admit that Brazil was becoming
Americanized. "Americanization" was a perennial topic of discussion and
was transformed into a polemical issue almost always associated with

modernization. Academics, intellectuals, and artists argued extensively pro or con. The ties between culture and economic dependence are evident in the analyses. Manichaeism was irresistible in the studies of the "Americanization" of Brazil. The quotation marks are significant. The phenomenon is sometimes interpreted as a great destroyer of our culture, a negative influence; sometimes, on the contrary, it is seen as a paradigmatic and mythical force, capable of liberating us from cultural and economic lethargy and having a modernizing effect on Brazilian society.

Monteiro Lobato, a Brazilian popular writer who lived in New York in the late 1920s, was one of those who were enamored with the idea of the American way as a way for Brazil to surmount its underdeveloped position and move toward a developed situation. Protective boots on the feet of the hillbillies and a tractor sufficed to create a new man: a positively strong and healthy Brazilian, capable of leading the United States of Brazil to be comparable to the United States of America.[2]

The current of thought that blames Americanization for the deconstruction, or even destruction, of our culture entails a Marxist theoretical arsenal based on socioeconomic models that almost always relate cultural and economic dependency. A book that made history analyzes in a generalized way the Americanization of Latin American culture. It is called *How to Read Donald Duck: Imperialist Ideology in the Disney Comic* by Ariel Dorfman and Armand Mattelart, which at the beginning of the 1970s—for obvious reasons (Brazil was ruled by a military dictatorship)—was circulating in a semiclandestine fashion in its Spanish edition among Brazilian leftist circles. Donald Duck, Mickey, and the other Walt Disney characters were interpreted as agents of destruction of Latin American cultural traditions. The authors conclude that, through the adventures of the Disney characters, Latin American youth absorb North American teachings on greed, individualism, and materialistic consumption.

In Brazil, José Ramos Tinhorão, a polemic historian and researcher, is one of the most fervent critics of the Americanization of Brazilian popular music. For Tinhorão

the singer Farnésio Dutra, who had symptomatically chosen the North American pseudonym Dick Farney, had been in the United States . . . in the naïve belief that he could make a career in that country by singing American music.

In the case of this singer—who, by the way, was a good piano player—the process of alienation of mentality had reached an alarming point: his voice was almost a replica of Bing Crosby's. . . .

Upon his return to Brazil, Farnésio Dutra, transformed into Dick

Farney, decided to sing what sounded closest to Bing Crosby: "fox-blues" . . .

The success was almost immediate with a public that was also alienated.[3]

To use the terms used by Umberto Eco to describe the attitude of intellectuals toward the impact of mass communication, both the "apocalyptics" and the "integrated" have contributed to keeping the discussion lively. But they also have hindered a more substantial investigation of the nature of American cultural influence through the mass media. We cannot always blame the imperialism of the media for the influence and the superiority of other cultures over ours. By doing so we run the risk of fetishizing these same media.[4]

Although Carlos Drummond de Andrade, a Brazilian modernist poet from the state of Minas Gerais, did not point directly to the media, he was intrigued by the national imperialism-culture connection when he attended a luncheon with American professor William Berrien, assistant director of the Rockefeller Foundation, who visited Brazil during the war. As a result of the lunchtime discussion, Drummond concluded that "any conception of cultural relations based on the inoculation of a weaker culture by another more powerful one, one better equipped with means of expression, would be an imperialist conception at the service of inexcusable economic and political goals." The poet could not perceive the planned imperialist intentions of a "more powerful culture," even by paying very close attention to the discourse of the American, that is, Berrien. According to Carlos Drummond de Andrade, the interest of the likeable American in Brazil was indeed of an intellectual and humanist character.[5]

During that same period, Sérgio Buarque de Hollanda also participated in the discussion:

Our increasing contact with the United States is at the same time unsettling and a suggestive subject for the imagination: It is no longer only economic and political, but also cultural. There are some who are frightened by this increasingly closer interchange, and where the idea already plays a considerable role—I might even say a prominent role—[fear it] as a mortal danger to our authentic traditions, our national character, our rhythm of life, our own reason to exist. . . . We would easily accept a new form of colonization, a little more tolerable than the old one—colonization of ideas, manners, and even enthusiasms and hatred—abandoning the venerable conventions of the past.

I have just returned from a trip to North America that lasted a few weeks, over the course of which I learned to better judge such an opinion. It demands of us a spiritual exchange that promises broad and lasting consequences, exactly the opposite of a simple consent. It is at least for this reason worthy of attention and respect. No great benefit can come from a hemispheric patriotism that is the result of abdications and compromises.[6]

From French to English

In the early 1930s, the Carioca (resident of Rio de Janeiro) musician and composer Lamartine Babo composed the fox-trot "Song for Englishman to See." The majority of the words in the verses are homophonic with English:

> Ai love iú
> Forget isclaine maine Itapirú

Lamartine was known for the critical irony of his lyrics. The title itself, "Song for Englishman to See" (Canção para inglês ver), is connected to the traditional relationship between Luso-Brazilian people, on the one hand, and the English, on the another. It is believed that the expression came from Dom João, the governing prince, in the first decade of the eighteenth century, who said, when he arrived in Salvador, which was all lit up for his reception:[ii] "It is good for Englishmen to see."[7]

The spelling of the words in the Lamartine song is in "Portugenglish," following a trend of the 1920s that was critical of foreignisms, as, for example, in the poetry and chronicles of Juó Bananére.[8] The meaning of some words that Lamartine Babo used in this song cannot be found in an English dictionary. The critical view of foreign expressions acquires a character that is almost anthropophagic in the modernist sense: The whiskey was produced from *chuchu* (chayote), a vegetable used as an ingredient in popular dishes, and not from Scottish malt or American corn from Kentucky. "Ai love iú" (I love you) rhymes with the Itapirú word, of Tupi-Guarani origin.[iii]

In 1933, it was Noel Rosa's turn. Rosa, one of the most popular samba authors, criticized foreign influence in Brazilian culture in a famous tune of that time. He attacked Americanization in the song "It Is Untranslatable" (Não tem tradução), a samba that shows the tensions and resistance of popular culture at a moment when an increased use of foreign expressions was noticeable in the media:

E as rimas do samba não são I love you	The rhymes of the samba are not I love you

THE SEDUCTION OF BRAZIL

Depois o malandro deixou de sambar[9]	Afterward, the scoundrel stopped dancing samba
Alô boy, Alô Jone,	Hello boy, Hello John
Só pode ser conversa de telefone	Can be only telephone chat

Both Noel and Lamartine—each in his own way—criticized the Americanization of Brazilian society. They also criticized the traditional French influence, which was starting to diminish around that time. In the mid-1930s, a change of paradigm was emerging. Liberal Europe was related to things out of fashion. Modernization came from North America or, for some, from Germany.

The liberal state, a minimum requirement for Americanization, according to Gramscian theory,[10] was far from Brazilian reality of the 1940s. The "apocalyptics" and the "integrated" had not taken into consideration that the "Americanization" of Brazil has its genesis in the nonliberal Vargas state of the 1930s and 1940s. This was a paradoxical Americanization.

Excluding the quotation marks, the questions remain: What exactly was the meaning of the Americanization of Brazilian society? Is it possible to determine the moment when this process began?

Americanism as a Paradigm

In 1940, a minor incident that occurred in Brazilian show business demonstrated that Americanization had to overcome resistance being shown by an important sector of Brazilian society. On the night of July 15, the Carioca elite gave Carmen Miranda the cold shoulder during her show in the Urca Casino in Rio de Janeiro. She had just arrived from New York, where she had performed on Broadway, on the radio, and in the movies.

At the beginning of the show, Miranda greeted the audience: "Good night, people." The public did not even react to her incorrect English. The proper greeting would have been "Good evening." Even the joking attitude of the singer, known as the Brazilian Bombshell, was not accepted by the public. The atmosphere worsened later when she sang "The South American Way," a rumba by Jimmy McHugh and Al Dubin, which, in her interpretation, resembled a samba. Dead silence was the reaction of the audience that had gone to the Urca Casino to see Miranda.

Perhaps the audience did not react solely in defense of both Brazilian nationalism and popular culture, which were being bombarded by one of its most popular representatives. The reaction was indeed closer to the attitude of the *mazombo*, to use the expression restored by Vianna Moog in his book *Bandeirantes e pioneiros*.[11] Since colonial times, the mazombo has been a symbol of the Brazilian character. Mazombo, the son of a Portuguese born in Brazil, suffered from an eternal longing for what he had never been, that is, an urbanite of the great cultural centers of Europe.

To those Brazilians, any cultural manifestation, even if it was popular, could not come from America and, much less, from the United States, which always had been identified with "barbarian" mass culture. The Portuguese writer Eça de Queirós synthesizes the thinking of the mazombos: for them, there was much "more civilization in a Parisian alley than in all of New York."[12] The paradigm was Europe, mainly France. The audience at the Urca Casino on July 15, 1940, found Carmen Miranda Americanized and somehow vulgarized, very distant from the "civilized alleys of Paris."

Two months later, the offended Carmen Miranda retaliated for the cold reception of the mazombos. In the same Urca Casino, she performed the samba "They Say I Returned Americanized" (Disseram que voltei americanizada), composed with typical Brazilian molho ("soul," literally, "sauce") by Vicente Paiva and Luís Peixoto:

E disseram que voltei americanizada,	They said that I came back Americanized,
. . . Eu digo mesmo eu *te amo*	. . . I really say *te amo*
E nunca *I love you*	and never *I love you*

Carmen Miranda sang in the most traditional style of the Carioca samba singers, the style that had characterized her as a typical Brazilian performer. In the second part of the samba, she changes her tone, giving to her voice a touch of the malandro. At the end of the song she pronounces the word "Brasil" as southerners—such as politicians like Pres. Getúlio Vargas—do, by stressing the letter "l."

However, the singer, who had reaffirmed her genuine Brazilian identity, returned to the United States and was swallowed up by the Hollywood machinery. She made films, performed in Broadway shows, sang, and, obviously, filled her pockets with money. She was, in the end, Americanized.

The world situation of the 1940s suggested to North American foreign-policy makers that attitudes such as those of the audience at the Urca Casino on July 15 needed to be examined carefully. Brazil was seen as an important partner in the hemisphere, and the safest way to guarantee this partnership was to Americanize Brazil by peaceful means.

The Americanization of Brazilian society could minimize some resistance to political ties between the United States and Brazil. Roosevelt's Good Neighbor Policy was an instrument with wide scope for the execution of the Americanization plan. The fine-tuning of the operation was carried out, as we will see, by a true "factory of ideologies" created by the American government.[iv]

Inside this "factory," Americanism was redefined with specific "raw materials" in which the suffix "ism" was transformed into a powerful, intentional tool with the clear objective of replacing other isms, whether indigenous or not. Americanization was the process of imposition of this ideology on the "weaker" cultures of Latin America.

Americanism can be better understood if we analyze some of the more important elements that took shape in the United States mainly during the first half of the twentieth century.[13] One of them is democracy, always associated with American heroes and especially with the ideas of freedom, individual rights, and independence. Democracy, freedom, and individual rights, prevailing over differences of social class, religion, and race, were guaranteed for all Americans.

However, the more important ideological component of Americanism is progressivism. Strongly rooted in American culture, it is related to rationalism and to the idea of abundance, as well as to creative ability better known as American ingenuity. This dimension of Americanism exalted the free and energetic man, who was capable of transforming the natural world. Thanks to this, the market could offer some useful and attractive products in abundance, creating a new form of pleasure: the pleasure of consumption. As these products became available to all, independently of their class in society, life would be easier, more pleasant and enriching. As Charles Maland points out, "economic growth provides the opportunity to meet social needs, to defuse class conflict, and bring blue-collar workers into the middle class."[14]

The same could be said about music. The channel was the market. Luís da Câmara Cascudo was correct when he identified in the syncopation of George Gershwin's songs the incessant rhythm of the assembly lines at Ford or other big American corporations.[15] The rhythm of swing and Glenn Miller's Big Band was much more attractive than German martial music of the military bands, or the SS goose-step. Or, as pointed out by Prof. Richard Morse, Americanism is simpler because you can tap your foot to it.[16] Almost everything was dictated by the rhythm of money-generating capitalism. It was irresistible. Once the difficulties of modern life were eliminated, the roots of social dissatisfaction would be removed. Social peace would be achieved by generalized consumption. Some key words had acquired a mythical meaning in the ideology of Americanism: "progress," "science," "technology," "abundance," "rationality," "efficiency," "scientific management," and the "American way of life."

Traditionalism is another important element in the ideology of Americanism. The myth of the pure and healthy life on the farm, the close relationship with nature, the small town, the high regard for family values, individual courage, fear of God—everything, in reality, had validity only for white Americans, Anglo-Saxons, fundamentalists, anti-Communists, and passionate imperialists.

The democracy-slavery paradox—present in the origins of Americanism—was, at least legally, swept away by Grant's and Sherman's troops at the end of the Civil War. In behalf of the Union, slavery was destroyed and a more dynamic market economy was put in place by force through the Reconstruction policies of the businessmen of the North.

Regional differences diminished through the implacable advance of the components of dynamic and standardized American modernization, such as the railroads, the telegraph, the telephone, the newspaper, and photography. Standardization took place at all levels. The cinema, the greatest of all American innovations in the area of entertainment, disseminated the American way of life more than any other medium. The movies Americanized the United States of America first and then the other American countries. It disseminated the bucolic image of the past of pioneers, farmers, small towns, the simple life—in sum, traditionalism—by means of modern and complex mass media.

Movie-made America is the title of Robert Sklar's book. It was a commercialized Americanism. In the first half of the nineteenth century, Alexis de Tocqueville had already foreseen the power of Americanism:

> It is unquestionable that the North Americans will one day be called upon to supply the wants of the South Americans. Nature has placed them in contiguity and has furnished the former with every means of knowing and appreciating those demands, of establishing permanent relations with those states and gradually filling their markets. The merchant of the United States could only forfeit these natural advantages if he were very inferior to the European merchant; but he is superior to him in several respects. The Americans of the United States already exercise a great moral influence upon all nations of the New World. They are the source of intelligence, and all those who inhabit the same continent are already accustomed to consider them as the most enlightened, the most powerful, and the most wealthy members of the great American family. All eyes are therefore turned toward the United States: these are the models which the other communities try to imitate to the best of their power; it is from the Union that they borrow their political principles and their laws.
>
> The Americans of the United Sates stand in precisely the same

position with regard to the South Americans as their fathers, the English, occupy with regard to the Italians, the Spaniards, the Portuguese, and all those nations of Europe that receive their articles of daily consumption from England because they are less advanced in civilization and trade. England is at this time the natural emporium of almost all the nations that are within its reach; the American Union will perform the same part in the other hemisphere, and every community which is founded or which prospers in the New World is founded and prospers to the advantage of the Anglo-Americans."[17]

In the world situation of the 1940s, the Tocquevillian idea of the propensity of the Americas for Americanism was more real than ever. A considerable part of the world was practically inaccessible to the United States. Nazi Fascist–dominated Europe was, in a sense, out of reach of the Americans.

Of all the ideological components of Americanism, Progressivism was the best suited "to conquer" the "other Americas" because of its simple and direct character, that is, to work, to produce, to earn money, and to consume. The other ideological components of Americanism were inherent and present in Progressivism in an abridged form.

Germanism as an Alternative Paradigm

To strengthen Brazil's sovereignty, many Brazilians tried to point out paths to the country's future. During the administration of Dom Pedro II, emperor of Brazil, who reigned from 1831 to 1889, some liberal thinkers, such as Tavares Bastos and André Rebouças, exalted the republican American formula. On the opposite side was Eduardo Prado, a conservative thinker, who, inspired by the country's past and the British regime, repudiated the American formula and defended the monarchy soon after the proclamation of the Republic in 1889. At the time of World War I, a book intended for "active Brazilians with courage and strong will" suggested Germany as a "third way," in order to avoid British and Yankee influences. Dunshee de Abranches, an outsider thinker, in *A illusão brazileira* (The Brazilian illusion) wrote: "Germany, which after 25 years of wise and happy internal reconstruction, had changed from a third-ranked country to a *leading power* [original emphasis], was worthy of being imitated by us, who possess the vastest and most productive territory in the New World."[18] Abranches emphasized that, compared with other European countries, Germany had shown its superiority in all fields. He believed that we in Brazil, who had more resources, could do as well as or even better than Germany by putting an end to the perennial extortion caused by the association with "perfidious Albion," as England was termed by the French.

In the United States, the formulation of Americanism was the ideology that explained the modernization of the nation in the New World. In Germany, through Germanism, the ideological justification for expansion and modernization was sought in a conservative manner. Abranches saw Germany as a model country during World War I. This concept was echoed among certain Brazilians who were part of the power structure in Brazil at the time of World War II. During the 1930s and early 1940s, many Brazilians who were thinking about the future of the country were attracted to the ideology of Germanism. Germanism was another paradigm that presented an alternative to dependence on England and the increasing influence of the United States. Therefore, the North American republic, with its Americanism, would have to supersede the Germanic paradigm. The United States would have to be accepted as a more viable model than the fascinating Germanic model, at that moment a well-oiled and apparently invincible war machine.

The technological and consumerist aspect of Americanism was not appreciated by a significant sector of the officers of Brazil's armed forces. The military identified the mass production of gadgets by North American industry with the wastefulness of an excessively materialized and commercialized society. For many Brazilian military officers, the autarchic Nazi Germany model was apparently a more appropriate paradigm at that moment. The relentless advance of the Nazis in Eastern Europe during the first half of the 1940s engendered enthusiasm not only at high levels of the Brazilian government, but also among the population of Germanic origin from the south of the country, who were not properly integrated into Brazilian society. The German colony in the southern states of Rio Grande do Sul, Santa Catarina, and Paraná had already been reached by Radio Berlin and its emphasis on Germanism.

The "fascinating" side of fascism gave more luster to the Germanic model. The power of attraction of the elegance and sensuality of fascism was felt by a character in Sartre's novel *La mort dans l'âme* (Troubled sleep). While watching the march of German soldiers into Paris, Daniel was "delighted by their beautiful hair, their tanned faces, with eyes that looked like iced lakes, their slender bodies, their incredibly long and muscular hips. . . . A delicious, unbearable sensation, spread all over his body . . . he repeated, gasping: 'As if they were butter—they are entering Paris as if they were butter.' . . . He would have liked to have been a woman to toss them flowers."[19]

If some masochistic Frenchmen were delighted by the Nazi victory, what can be said about the population of Germanic origin from the South of Brazil? Could it be that in the eyes of Brazilian officers, the German soldiers seemed to be more elegant and better fighters than the French with their khaki uniforms? For Susan Sontag, the Nazi soldiers were aesthetically more attractive, especially the SS soldiers, with their well-cut uniforms, black boots that seemed to compel the soldiers to stand erect, and white gloves hiding their hands. This elegance made the American soldiers look like salesmen in civilian clothes, with their neckties and shoes with laces.[20] Thus, Brazil's aesthetic-military paradigm became Germany.

Even Frank Capra, considered to be one of the most distinguished "manufacturers" of the American dream, was impressed with the aesthetic side of Nazi ideology. In April 1942, Capra and Anatole Litvak went to MoMA, the Museum of Modern Art, in New York and in a special screening watched *Triumph of the Will*, the already famous film by Leni Riefenstahl. Capra was astonished: "It scared the hell out of me. My first reaction was that we were dead, we couldn't win that war . . . just exactly as the Austrians did and the Czechoslovakians did and the Channel countries did. That picture just won them over. . . . When I saw it, I just thought, 'How can we possibly cope with this enormous machine and enormous will to fight?' Surrender or you're dead—that was what the film was saying to you. I sat there and I was a very unhappy man. How can I possibly top this?"[21] Frank Capra, who was terrified by "fascinating fascism," was the aesthete momentarily distanced from American cultural and marketing reality. The film transformed power into spectacle, politics into aesthetic: a demonstration of camaraderie, youth, willpower of the people (*Volk*), and blood.

But outside the deeply idealized context of that historical German moment, the marches, the speeches, the parades, the torches, and the references to the heathen cults of the primitive Germanic tribes had almost no significance. The parades, and so on, touched the heart of some *integralistas* and isolated Brazilian army officers,[22] but only for a short time. It did not take them long to convert to Americanization.

When Capra recovered from the impact, he retaliated with the series he produced together with Litvak, *Why We Fight*, aimed at the soldiers on the front, a documentary with propagandistic intentions sponsored by the Office of War Information and the Signal Corps, a movie company linked to the American Armed Forces. The series had little impact beyond the barracks. It is currently an integral part of the archives on World War II. Capra's commercial films, such as *Mr. Deeds Goes to Town* (1936), *Mr. Smith Goes to Washington* (1939), and *Meet John Doe* (1941), were a much more efficient vehicle for Americanization. In other words, the market was the best road to Americanization.

The German model was not easy to understand, and it was difficult to adapt to Brazilian reality. The Nazi autarchic pattern was rooted in the remote past of German history, mixed with fragments of conservative imperial culture and the modernization of the Weimar age. In sum, Nazi Germany was based on the project of self-supported expansionism. The ideological project was strengthened by a combination of traditional culture, racism, and enlightened rationalism.[23]

Furthermore, one has to add all of this to the idea developed at that time by a vast war literature, the result of *Fronterlebnis* (war experience at the front), which portrayed Germany with a more masculine culture. A generation was forged capable of fighting *Amerikanismus*, which was seen as a "veritable plague" with its Taylorism, its mass production and consumption, the rationalism of its industry, and as a threat to the German spirit. For the German right wing, Fronterlebnis produced strong souls to fight the American way of life and its escapism.

This formulation, which seemed to transform Nazi Germany into a significant world power, captured the attention of some Brazilian army officers. Gen. Pedro Aurélio de Góis Monteiro was invited to attend one of the many huge military parades in Berlin. Góis Monteiro did not manage to visit Germany, but in one way or another, a self-supported developing economic project remained in the thinking of the military officers of the 1930 Revolution. Although we did not have the past technical experiences that came from schools of engineering,[24] we had more natural resources than Germany.

Until Brazil achieved technical independence, it could buy weapons and machines produced by the great German industries under the system of compensation offered by the Germans. In these transactions, money was not used, but products were exchanged. By 1935, "the Brazilian government made an informal compensation (aski) arrangement with Germany, in spite of having signed a reciprocal trade agreement with the United States in February of the same year. Finance minister Arthur da Souza Costa, in defending this move, stated that certain Brazilian commercial interests depended on the compensation system to export their products to Germany, while others used it to import German goods."[25]

The manifestation of the Brazilian government's autonomy caused the Americans to protest. But for the more nationalistic military sector, such attitudes of independence in our commercial relations strengthened the idea of distancing Brazil from the excessively commercialized orbit of the American economy. At the same time, we would divest ourselves of the feminine image of Latin America portrayed by the North American press starting at the end of the nineteenth century.[26] This image would change through a Fronterlebnis transposed to Brazilian reality and forged in the remote Paraguay War (War of the Triple Alliance, 1865–1870), in Canudos

THE SEDUCTION OF BRAZIL

(the backland peasants' rebellion in Northeast Brazil at the end of the nineteenth century); in the Contestado (the peasants' rebellion in southern Brazil at the beginning of the twentieth century); in the military upheavals of 1922, 1924, and 1926–1927; in the movement of 1930; and in the brief battles against leftists in 1935.

However, the formulations of the military were hindered by our historical-cultural reality, which demanded different mechanisms from the German model. Pres. Getúlio Vargas seemed to better understand our formation. On the international level, he tried to maintain equidistant relations with "mercantile Yankee imperialism" and "romanticist Germanic imperialism." This game was not easily understood by the general staff of the armed forces. Some of President Roosevelt's skillful and sensible advisors on American foreign policy were paying attention to the conflicts of Brazilian internal politics.

As previously mentioned, German expansionism threatened the hemisphere and the equilibrium set by the interests of the United States. Three days before the swastika flew from the Eiffel Tower, President Vargas took advantage of the situation. His speech on board the battleship *Minas Gerais,* delivered on June 11, 1940, is known for its dubious message: "We march toward a different future . . . the time for short-sighted liberalisms, sterile demagogies is over . . . The energetic peoples fit for life need to follow their aspirations."[27]

He commented on the repercussions of the speech in his diary.[28] Many saw the speech as Germanophile; at least that is what it sounded like to England. The United States was initially surprised. A diplomatic discussion took place involving Chancellor Oswaldo Aranha, American Ambassador Jefferson Caffery, and Undersecretary of State Sumner Welles. The tense situation was evaded.[v]

A few days after having criticized the democracies, Vargas had been skillful enough to show his support for the policy of Pan-American solidarity proposed by President Roosevelt. On June 12, Vargas recorded in his diary: "We began the talks on our war planning with the head of the American military mission, our military people, and the minister of the exterior."[29] The game of Brazil's head of state yielded its first results.

The Good Neighbor Policy, the Intellectuals, and Americanism

There is no denying that World War II was the turning point in the history of cultural relations between Brazil and the United States. However, the idea of the Good Neighbor Policy, which included culture in the international agenda, was developed a few years earlier, during the government of Republican president Herbert Hoover. Elected in November 1928, President Hoover embarked on a trip through Latin America before taking office that, according to him, was not exactly a recreational trip. He intended to change some important aspects of American foreign policy. As soon as he arrived in Honduras, President Hoover gave a speech in which the expression "good neighbor" was used;[30] this expression would be adopted by President Roosevelt in 1933.

Hoover was preparing the ground for his Latin America foreign policy. However, he was not well received in all the countries he visited. Argentina and Uruguay showed little enthusiasm. In Buenos Aires there were protests against the presence of the American president. But when President Hoover arrived in Rio de Janeiro on December 21, 1928, he received a warmer welcome.[31] The poet Oswald de Andrade also welcomed the North American leader in his own way: "Hip! Hip! Hoover! Poetic Message to the Brazilian People."

Oswald de Andrade's verses reflect the critique by sectors of the Brazilian intelligentsia of the growing presence of Americans in Brazil. They also reflect the disagreement on racism, as does Mário de Andrade in the "Nova Canção Dixie" (New Dixie song): "No, I'll never be in Color Line Land."

For a long time, Americanism had forged a discrediting image of Latin America. The white Protestant man was valued. He was always mentioned as leading progress in the fight against uncivilized life and created an opposite image for Latin Americans. According to this concept, to the south of the Rio Grande was the America of the Indians, the blacks, the women, and the children. This America needed to learn the lessons of progress and capitalism to abandon this "inferior" position. This America needed, ultimately, to be domesticated.[32]

Some American intellectuals began to criticize this image of superiority, a trend current mainly after World War I. Those were the 1920s—in reference to the United States, already described as "splendid drunken years," the years of nonconformism, with flappers, as young women of free behavior who liked to dance were known. The Brazilian name for flappers was *melindrosas*, the young women whom Monteiro Lobato described as "these charming creatures, unique in the world, American girls whom European painters proclaimed the prettiest beings on Earth, most perfect body, physically slim, solid as Helen Wills, the tennis queen, self-assured, friends of whiskey in massive doses after Prohibition proclaimed the use of alcohol a crime, these flowers of flesh . . . who trot in the street to their clerical work, where they walk out on men, and who keep a series of boyfriends."[33]

The February 1920 issue of *Life* magazine had on the cover a flapper, that is, a slim "Lobatian" melindrosa. Wearing a big necklace, garters showing, full of bracelets, face painted, she was dancing with an old man wearing a tuxedo and eyeglasses on the tip of his nose. A small caption read: "Teaching old dogs new tricks." The old gentleman who danced with the flapper represented traditional America, which could not resist the appeal and pleasure of an America that was almost its opposite. It was a time when the paradigm of the puritan and honest American was shaken: a moment of cultural disturbance. As Warren Susman mentions:

> Too often the decade appears as Ishmael Reed describes it in his recent (1972) brilliant and provocative literary tour de force *Mumbo Jumbo*: "That decade which doesn't seem so much a part of American history as the hidden After-Hours of America struggling to jam. To get through. . . . If the British prose style is Churchillian, America is the tobacco auctioneer, . . . the traveling salesman who can sell the world the Brooklyn Bridge and convince you that tomatoes grow at the South Pole. If in the 1920s the British say 'The sun never sets on the British Empire,' the American motto is 'There's a sucker born every minute.'"[34]

But it also was a time dedicated to the material prosperity of the interwar period. Calvin Coolidge, the Republican president (1923–1928), had close ties to big business. President Coolidge had a "religion": wealth and work, in the deepest puritan and individualistic sense. The factory was its temple.

The decade of the 1920s is well known in the history of the United States as a moment of great economic expansion. It was an era of intense mechanization of production and a vertiginous growth in the market. Profit was the motto of the big investors who preached in Coolidge "temples." The high priests were Frederick W. Taylor and Henry Ford. It was a market that produced everything en masse: cars, vacuum cleaners, radios, refrigerators, and food. There would always be a sucker ready to buy any thingamajig produced. The progressivism and reformism that had marked the government of Pres. Theodore Roosevelt had been covered, after President Coolidge, with a mask, a sort of stingy caricature, reduced to a concept of productivity and enterprise. Morality walked hand in hand with the religion of production and consumption. Ford was publicly opposed to tobacco, alcohol, and dancing. The blame for the vices of society fell on immigrants, Jews, and blacks.

For the provincial attitude of the moralists-fundamentalists, beer was always related to the temptation of the devil and the immigrant. The same was true for sex and music. This attitude gave birth to the constitutional amendment that established Prohibition, which came into effect in 1919. It was a time of moralism and greed. It was a time to flout strict laws. A lot was drunk during these "drunken" years, a time in which it was forbidden to drink alcohol.

The breaking of the law produced a specific type of culture and behavior. Speakeasies were established, in which there was no restriction on alcoholic beverage consumption; bootleggers, traffickers, and rumrunners, a Latin-Caribbean variation of traffickers, brought rum from the Caribbean to the thirsty American market.

This morality imposed during the Coolidge-Hoover years could not control the sexual appeal of the advertisements of the big companies. For instance, it was impossible to prevent a cigarette manufacturer from advertising its products outdoors with a poster of a pretty young brunette whose seductive lips longed for an imaginary Lucky Strike, or perhaps even a kiss. Sex appeal was not used only in commercials. The cinema, still silent, showed the curves of the "It Girl," Clara Bow, or the "masculine sexual symbol" of the time, Rudolph Valentino.

It was not easy for the puritan and moralist soul of the average American to control its so-called primitive instincts. The abundance and offers were such that sex and alcohol—integral parts of the market—could not be abolished by the force of law alone. Evidently, moral and religious limits were present. The pleasure-seeking white man found himself exceeding the limits established by law and morality. Literally leaving his territory, he searched for a kind of anticipated forgiveness of his sins. Harlem, the black neighborhood of New York, represented a truly free territory for part of the white population.[35]

They searched in other "territories" for what was forbidden in their own. White Americans had discovered the sensuality of black American music in Harlem. There was no sin in Harlem. Even if there was, when the white man returned to his territory, the guardians of puritan morality would not take into account the sin committed in another spiritual "jurisdiction."

At this time, almost simultaneously with Latin Americans, a generation of American intellectuals started to question the segregation and materialist-consumerist character of American society. They criticized, above all, the prejudiced interpretations formed in the "drunken '20s" and during the depression that some periodicals made of Brazilian cultural peculiarity. These intellectuals believed that it was essential to understand what were commonly regarded as negative qualities: the "savage" and "natural" aspect of certain social groups in their own country and of the Latin American peoples. It was an introspective phase for these intellectuals. It was necessary to understand the savage forces and not deprecate them. This was a route to a more spiritual America, in which nature was the source of regeneration.[36]

This approach tried to keep alive the idea that the Wild West, the frontier, had not died. Many went looking for the pure and genuine values of the Pueblo Indians in New Mexico. They learned their customs, their dances, their food, their music, and even slept with them, with the intention of criticizing the American way of life. The idea of going to the origins was what guided young Americans such as Mary Austin, Franz Boas, John Collier, Robert Herrick, and Lewis Mumford. All of them in a certain way contacted the Indians and criticized the addicted, capitalist, and materialistic American culture. Perhaps this is one of the bases of "Freyrian" Brazilian sociology: Gilberto Freyre had strong connections with Franz Boas.

From Indians to women, from women to children, from children to blacks and their folkloric music. From there to jazz, which white people such as George Gershwin took upon themselves to incorporate into concert music. It is "natural" that Latin America was the next step. According to Pike, "Latin America's cultural and racial mestizaje instead of being taken as a badge of inferiority became now a symbol of hope to a generation intent upon synthesizing culture and nature, rather than obliterating nature so as to safeguard cultures."[37]

One of the intellectuals who had searched for this synthesis most intensely was Waldo Frank. According to Fredrick Pike, Frank has to be understood as an integral part of a generation of East Coast Jewish intellectuals who stood for a messianic and millenarian concept of history. The idea of the American melting pot, according to Frank, should be carried beyond American borders. The cabala supplied the bases for a curious theory of integration between the north and the south of the continent: the feminine aspect of God (Shekinah) had been separated from its divine head; later, a sacred marriage joined the parts again, forming a union of God with the feminine principles. Frank drank from this source and re-created the popularized interpretation according to which the United States always had been seen as the masculine part and the Latin peoples as the feminine part of the Americas.[38] For him there should be a union between the feminine and the masculine parts of America, and not the domination of one over the other.

Frank and other intellectuals of the time believed that Latin America should not follow in the steps of American historical development, which had produced an excessively materialistic society. With the help of its intellectuals, Latin America should deepen its mystical sensitivity and help Americans recover their lost spirituality, their pioneering past. In 1942, during a trip through Latin America, Waldo Frank spread his interpretations. It was not by chance that the Good Neighbor Policy was understood by some sectors in Latin America as the first phase of sincere relations with the United States.

However, in the 1940s, Waldo Frank was not the true "messenger" of the Good Neighbor Policy, nor did this represent the type of closeness that those ingenuous and sincere Anglo-American and Ibero-American spirits had hoped for. The Americanization of Brazil was the achievement of a United States more interested in keeping the continent as part of its market. The traditional Protestants were little influenced by the activities of outsiders such as Frank. In reality, by disseminating a morally favorable image of the materialistic and consumerist aspect of Americanism, they were trying to isolate the influence of these young opponents of the "extreme materialism" of North American society.

The idea of Americanizing the United States itself was translated into a pedagogical and disciplinarian politics following the precepts of the Protestant Anglo-Saxon white elite. The target of this politics was a mass of immigrants who had recently arrived in the country. The heterogeneous, undisciplined, and even anarchistic culture of the immigrants needed to be controlled in order to protect the basic "pillars" of "Christian civilization."

Let us focus on the name of the country called the United States. It is one of the few countries—if not the only country—in the world that does not have a specific substantive name. One has the impression of an abstract being with political qualities. It seems to be a group of independent states that decided to become united around a few common ideals. It was the state of New York that joined the state of Maryland that joined the state of Virginia that joined the state of Massachusetts, and so on. Keeping the idea of independence, the set of states adopted a common name, the United States of America: a sociological and political concept. Because of this development, the notion of nation was not immediately formed. The English language lacks a word to define people born in the United States. Or, better, the word exists: "Americans."

From the beginning, there was an unconscious desire that was translated into the idea of "Manifest Destiny": the United States would appropriate the word "America" to identify the country. The intriguing part is that, in all State Department documents I have examined, the expression "Other Americas" is used for all the American countries except the United States. However, this does not include Canada, for obvious cultural and racial reasons. "Other Americas" sounds like a paradigmatic truth. Thus, an America existed, that is, the United States, in short, a grand country with an industrial revolution, magnates, laborers, Hollywood, skyscrapers, modernity. And then there were the Others, with none of the above.

Partly owing to negligence, Brazil and the other Latin American countries became accustomed to these denominations when referring to the United States and to people from the United States. Immigrants, in turn,

Americanized themselves within a generation. Some of the cases of resistance were restrained or seen as colorful manifestations. Many immigrants in Brazil, especially the Germans, had been isolated for a period of time. This preserved the German language and culture in Brazil, facilitating the dissemination of Nazism in the colonies of the South.[39] German-Americans, in contrast, quickly adapted to the Anglo-Saxon Protestant community.[vi]

A simpler project would be necessary to Americanize the other Americas. Some of the issues expressed by dissident intellectuals—the critique of segregation and the idea of the superiority of the white Protestant—had undoubtedly been incorporated, but only to consolidate a model condemned by outsiders, that is, to elevate the idea of material progress and the insertion of the Latin American countries into the mercantilist sphere of Americanism. The "outsiders" had been used, in a certain way, to carry through the Americanization project, at least on the representational level.[40] The conditions that would be used as the basis for relations with Latin America were created during the government of Pres. Franklin Delano Roosevelt.

The depression surprised a euphoric and "drunken" America. The national income fell from $81 billion to $49 billion, and millions of unemployed people took to the streets. The middle class began to lose its savings, insurance, and income from small investments. Unable to pay their mortgages, members of the middle class lost their own homes, one of the most important symbols of the American way of life. The slums, known as Hoovervilles, and breadlines, ironically, seemed to have become the new symbols of an impoverished America.

After 1933, the new government of the Democratic president, Franklin D. Roosevelt, introduced the New Deal. Along with it, a feeling emerged: the 1920s had been years of sin and, therefore, needed to be forgotten; a great effort of reconstruction had to be marshaled. The country acquired the shape of an immense family congregated around a "father," who, by the way, entered American homes on a weekly basis through his "fireside chats" on the radio.[41]

One of President Roosevelt's first acts was the abolition of Prohibition. Wine and beer, now legal, boosted an important and lucrative sector of the economy. Aside from the lack of money, it was a time concentrated on the arduous work of rebuilding the nation. The time and space for pleasure had been reduced or, at least, disciplined and domesticated.

The disciplinary characteristic was also noticeable in the music. In the 1920s—baptized by Scott Fitzgerald as the "Jazz Age"—a great number of talented musicians were known for their individual virtuosity and distinguished themselves in small groups, such as in the house-rent parties of Harlem, or on the South Side of Chicago. But the New Deal period was marked by the birth of the big bands, the age of swing. In the formation of the orchestras at the time of the New Deal, "the individual musician had to work harder than ever before. He had to be able to 'swing' separately as well as with his section. And then the sections had to swing together, too. It meant endless rehearsals, a comparative loss of identity (except for the solo stars), and high-level teamwork."[42]

Jazz also was moralized and disciplined. One could say that it was a moment in which there was a kind of informal morality. In other words, it was a morality that was more politico-economic than cultural. Some years later, in the early 1940s, bebop was a reaction to the "disciplining" of the music. In spite of this, for "millions of common Americans, especially workers and farmers . . . the New Deal was a huge moral crusade capable of restoring the values of justice, fairness, democracy and equality in the economic life of the Republic."[43]

From Anglo-Saxon America to Ibero-America

"Por muy bien cortado que esté un frac, puesto sobre el lomo de un yanqui parece siempre un frac de prestidigitador" (a tuxedo—no matter how well cut—once put on the shoulders of a Yankee always looks like a magician's tuxedo). This conclusion of the cultured dictator of *El recurso del método* (Reasons of state) by Alejo Carpentier, summarizes well how Latin American aristocrats saw the Yankees: as uneducated and inelegant. Also, José Enrique Rodó in *Ariel* bitterly criticizes the utilitarianism, the materialism, and the mediocrity of American culture in order to emphasize the "aristocratic" culture of Latin American thinkers.[44]

Public opinion on the subcontinent had always associated Americans with the arrogance and superiority of the Uncle Sam image with its Mephistophelian goatee. Uncle Sam was a simultaneously ridiculed, comical, and fierce figure, with his flawless top hat threatening the Latin American peoples.

New times introduce new images. By 1938, arrogance was coming from German ambassador Karl Ritter,[vii] who insulted Chancellor Oswaldo Aranha.[45] The old image of the Americans contrasted with the European elegance of Amb. Jefferson Caffery. The refinement of this southern gentleman belied the association of the tuxedo he wore for official ceremonies with the image of any magician. Rockefeller was one of the few responsible for this change by "delivering the message to Latins that Yankee men and women of affairs had a genuine interest in promoting the better things of life: They were not the cultural barbarians that Latin-American pensadores so often assumed them to be."[46]

In a photograph taken in Rio Grande do Norte in January 1943, after President Roosevelt returned from the Casablanca conference, he is sitting in a Jeep, smiling, dressed in a white linen suit and a Panama hat, in the company of President Vargas, also smiling and confident (see cover illustration). This is a new seductive image transmitted by President Roosevelt to the Brazilians.

In this new phase, Latin America could still be represented as the feminine part of America, but not in the same mold as before. To the American, who was living the "informal morality" of the New Deal era, the Latin America represented in this feminine image started to become, on the plane of pleasure, a liberated territory, a kind of international Harlem. Generic and hypothetical Carmen Mirandas had taken the place of the flappers. What was difficult to find in the United States could be found easily in Brazil. The religious chronicler of the sixteenth and seventeenth centuries had written about the absence of sin to the south of the equator. Americans seemed to have discovered the old writings, interpreting them according to a naughtier concept. Waldo Frank would prove this thesis with a mulatta from Belo Horizonte in 1942.

In the same year, Orson Welles produced a radio program with Carmen Miranda in which she taught him how to sing and dance. When one listens to the program, the relationship of exchange established between the two is noticeable: it discloses the delicate malice of the woman-America— seducing the man-America—at the same time as she is seduced by him.[47]

1. A True "Factory of Ideologies"

The Office of the Coordinator of Inter-American Affairs

A coordinator is someone who can keep all the balls in the air without losing his own. NELSON ROCKEFELLER TO HENRY WALLACE

Latin America: Nelson Rockefeller's Manifest Destiny

The success of German forces in Western Europe, which conquered Denmark, Norway, Belgium, Holland, and later, France, was evidence enough for the United States that the West was threatened. Central America as well as South America were also included in the plans of the Axis. It was believed that England alone would not be able to hold off the powerful Nazi war machine.

U.S. foreign policy, until then guided by isolationism and neutrality, began to be the subject of an intense debate in the political circles of the country. Since the end of World War I, American society had rejected any involvement in European politics. It was said that the Americans no longer wished to play the role of "merchants of death," referring to the sale of arms to Europe that enriched big corporations. In 1935, Congress approved the Neutrality Act, which forbade the sale of weapons to countries at war. President Roosevelt signed the new law with restrictions. When, in 1937, China was attacked by the Japanese, Roosevelt found a way to interpret the Neutrality Act to allow the sale of American weapons to the Chinese. At the end of that year, tensions rose in Japanese American relations after the Japanese bombed an American gunboat that was protecting Standard Oil's tankers.

In March 1939, before the German advance in Western Europe, Roosevelt sent a peculiar message to Hitler in which he asked Germany not to invade twenty countries, each of which he named. In a movie newsreel of that period, Hitler appears reading the American president's message in the Reichstag while high-ranking Nazis burst out laughing. In spite of an official declaration on September 5, 1939, which reaffirmed the country's neutrality, American public opinion's isolationist profile changed between the time of the invasion of Poland in September 1939 and the defeat of France in June 1940. In a radio announcement, President Roosevelt stated that the country would remain outside the conflict, but that he could not demand the neutrality of all Americans.

On June 10, 1940, as France's dying government left Paris, the prime minister, Paul Raynaud, made a dramatic request for President Roosevelt's help, which strongly indicated that the Americans could not remain neutral much longer. The isolationists, led by such people as Charles Lindbergh and Herbert Hoover, organized in the so-called America First Committee, lost ground.

In the same month in which Roosevelt reinforced the declaration of American neutrality, the U.S. Congress approved the Burke-Wadsworth Act, which created the first peacetime draft in U.S. history. In early 1941, the United States already had called up and was training 1.6 million soldiers. At the same time, Roosevelt honored Churchill's request, sending fifty WWI-era destroyers in exchange for English bases in Bermuda, the Caribbean, and Canada (Newfoundland). At the end of 1940, in another fireside chat, Roosevelt announced the Lend-Lease Bill, approved in March of the following year. According to this law, the United States could lend resources, basically without any guarantees, to finance England's resistance against Germany. In the following year, the involvement of the United States in European matters increased even more, after the meeting between Churchill and Roosevelt in Newfoundland, where they signed the Atlantic Charter, full of promises of mutual aid to defeat Nazism.

Acting against American political tradition, President Roosevelt ran for a third term in the presidential elections of 1940. Latin America had an important function in this process. In the campaign, President Roosevelt gave increasing emphasis to defense and continental cooperation, which guaranteed the support of certain Republicans. This approach bolstered the sectors that advocated strengthening relations with Latin America.

The most agile and dynamic of the nonofficial groups that were urgently proposing closer relations with Latin America was led by the multimillionaire Republican Nelson Rockefeller, who, according to some sources, had donated $25,000 to the Democratic Party campaign.[1] The Republicans had been weakened without the support of people such as Rockefeller, and Roosevelt was reelected with 54.8 percent of the vote.

IN THIS CONTEXT, the American government developed, not without major controversy, its policy for Latin America. The destiny of the evangelist "missionary" Nelson Aldrich Rockefeller was to play an important role in this policy. Nelson was the second son of John D. Rockefeller, Jr., of the well-known family of multimillionaires who owned the Standard Oil Company, which had a presence in many Latin Americna countries. He graduated in economics from Dartmouth College in 1930. He was not an above-average student nor did he have a vocation for business, as he confessed in a few letters to his father. However, he had an interest in the arts, which he seemed to have inherited from the Aldriches, the maternal side of the family. Familiarity with the arts was used skillfully by Rockefeller to navigate between politics and business.

Rockefeller was educated with evangelistic precepts. Every morning at 7:45 A.M. the family congregated around the breakfast table for first prayers and to eat. This ritual was repeated in the evening before dinner. Following the same religious principles, the Rockefellers adopted a philanthropic policy aimed at changing the image of its companies, known for violence in the treatment of their workers. According to Brazilian writer Monteiro Lobato, they had transformed themselves into "capturers and redistributors of money. They carried out a work of socialization that constituted a dream of the Russian radicals."[2] The philanthropic acts of the family were coordinated by the Rockefeller Foundation, directed by Raymond Fosdick, a dedicated evangelistic employee, who knew how to manage the resources that came from the oil company and railroads, among other companies.

Abroad, the religious and cultural missions of the foundation used the Rockefeller family companies as bases. In Mexico and Guatemala, for example, its religious health-care workers fought malaria and yellow fever with the same zeal they employed in antirevolutionary efforts. The revolution was seen as a social illness that needed to be fought with aid, donations, and propaganda. In short, to avoid revolutionary "contamination," the foundation promoted social welfare by fighting malaria and yellow fever. For many liberals, intellectuals, Democrats, and even for the American Left, Rockefeller "philanthropic diplomacy" was preferable to the "big stick" policy of the beginning of the century.[3]

Nelson Rockefeller's involvement with economic activities began in the Foreign Department of Chase National Bank. The department was headed by the bank's vice president, Joseph Rovensky. From his work with Rovensky a strong friendship developed that later was important for Rockefeller's political career. Rockefeller worked in the clan's headquarters located in Room 5600 at 30 Rockefeller Plaza, in the Rockefeller Center, an art deco–style set of buildings on Fifth Avenue in New York City. Thanks to the intervention of his mother, he became president of the Museum of Modern Art and trustee of the Metropolitan Museum. MoMA was gradually transformed into a truly free space for Latin American artistic expression and acquired great importance for the new North American policy for the subcontinent.

Rockefeller's position at Chase National Bank required that he travel frequently, especially through Latin America. In 1935, he made his first trip to Venezuela, where he financially supported a group of plastic artists exhibited at the local Museum of Modern Art.⁴ This trip connected him more closely to the international division of the Rockefeller Foundation, which developed a health-care program in some Latin American countries.

In 1937, he traveled again to South America, starting his trip at the Orinoco River, in Venezuela. The splendor of the jungle seen from the Standard Oil yacht contributed to the young millionaire's increased interest in the subcontinent.⁵ The main objective of the trip was to inspect areas of exploration for the Creole Petroleum Company, a subsidiary of Standard Oil in South America. He noticed, above all, that the employees of the company lived in isolation, literally separated from the local population by barbed-wire fences. To change the image of the Rockefeller companies, on his return to New York he proposed to his executives that they initiate a sanitation policy through the foundation by sending teachers, doctors, and missionaries. He had a sufficiently practical grasp of the situation, and with this social welfare policy he wanted to prevent a wave of anti-Americanism that certainly would affect the companies. He also visited Brazil, Argentina, Chile, Bolivia, Peru, and Panama. In May 1937, he interrupted the trip to attend his grandfather's unexpected funeral.

In the same year Rockefeller traveled to Venezuela, the United States was plunged into the so-called Roosevelt Depression. Millions of unemployed filled the streets again. The desperate scenes witnessed after the 1929 crisis seemed to be repeating themselves. Also during this year, after the conflict between Japanese ships and American gunboats escorting the Standard Oil tankers in China, Roosevelt's foreign policy began to change direction.

According to President Roosevelt, the Americas, not just the United States, had to be transformed into the stronghold of the hemisphere. At the Pan-American meetings in September and October 1939, American countries, urged by the United States, formed a commission that founded the Inter-American Economic and Financial Council. The U.S. representative also obtained approval for the formation of a neutrality zone of three hundred miles around the American continent. This measure proved ineffective. At the end of the year, the Prata estuary was the scene of a naval battle involving the German ship *Graf Spee* and a British squadron.

After the Nazi army invaded Denmark in April 1940, U.S. foreign-policy makers needed urgently to find formulas to guarantee the continent's security. The misery caused by the economic backwardness of the Latin American countries could foment revolutions led by nationalists, socialists, or sympathizers of Nazi Fascism, movements that would jeopardize U.S.

THE SEDUCTION OF BRAZIL

interests. In mid-1940, the Inter-American Development Commission was founded, with the objective of promoting the economic potential of the "other American Republics." In the eyes of U.S. strategists, the economic, social, and military weakness of the Latin American countries was a direct threat to the United States.[6]

During the 1940 election campaign, two groups had formulated different proposals for a Latin America policy. The first was led by Sumner Welles, undersecretary of state, assisted by Adolf Berle, the secretary's assistant, and by the leader of the Pan-American Union, Leo Rowe. The second, organized by Nelson Rockefeller, was not as well known or official, but politicians began to notice it. The group called itself the Junta, in a reference to Latin American dictatorships. The Junta's most prominent personality was Beardsley Ruml, the treasurer of Macy's, who became the link between Rockefeller and Washington. Harry Hopkins, the secretary of commerce and President Roosevelt's alter ego, introduced Rockefeller to the president, who, with an eye toward reelection, accepted the magnate's invitation to participate in a shortwave radio program transmitted to Latin America directly from MoMA.[7] From then on, Nelson Rockefeller's political trajectory was remarkable.

A plan with economic and political measures for Latin America was formulated in the Junta's meetings in Rockefeller's luxurious apartment on Fifth Avenue. The objective was to impede the increase in trade and influence of the Axis on the subcontinent. To achieve this, the United States would have to adjust its policies concerning the rising nationalistic movements instead of fighting them. As mentioned earlier, three days after Vargas's speech on the ship *Minas Gerais*, and while Paris was being taken by the Nazis on June 14, 1940, Nelson Rockefeller arrived in Washington and presented his plan to Harry Hopkins, who suggested that he send it to President Roosevelt. The next day, Roosevelt submitted Rockefeller's proposal to the secretaries of state, agriculture, commerce, and treasury. The memorandum was accompanied by a note from President Roosevelt in which he said he was anxious for a rapid response to the proposals related to Latin America, which he hoped to obtain by June 20.[8]

The memorandum, "Hemisphere Economic Policy," was a synthesis of the text written by Nelson Rockefeller and his Junta. It criticized bureaucratic formulas developed in several long Pan-American meetings. The only and the most efficient way to fight totalitarianism was, according to the document, to adopt measures to make the Latin American economy more competitive. The security of the United Sates depended on close economic and cultural cooperation with all the governments of the Americas. It would be possible to make a qualitative leap in the living conditions of

Latin America's peoples with emergency measures such as the purchase of the agricultural and mineral production of the region.

Rockefeller was putting into practice the experience he had gained during his trips with Rovensky to the Standard Oil fields. During these trips, he realized the urgent necessity of modifying the relationship of the company with the inhabitants of the "host" countries. The objective of this Realpolitik was to control anti-Americanism by peaceful means, because armed intervention by the United States was not part of the Good Neighbor Policy promoted by President Roosevelt and his closest advisors.

The Rockefeller group's proposal had a big advantage over the others that came from government organisms: it was supported by Rockefeller's fantastic financial power and was independent of the bureaucracy.[9] The Junta's program was very bold: suggestions that the United States reduce or eliminate taxes on products imported from the "other Americas"; the development of a more appropriate transportation system for the distribution of the products of Latin American countries; and incentives for investments, with the objective of assuring production of raw materials, for example. External debt should be analyzed according to a realistic point of view, that is, according to the possibilities of the debtor instead of the requirements of the creditor. It criticized the American functionaries who worked in Latin America as lacking knowledge of local culture and needs. To be successful, the program would have to promote the integration of the federal government and private initiative. An interdepartmental commission, assisted by representatives of private companies, would be in charge to assure the successful realization of the project.

The Creation of the Office of the Coordinator of Inter-American Affairs

To prevent possible rivalries between departments, Nelson Rockefeller was skillful enough not to openly suggest himself to coordinate the program, even though he was eager to occupy a political position in the government. The intense conflicts of interest among the New Dealers hindered the peaceful choice of a leader for the new agency. Therefore, the president preferred Nelson Rockefeller. Not having any official relationship with the Roosevelt government, Rockefeller had created the conditions necessary to have his name put forward: He was "neutral" and a Republican.

This is exactly what happened. At age thirty-two, Nelson Rockefeller was hoisted into the political machinery of the Roosevelt government. The Office for Coordination of Commercial and Cultural Relations between the Americas was created on August 16, 1940, and its direction was assigned to the young millionaire. In the following year, as we will see, the agency would change its name to the Office of the Coordinator of Inter-American Affairs (OCIAA), which clearly reflects the increase in Rockefeller's authority: from an office of *coordination*, it was changed to the office of the *coordinator*.

The newly created office encountered serious obstacles. The most serious of them came from inside the State Department. Undersecretary Sumner Welles, known for his shrewdness, was certain that the eager magnate would collide mainly with the cultural policies of the Department for Latin American Countries. Welles's predictions materialized, but, as we have seen, Rockefeller's plan was feasible, and the undersecretary ended up accepting Rockefeller's presence within the State Department bureaucracy. The Rockefeller Junta moved to Washington.

The routine to organize the OCIAA was intense and demanding from the start, as might be expected of a Protestant for whom work was an article of faith. Rockefeller and his family's day began as in his childhood, with the difference that now he was seated at the head of the table. He woke up at 6:00 A.M. and engaged in some kind of physical exercise, which, at times, included a tennis match with Henry Wallace, Roosevelt's "leftist" vice president. Afterwards, he had breakfast with his children. After a brief prayer, he read the news to his family, thus substituting the daily newspapers for the Bible.[10]

The OCIAA's offices were located in the same building as the Department of Commerce, headed by Harry Hopkins. There Rockefeller installed his general headquarters. The word "headquarters" may seem exaggerated, but in this case it came close to reality. The Rockefeller Foundation's semimilitary organization shaped the office commanded by Rockefeller. He was the center, and he did not allow anyone to diminish his leadership. When it happened, the young Rockefeller, conscious of his power and backed by one of the biggest fortunes on the planet, mobilized all his resources to control his potential opponent. The apparently democratic organization of the OCIAA's meetings was actually controlled solely by Rockefeller in an almost authoritarian fashion.

The Office for Coordination of Commercial and Cultural Relations between the Americas was composed of three divisions: the Commercial and Financial Division; the Division of Communications; and the Division of Cultural Relations. Political and economic objectives were at the heart of the office's agenda regarding a "hemispheric economic policy." However, to reach this objective, cultural activities and communication received highest priority.

From the beginning, Rockefeller hoped that, with financial aid, he could politically stabilize the region south of the Rio Grande. Without a doubt, he was involved in the fight against the Nazi expansion, but the political vision of the entrepreneur prevailed: he wanted to bar from Latin America German products that competed with American products. Simultaneously, socialist proposals that pointed out the capital-labor antagonism could be fought with the propaganda of the American model: consumption of wonderful products, material progress, and good salaries.[11] The industrialization of the subcontinent would, therefore, have to be stimulated and linked with the intensification of trade relations. In order to expedite these relations, the implementation of a communications network was deemed necessary.

When France was invaded by the Nazis, the English blockaded the European continent. Consequently, an important market for Brazil and other Ibero-American countries disappeared. Initially, the United States alone was not able to absorb Brazilian exports. The men of the office foresaw an economic collapse that would transform the whole subcontinent into a fertile field for the germination of Nazism, which represented itself as opposed to liberal capitalism. Faced with this scenario, President Roosevelt gave Nelson Aldrich Rockefeller a "blank check."

On September 27, 1940, the president of the United States sent a letter to the National Defense Council, stating the following:

> Because markets for forty percent of the normal exports of Latin America have been lost due to the war, there is grave danger that in some of these countries economic and political deterioration may proceed to a point where defense of the western hemisphere would be rendered much more difficult and costly.
>
> In the interest of hemispheric solidarity and as good neighbors the United States Government must do what it reasonably can to prevent any such development.
>
> One thing we can do is to give sympathetic consideration to Latin American products in the procurement of strategic and critical materials for the defense program. Among such products may be mentioned hides, wool, nitrates, manganese, tin and numerous other commodities.
>
> When buying in foreign markets for defense needs, it is my earnest desire that priority of consideration be given to Latin American products and I so request.[12]

Latin America would be incorporated into the U.S. market, offering the immense potential of its natural resources and contributing to the construction of the powerful war machine that was part of the still not very explicit plans of Roosevelt's government. Unemployment would disappear

THE SEDUCTION OF BRAZIL

from Latin American countries and, with it, the opportunities for Nazis and socialists to spread their ideas.

In the months following the creation of the OCIAA, many projects in the economic realm were in progress. One year after its formation, the coordinator wrote to Vice President Wallace stating that all the energy of the group had been spent in the construction of solid economic relations between the north and the south of the American continent. The flow of trade between the United States and Latin America had grown noticeably. In this short period, Eximbank (Export-Import Bank) loans to Latin American countries had jumped by more than $200 million to $700 million. U.S. strategists began to stockpile Latin American products. After the Japanese attacked Pearl Harbor and the United States joined the war against the Axis, the range of products bought from Latin America increased. Brazilian rubber and quartz acquired a vital role in the continent's defense.

In the area of cultural relations, a lot of work remained to be done. Culture and propaganda began to be accepted as equally strategic. Social and political stability would be the best defense for the whole continent. Germanism would have to be fought by increasing Latin American markets.

Nelson Rockefeller had powerful allies in the Roosevelt administration who helped him realize his ambitious project. One of the most important was Henry Wallace. A passionate proponent of the New Deal, Wallace was Roosevelt's first secretary of agriculture, and, later, as vice president, he defended, almost religiously, the idea that the Americas could be united through agriculture, especially through corn, the American cereal par excellence.[13] According to him, corn "culture" would win out over other cultures that were strangers to American reality. Thanks to the connections Rockefeller cultivated, he often came out on top against those who opposed his project. This was the case in the conflict between Rockefeller's office and other information agencies of the Roosevelt government.

Communication and Information

Rockefeller's information service disclosed in a 1941 report that several American businesses were represented in Latin America by Germans and/or Nazi sympathizers. Ironically, these representatives used advertising and propaganda by their companies to disseminate, though veiled, anti-American messages. Rockefeller believed that the future of these enterprises in Latin America depended not only on the sale of American products, but also on the dissemination of the "American way of life." He was, therefore, conscious that success in the economy had to be rooted in a solid ideological base. Thus, for Rockefeller communications included the intelligence service. Rockefeller's friendship with J. Edgar Hoover, the feared head of the FBI, was not an accident.

All means necessary would be used to consolidate the image of the model to be followed, which meant that U.S. liberalism and democracy would have to be a paradigm. The formula, even though inadequate for countries with an Ibero-American foundation, needed to be made attractive to Latin American cultures with different roots.

The press and propaganda were important means of disseminating the principles of Americanism, which were reelaborated and presented in a more acceptable way. The Press and Publication Division was the spine of the OCIAA, which, together with the Divisions of Radio, Cinema and Information and Propaganda, among others, formed the Division (or Department) of Communications. It had two objectives: (1) to disseminate positive "information" about the United States by means of a communications network maintained by the OCIAA in close collaboration with the countries of the continent; and (2) to counterattack Axis propaganda. It also wished to propagate in the United States a favorable image of the "other Republics."

Theoretically, Rockefeller's projects had to be approved by Secretary of State Cordell Hull. In practice, however, Rockefeller enjoyed enormous autonomy. His advisors often traveled without the knowledge of the State Department, creating friction with career diplomats.

With headquarters in New York and Washington, the Press and Publication Division was led by John M. Clark of the *Washington Post*. He was succeeded by Francis A. Jamieson of the Associated Press. Everyone came from the world of big American newspapers and news agencies. The professionals in this area had to counterattack the German propaganda service, represented in Latin America by the German Transoceanic Agency, which supplied news and photographs at low prices.

High-ranking employees of the office never used the word "propaganda" in documents prepared for distribution. The United States differentiated itself in this way from Nazi Germany. The Nazi government not only made constant use of the word, but its famous Reich Ministry for Public Enlightenment and Propaganda was one of its more important organisms.

The propagandistic strategy of the office included the publication of brochures, pamphlets, and magazines. The most widely distributed among these was *On Guard*, a magazine in the style of *Life* magazine, published in Portuguese, Spanish, and English. Initially (at the end of 1940), the publication was called *On the March*, but Cordell Hull, being more in tune with diplomatic relations, vetoed the name as being excessively aggressive. The name *On Guard*, on the other hand, suggested defense rather than attack.

The magazine propagated an image of the United States as the fortress of continental democracy, a stronghold from which the countries of the American continent could request support whenever necessary. The subjects of the news articles varied: the production of war matériel; the excellence of a tank; how to take care of a vegetable garden; the efficiency of the U.S. nursing service; notice of Allied victories, and so on. In 1945, the magazine had reached a monthly circulation of more than 500,000 and was distributed in many Latin American countries.

The Press and Publication Division was one of the biggest in the OCIAA. In the United States alone, it had about two hundred full-time employees. Among them were some Brazilians, such as Orígenes Lessa, Marcelino de Carvalho, Raimundo Magalhães, and Carlos Cavalcante. They performed almost all tasks, from sending photos to Brazil's biggest newspapers, to helping distribute official documents, speeches, and pamphlets. There were more than fifteen million copies of "Why We Bear Arms," a speech delivered by Roosevelt when the United States joined the Allied Forces in World War II, and more than two million copies of illustrated booklets such as "The United States in the War" and "True Heroes," which described the performance of U.S. soldiers at the front. For the magazine's marketing and distribution in Brazil, the office enlisted young idealists who wished to be active in the anti-Nazi front.

During the first half of 1942, ads placed by American companies in the Brazilian mass media (radio and newspapers) began to diminish, because the most heavily advertised products, such as tires, refrigerators, and automobiles, practically did not exist in the market anymore. The factories were occupied by production of war matériel. The great Moloch that was the war machine of American democracy was in need of everything that was produced with a voraciousness unparalleled in history.

Nelson Aldrich Rockefeller used all his influence to persuade his partners at Ford, General Electric, and General Motors to continue to invest in advertising, even though there were no products available for sale. From then on, big U.S. companies increased their advertising expenses, from $4 million in the first year of the war, the total surpassed $8 million in 1942, $13.5 million in 1943, $16 million in 1944, and $20 million in 1945.[14]

Even though *Reader's Digest* was not directly part of the Rockefeller project, it played an important role in the dissemination of Americanism in Brazil. The magazine had a worldwide circulation of five million. In Brazil, it was launched as *Seleções* in the first half of 1942, the same year that Coca-Cola and Kibon ("Very Tasty!") ice cream arrived.

The word "Seleções" was written on the cover just above the words "from Reader's Digest." With *Seleções* the Americans hoped to conquer the average urban Brazilian through advertising and articles that celebrated the American way of life. The name of the magazine itself was indicative of its function: a monthly selection of articles from the U.S. press. The main idea, the philosophy of the magazine, was revealed in its subheading: "Articles of Permanent Interest." There was redundancy. Translating: "digest" means a selection of texts but also "digestible." The key was this: selected texts easily assimilated. The magazine's business notice was "Selections from *Reader's Digest*—copyrighted—Published monthly by Reader's Digest Association Incorporated in Pleasantville, New York, U.S.A."

In one of the first issues of *Seleções* published in Brazil, the publishers gave information on the location of the magazine's headquarters. *Reader's Digest*, already famous in the United States, had headquarters in a building constructed in an austere and traditional style of classic red bricks. The house had a bell tower and was located about thirty miles from New York City. Readers could, thus, trust the solidity of its publications. In short, they could trust the "moral image" of the text. It was edited in Portuguese in the United States and printed on paper that guaranteed the quality of the illustrations.

The common enemy, temporarily represented by the Axis, allowed *Seleções* a freedom that we would not see later. "Einstein: An Example of Simplicity" was the title of an article reprinted from *The Nation*, the liberal and leftist American weekly. Articles by John Gunther, the semiofficial historian of the New Deal, and Bertrand Russell could be read, as well as articles reprinted from *Collier's, Esquire, Forbes, Harper's*, the *New York Times Magazine, Fortune*, and *Scientific American*. However, the most popular part of the magazine was the book section. It simplified and condensed novels to make them easier to read, while "keeping the gripping power of narrative," as stated in the introductory section. The popularity of the magazine in Brazil was analyzed on the inside cover of the May 1942 issue: "The readers of *Seleções do Reader's Digest* will certainly have the pleasure of knowing that, upon reaching its third issue, this new magazine already has one of the largest circulations in Brazil. The Brazilians bought more copies of the first issue of *Seleções* than all of Spanish-speaking America collectively bought of *Selecciones*."

Thus, *Reader's Digest* from November 1943 announced "Our export model for 1943" next to a photograph of a machine gun bringing down enemy airplanes. Soon thereafter, another photo showed a housewife using a washing machine, and the text next to it read: "Today military production, washing machines tomorrow."[15] In January of the following year, General Electric guaranteed that "electronics will bring television into our home." Although there were not any goods to consume, the electronic and mechanized future was offered as a beacon of hope in difficult times, a happy, electrified, standardized future.

The system was sold on the symbolic level. In behalf of the Good Neighbor Policy, the companies would have to make the sacrifice of advertising without immediate return. Realpolitik masked marketing under the democratic-liberal image of the fight against Nazi Fascism and totalitarianism. There were both ideological and marketing reasons: "The advertiser reaped multiple advantages, and was motivated not only by the prospect of good future business, but also by patriotism."[16]

A few more examples from *Reader's Digest*: from RCA-Victor, there was a symbolic promise of "forging swords into plowshares." Philco, the world's largest manufacturer of radios, "showed how to work . . . with Brazilian rock crystals for radio with an exactness of 40/1000000 of an inch."

Even the OCIAA advertised its shortwave radio programs in magazines. Westinghouse argued that the war had "its good side . . . [because] out of its ashes marvelous things would rise—things that promise enormous benefits to humanity"—such as electronics, the science that would illuminate the progress of humankind. There was "no reason that we could not produce during peacetime as we did . . . during wartime." This was the promise of Ford Motor Company in an advertisement entitled "When calm returns." Johnson, the producer of outboard motors, temporarily discontinued its leisure-oriented production and went to war. Even Michel lipstick, which offered "eight seductive shades," was "on guard to protect beauty; to protect our hemisphere." Goodyear recommended: "For the victory of Brazil and its allies, do not waste rubber: Stop and start cars slowly."

Nonetheless, the work ethic was the theme of advertising. Westinghouse had an "ad" that said "We work day and night." "I enjoy my work as a foreman at Westinghouse, because it gives me the opportunity to speak with new employees. Many of the recently hired workers think that big companies are impersonal and that by working for one of them they will lose their own individuality." The ad continues by narrating the history of the company, which had started small in 1886, and highlights the spirit of camaraderie among the workers: "We all are working for that day when our hands can return to creating goods for a world without wars." A notice followed: "Readers, tune in to the WBOS stations to hear news about the war."

When Waldo Frank was in Brazil, he had the impression that Brazilians in general were fond of Americans. The Brazilian readership of *Seleções*, surpassing that of the Spanish-speaking countries, seemed to prove Frank's point. The digest character of the culture of *Seleções* was also highlighted by many intellectuals. Afrânio Peixoto found: "I am glad if, in a book or magazine there is a page to capture one's attention, and on a page a sentence. In an issue of *Reader's Digest* there are dozens of these pages."

Rockefeller requested the assistance of George Gallup, the well-known public opinion researcher, to produce the necessary data for the expansion and consolidation of the office. From the United States, Gallup conducted an extensive poll in all of Latin America, and especially in Brazil, to find out about the tastes, the opinions, and the habits of Latin Americans. One objective of these surveys was to ensure that American envoys did not make mistakes when interpreting the cultures of the different countries. The biggest objective was to determine the best vehicle of communication to disseminate a positive image of the United States.

Simultaneously, another survey—tied directly to the previous one—was carried out in the United States to evaluate the attitude of Americans toward Latin America. There was an interest in finding out the opinion of the public in general and the corporations in particular. With the secret cooperation of the FBI, the surveys also tried to get information on the degree of Brazilian preference for the Axis countries and for the United States. Directly linked to this question, the reach of the Brazilian mass media was also analyzed. "Observers" (the quotation marks used in the official document tried to minimize the espionage aspect of the surveys) who worked throughout Brazil had carefully evaluated the editorials of the big newspapers and the number of radio listeners and had bought space in newspapers and on the radio.

The report of these surveys included in its heading the expression "cultural relations," an expression broad enough to cover the exchange of university professors, the development of systems of information, and all the branches of mass communications. However, Rockefeller dedicated special attention to two media: the cinema and radio.

The Motion Picture Division

John Hay Whitney, a refined millionaire friend of Rockefeller, was put in charge of the Motion Picture Division. Known as "Jock" Whitney, he had a curriculum vitae that justified his choice to supervise the division. As one of the entrepreneurs who had financed the lucrative film *Gone with the Wind,* he enjoyed great influence in Hollywood. Rockefeller himself was a shareholder in RKO Pictures. One of the great achievements of the Nelson-Jock duo, as we will see, was to win over artists such as Walt Disney and Carmen Miranda to the cause of "freedom" of the Americas.

Compared with German film production, even taking into account the tradition of cinema during the Weimar Republic, the U.S. film industry was in a privileged situation. Because of the war, German films no longer reached South America, especially after the British blockade. Since American movies had no competition, they reigned absolutely. The OCIAA tried to consolidate the role of movies as a propaganda vehicle for the Allied cause. The Motion Picture Division was considered one of the most important departments of the office. However, in 1944, only forty people worked in its offices in New York, Washington, and California. Nonetheless, this small number of employees accomplished great work, because a large part of the material arrived completed from Hollywood.

The films were divided into two branches: those intended for screening in movie theaters; and the noncommercial films presented in schools, clubs, or outdoors. The nerve center of the division was located in New York City and included three sectors. The Production and Adaptation Section selected films produced by other departments and by Hollywood and adapted them to Portuguese and Spanish. In this section, scripts were also produced. The Short Feature Films Section was responsible for newsreels, documentaries, and cartoons related to the United States' inter-American policies. Even though many of these materials were intended to be shown in Latin American countries, they were also screened in the United States, with the objective of spreading a good image of Latin American countries. And, finally, there was a section that supervised the distribution of the 16-millimeters. The commercial circuit was in charge of the 35-millimeter films.

Noncommercial production was directed at educational institutions, clubs, churches, companies, unions, and rural organizations.[17] For example, *Americans All*, a black-and-white twenty-minute film on the work of the young in each American country, was shown in Brazil, as was *Defense against Invasion*, a Disney animated film in color on the benefits of vaccination. On the other hand, U.S. Americans could see Brazil in an eleven-minute short feature in color of scenes from Rio de Janeiro, the Amazon rain forest, and the port of Santos. They also saw a ten-minute film telling the story of Brazil's fishing school, created by President Vargas. They saw *Brazil Gets News*, a ten-minute film in color explaining the functioning of a big São Paulo newspaper. In addition, they saw films with Carmen Miranda, Charlie Chan, and Bette Davis, commercial Hollywood productions supposedly set in Brazil.

For obvious reasons, the Motion Picture Division had an important branch office in Hollywood, which was responsible for contact with big producers and which assisted the main office in significant ways. It promoted the inclusion of Latin American artists in big studio productions, but mainly it worked on changing the "bandit" image that Hollywood had forced on Latinos, especially the United States' Mexican neighbors. Whenever possible, the division suggested that the big producers research Latin American customs before making their films. This way they would avoid problems of interpretation, and some diplomatic friction, as had been the case with *Down Argentine Way*, Carmen Miranda's first film produced by Darryl Zanuck. In this film, Carmen sings a rumba in Portuguese, and another actor uses castanets. The problem was that the film was set in Argentina, where there are neither rumbas nor castanets.[18]

For these and other reasons, Nelson Rockefeller sent Jock Whitney on a reconnaissance trip through Latin America. In August 1941, Whitney, who had traveled with Walt Disney, sent a report to Rockefeller from Rio de Janeiro:

> The trip thus far seems very successful and certainly justified. Everything we have been trying to do for these months falls into plan and perspective when the frame is put in place. . . .
>
> The people of Rio are friendly and hospitable and also thoroughly critical. You feel that they want you to like them and to like you, and if it doesn't work out, that's your fault, which it is. . . .
>
> Walt Disney is far more successful as an enterprise and as a person than we could have dreamed. His public demeanor is flawless. He is unruffled by adulation and pressure—just signs every autograph and keeps smiling.[19]

From Brazil, Whitney suggested that Latin American subjects would have to appear more frequently in Hollywood productions. And the use of artificial scenery of known places such as Christ the Redeemer on Corcovado, Sugar Loaf, and Copacabana in Rio de Janeiro had to be avoided.

Artists began to arrive in Brazil and other Latin American countries. In Hollywood, a group was organized to help the Latin American cinema. It was formed by committees of artists and representatives of the Academy of Motion Picture Arts and Sciences. In April 1941, Douglas Fairbanks, Jr., who had been fighting isolationism since 1939, became one of Roosevelt's closest allies and was invited by Roosevelt and Sumner Welles to go on a trip to Latin America. The official objective of this trip was to research the situation of the American cinema, but in reality it was to verify the relationship between the nationalistic tendencies of some Latin American governments and Nazism.[20] Fairbanks was received enthusiastically in Rio de Janeiro. According to him, Alzira Vargas, President Vargas's daughter, taught him to dance the samba at a party.[21]

RESPONSIBILITY FOR THE Motion Picture Division's operations was under the Film Library, Inc., of the Museum of Modern Art in New York, not coincidentally Rockefeller's territory. It was in the museum that the films were completed, that is, turned into a political and culturally correct version for Latinos.

The functions of the Motion Picture Division were very clear: to promote the U.S. production of short and long features as well as newsreels about the United States and the other Americas; to distribute them to the whole Western Hemisphere, that is, to all the Americas; to produce and stimulate the production of short feature films and newsreels in Latin American countries that could be shown in the United States in order to counterattack the films produced by the Axis; and to convince the big movie companies that it was not good policy to distribute films that conveyed a bad impression or compromised the U.S. image. Nothing should be shown that resembled *The Grapes of Wrath*, the John Ford film in which Tom Joad, the main character, and family leave the depressed dust bowl of Oklahoma to live in the slums of California, where he is exploited in degrading work. A short time after directing *The Grapes of Wrath,* Ford himself joined the crusade of moral recovery led by Roosevelt and Rockefeller and came to Brazil to film the Brazilian war effort.

The connection between Rockefeller's office and Hollywood was mediated by the Motion Picture Society for the Americas, a nonprofit organization created in March 1941 and directed by Walter Wanger, an important Hollywood producer: special treatment for a special moment. The office did not need to spend much money on production of the films, thanks to Rockefeller's and, mainly, John Hay Whitney's connections to big movie moguls. The patriotism of the film industry in helping the fight against the Axis was also a chance to make fantastic profits.[22] The European market was closed, and only the Latin American market remained. Walt Disney's well-known films sold notably well. Darryl Zanuck, in tune with the Good Neighbor Policy, produced Carmen Miranda's films, which helped 20th Century Fox get out of the red.[23] In spite of this, Disney complained that many of his contributions to the war effort, such as short films on the training of soldiers or tax payment (this one featuring Donald Duck and friends), did not provide enough return. Disney even had a legal dispute with Henry Morgenthau, the U.S. secretary of the treasury.[24]

There was a "solidarity" that diminished the cost of production. In a general way, this solidarity, when it came from artists' and musicians' unions, had a less-self-interested character. This was the case of the American Federation of Musicians and the American Society of Composers, Authors and Publishers, which declined royalties on behalf of the war effort. RCA also cooperated and granted rights to some music used in sound tracks of documentaries, short feature films, and newsreels.[25]

The graph below was published by the Motion Picture Division in 1944. By comparing the United States with Latin America, the audience growth for 16-millimeter films shown in public schools and institutions can be seen. In August of 1943, 113 projectors and 69 trucks with projectors were made available in the United States.

Beyond Hollywood, other sectors contributed to the production of films, mainly newsreels. This was the case of United Steel Export Corporation, Bell Aircraft, the Greyhound Bus Company, American Can Company, and Aluminum Corporation of America. Other departments of the U.S. government, such as the Department of Public Health, also contributed to the production of short feature films, which supplied important data on combating tropical diseases.

The production of newsreels by the Motion Picture Division became as important as the production of fiction films. Until the United States joined the Allies in the war against the Nazis, German newsreels, even though they were not numerous, always showed Germany as a military and moral model. The German army was presented as unbeatable in its advance in Eastern Europe. This success was attributed to the discipline of the troops and the organization of the new German state. Until then, U.S. newsreels had shown only picturesque things or negative occurrences (such as murders or

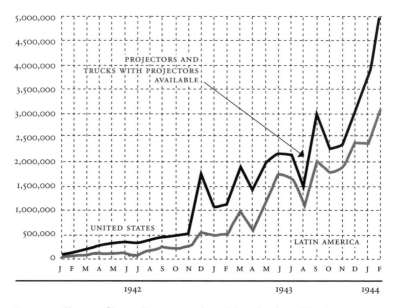

Sixteen-millimeter film audience growth, public schools and institutions

THE SEDUCTION OF BRAZIL

disasters), which did not contribute to the formation of a positive image of the United States. By creating the Newsreel Section in 1941, the Motion Picture Division had already begun to work intensively to change this image.

Documentaries such as *Brazilian Quartz Goes to War*, in 1943,[26] were presented to the American public to show Latin American countries' cooperation in the war effort. Brazil was presented as an important mineral supplier, indispensable in the production of radios for the planes and ships that were fighting in defense of democracy and Western civilization. Paramount News and United News made an agreement to produce newsreels. A chain of movie theaters agreed to show newsreels that dealt with subjects related to Latin American countries. In various newsreels, the progress in inter-American relations accomplished by the OCIAA was shown, from the arrival of Nelson Rockefeller in Rio de Janeiro in September of 1942 and his meeting with Getúlio Vargas, to the landing of the first contingent of the Força Expedicionária Brasileira in Italy.[27]

The educational short feature films produced by Walt Disney became very popular. One of them on malaria,[28] for example, opens with the bald eagle, the symbol of the United States, followed by the credits "A Walt Disney production—Filmed under the auspices of the OCIAA." To capture the attention of the spectator, the sound track is similar to that of a thriller, an indispensable element of film narrative. It focuses on a pole with a poster: "Wanted . . . dead or alive—public enemy number 1," which appears in most Westerns. The wanted figure pictured from the front and in profile is the mosquito, transmitter of malaria. An off-camera voice enumerates the dangers of the disease. The camera follows the mosquito, which flies to an obviously very poor mud and wood shack. The mosquito enters through one of the many holes in the walls of the house, lands on a bed, and bites a man of undefined "nationality," but certainly a Latin American. He could be an inhabitant of Paraguay, of the slums of Rio de Janeiro, or of a *palafita*, a stilt house in the Amazon rain forest.

The strange thing is that, didactically, the spectator in a way feels sorry for the mosquito and not for the man. In a well-constructed way, the narrator demonstrates that the mosquito is not infected, but the man is. The victim then becomes the mosquito, the executioner. The focus is the sucked blood "deposit" inside the mosquito.

With the same technique developed for Disney's animated film *Fantasia*, the Disney insect beats its wings in time with the allegro of the violins and flies over swamps until arriving at the house of a prosperous farm. The house, constructed in the colonial style of the American South, is inhabited by healthier people. A man, who seems to be the owner, is sitting in a rocking chair on the veranda and, according to the narrator, is enjoying the peace and quiet. The mosquito bites the arm of this honored citizen, infecting him with malaria: good blood infected by bad blood. Soon after the mosquito bites the man, everything around the house deteriorates: the plants, animals, and later, the house itself. Everything looks abandoned.

Faced with such misfortune, the narrator asks the audience for help. The film is being shown in a movie theater in some lost town in Latin America. Out of the hypothetical audience come seven volunteers to help the unfortunate man. The shadows of the volunteers that appear on the wall are familiar. They are none other than the imaginary Seven Dwarves from the also imaginary *Snow White*. Collective work for the collective good brings immediate results to the individual. Only with great effort does the spectator not abandon his or her armchair—or, in this case, chair or bench (because the films were shown only in popular public places) to help the untiring group of hard-working dwarves.

First, it is necessary to learn how the mosquito larva is reproduced. Walt Disney was a brilliant master of didacticism. Everything is very well explained: still waters first; draining of swamps; later, cleansing of wells, etc., etc., etc. "Okay, boys, now we can start the fight!" says the off-camera voice. The sound track is a military bugle sounding the charge: the battle will begin. The seriousness and the difficulty of the task are lightened by the familiar confusion created by the Seven Dwarves, especially the long-eared Sleepy and the other goofy one, whose name is lost in my remote childhood memory. They do everything. With the aid of the famous birds (I suspect that they are the same ones that helped Snow White and Cinderella get dressed to wait for their respective magic princes), they nail screens on windows to protect themselves from future enemies. In the place of the dilapidated farm, a new and vigorous property is born.

The war effort created an imaginary world divided into two parts: the good and the evil, that is, light and dark. Disney's educational cartoon follows the same pattern shown in the first film of the series, *Why We Fight*, by Frank Capra, where part of the world is illuminated by the sun of democracy and another part is kept in darkness by totalitarian regimes. We assume that the mosquito is part of the dark world, a kind of fifth column that has infiltrated the weak part of the infected new and bright word.

Of all the films planned for commercial distribution, *It's All True*, by Orson Welles, was the most controversial and highly anticipated. It would be a Pan-American saga: from the jazz of Duke Ellington to Jacaré, a *jangadeiro* (fisherman who used a raft) from Ceará. The adventures and misadventures of Welles in Brazil have been sufficiently explored and investigated already. It is worth remembering that the Motion Picture Division intended to produce a long feature film about Latin America, and Welles had a project at the ready. When John Hay Whitney was in Brazil, Lourival Fontes, then DIP manager, introduced the idea of producing a film on Carnaval, Brazil's biggest party. There was, therefore, a favorable confluence of factors for accomplishing the project.

Welles was already well known for the radio adaptation of H. G. Wells's *The War of the Worlds*, about the Martian invasion of Earth; the film *Citizen Kane*; and his theatrical production of Shakespeare. He was famous but was something of a pariah in Hollywood and an outsider, as he himself saw it. Critics regarded him as a genius, but he was misunderstood by the mass movie-going audience. There was a certain tension between him and RKO, the movie production company in which Rockefeller owned shares. However, when the gentlemen of the office called Welles to Washington, he was not yet considered an outsider, either by the studio owners or by Whitney, the head of the Motion Picture Division. The idea of a film about Carnaval was reborn and coincided with the expectations of the OCIAA and of Lourival Fontes.

Welles arrived in Brazil before Carnaval in 1942 as one of the ambassadors of Pan-Americanism. He began preparations for filming and decided to familiarize himself with Brazil on all its levels. Simultaneously with the disrupted production of the film, Welles gave lectures, organized a party in honor of President Vargas's birthday, and flirted with as many Brazilian women as possible. He went to Minas Gerais State and filmed in Ouro Preto. In Ceará, he filmed the daily life of a fishing village. The death of the jangadeiro leader Jacaré during the shooting of the documentary, who disappeared in the sea on arrival in Rio de Janeiro, complicated Welles's stay in Brazil.

The failure of one of his films, *The Magnificent Ambersons*, which was being shown in the United States, and the change in direction of RKO had left Welles without allies in the studio.[29] In addition, his situation in Rio de Janeiro was not very comfortable. The Motion Picture Division did not agree to his expenses, considered excessive, including indemnity payments made to the family of Jacaré: "As a matter of fact both Jacaré and his family were more than generously paid for all that they did. Mr. Welles paid Jacaré an almost fantastic salary during the filming of the picture, and after his death the family received about $2,000 in insurance. When it is considered that Jacaré in his life time probably never earned more than $10 per month, it is evident this payment was a very liberal indemnity."[30]

Welles was no longer celebrated by the Brazilian press, particularly the papers in the Northeast, which implied that he was responsible for the death of the jangadeiro Jacaré. His behavior in Rio de Janeiro was not considered that of a good neighbor because he was loud and even arrogant. Five months after arriving in Brazil, Orson Welles returned to the United States.

By 1942, one could see in Brazilian movie theaters Walt Disney's film *Saludos Amigos*, with the title in Spanish. Later on, the title was changed to an Americanized version, *Alô Amigos*, in spite of Noel Rosa's criticism, mentioned earlier. Disney made a profit and collaborated with the philosophy of the Good Neighbor Policy, propagating continental solidarity.

And Welles? He fought to save *It's All True*, which he never released. Today only fragments of the film remain, which can be seen in an excellent documentary about Orson Welles's lost three-part South American film. The aesthetics and production values of *It's All True* commendably contrast with the conventional Hollywood approach regarding race and Latin Americans. According to Ella Shohat and Robert Stam:[31] "Rather than displaying North American stars against 'exotic' backdrops, the usual practice in Hollywood films set in Latin America, *It's All True* was designed to promote local talent, much of it black: well-known carnival orchestras like Chiquinho, Fon-Fon, and Dedé; Brazilian composers and instrumentalists such as Pixinguinha, the composer of 'Carinhoso.' The key performer was to be the brilliant black actor Sebastião Prata (also known as 'Grande Otelo,' the future lead in *Macunaíma*, 1969), whose role would be to 'personalize' the carnival sequence." Welles continued collaborating with the war effort in a radio program called *Alô! América*. He interviewed Oswaldo Aranha, the Brazilian minister of foreign affairs, and produced a small show with Carmen Miranda.

Some films produced by Rockefeller's office, in cooperation with the Office of Strategic Services (OSS), the Office of War Information (OWI), and the Signal Corps, were intended for internal consumption. They were called staff film reports; that is, they circulated among employees who had come to work in Brazil. This was the case of *Brazil*, a film from 1945.[32] The film shows Jefferson Caffery, still in the embassy, Vargas with officers, medical services, the coffee harvest, the shipment of iron ore, American airplanes taking off from the Northeastern bases, rubber, and mining. This was information that interested the U.S. Secret Service.

But in 1945, the Office of Inter-American Affairs was no longer the same. Rockefeller occupied another position in the government. Jefferson Caffery was no longer ambassador; and the United States no longer had the same interest in Brazil.

The Radio Division

Although theoretically subordinated to the Department of Communications, the Radio Division—similar to the Motion Picture Division—enjoyed great autonomy. Initially, it was located in New York, but later it was transferred to Washington, D.C. The Radio Division did not produce programs directly, but it ordered them from different studios, many of them located in Manhattan. The Radio Division was directed by Don Francisco, a public relations professional. The objective of the Radio Division was defined by Don Francisco himself in a document sent to the coordinator's office and dated June 5, 1942: "Radio helps to create a dynamic public opinion in the Western hemisphere, continuously supporting the war effort of the American republics. Public opinion thus informed, will not accept or tolerate propaganda of the Axis aimed at the Americas."[33]

Until the beginning of World War II, the big radio stations had never bothered to expand their activities in Latin America, because there were no prospects for substantial profits. European radio stations, especially in the Axis countries, took advantage of this gap left by the Americans. In 1939, Radio Berlin broadcast varied programming in shortwave, from an "Entertaining Concert" at noon, to "Greetings to Our Listeners" at 10:50 P.M., to "Helma Panke Sings German Songs" at midnight. Soon thereafter, a Brazilian orchestra concert was broadcast, under the direction of Maestro Spartaco Rossi, with pieces by Brazilian composers such as Nepomuceno, Mignone, and Carlos Gomes, interpreted by soloist Christina Maristany. All of Radio Berlin's programming was sprinkled with economic and political updates. At 11:30 P.M. it aired the latest news and reports from Germany in Portuguese, and at 2:00 A.M., the same program in German.[34]

With a more ideological objective (they did not aim at immediate, material results, as American radio stations did), the German and Italian stations had specific programming for Brazil. The signals emitted from Berlin and Rome were much more powerful than those from the United States. Additionally, in these totalitarian regimes, the media were under the authority of the government, which used them for political ends, while in the United States the radio stations were independent and belonged to the arena of free enterprise, with commercial objectives. Therefore, it was more difficult to reach consensus.

The Germans continued aiming at Latin America, especially Brazil, with Radio Berlin shortwaves. About one million Germans or their descendants resided in Brazil's southern states. The airwaves would be the first battlefield on which Americans and Germans would have to match forces. Therefore, Rockefeller devoted special attention to the radio as a communications and propaganda medium. The Radio Division was Rockefeller's favorite area. His accurate reasoning was that radio could reach a wider audience from all social classes. Consequently, he sent Don Francisco to travel in Latin America to evaluate the conditions for starting up a broadcasting program.

The big American communications industries would have to serve the interests of combating ideologies contrary to liberalism. Thus, Brazil was an important target to be reached via American broadcasting's shortwaves. In reference to radio, Rockefeller also used his position to achieve his objectives. Powerful NBC had its studios in Rockefeller Center, which facilitated negotiations with the OCIAA. Although the connections Rockefeller had with NBC were significant, CBS was the first network to offer the radio sector for the Good Neighbor Policy. As we will see, the company's president, William Paley, traveled to Latin America and received an enthusiastic official welcome in Brazil.

Rockefeller's first suggestion—which revealed his expansive personality, and also his faith in the power of mass communications as a political weapon—was the distribution of extremely cheap radios throughout Latin America. Technical problems hindered the execution of the plan. Additionally, there was the objective of convincing Latin American countries that the genuine intention of the United States in Latin America was to create and not to exploit. Unable to influence the production of radios, Rockefeller concentrated on the task of making the broadcasting of the programs more efficient. In this he had the cooperation of the big broadcasting companies, which had lowered the prices of their services by approximately 50 percent. An NBC executive declared: "We have priced [our shortwave] service at about half what it actually costs us to operate, because we are trying to make a definite contribution to the public service of this country in the important field of foreign public relations. . . . Since the Axis success in Europe, another very important factor has entered the picture. It is the growing conviction of government officials and advisors, and of business leaders in this country that the country can be served in a very important way by broadcasting to Latin America in the interest of hemispheric solidarity."[35]

NBC was directed by David Sarnoff, one of the best examples of a self-made man, who, like other businessmen, did everything to keep his companies lucrative and had a mild influence on the Good Neighbor Policy and its radio programs. The "dictator" of American radio needed to bow before the new reality. Confronted with the German threat, U.S. entrepreneurs had become aware that, temporarily, they needed to abandon individualistic attitudes to confront Nazi expansion. To convince Latin Americans that the interest of the United States was *to create* and not *to exploit,* even a "hard-liner" like Sarnoff had to show his "soft" side in order not to perpetuate the image of the United States as arrogant.

The "radio-journal" was the first form of approved programming to receive funding: $50,000 in April 1941 for daily radio news transmission to all Latin American countries. The first editions of this news journal were produced in partnership with CBS, retransmitted by American Telephone & Telegraph, and distributed by International Telephone & Telegraph to local stations in Latin America. As we have seen, in order to fight Axis radio programming, U.S. communications corporations chose to collaborate instead of competing with each other.

In a CBS document dated June 5, 1940, the company announced the appointment of Luís Jatobá, "the reputed number one radio announcer of Brazil."[36] Jatobá was one of many Brazilians who had been working in the United States, and, as one of Brazil's most famous voices, he had been participating in the war effort.

Rockefeller's familiarity with the big entrepreneurs facilitated the formation of this "alliance" between NBC and CBS, the two big rivals in the United States. The alliance was valid only for shortwave transmissions in Latin America. Some newspapers and magazines, among them *Seleções* and *On Guard*, published the schedule of all the programming. The Brazilian radio stations all transmitted the programming sent from the United States: *Cruzeiro do Sul, Mayrink Veiga,* and *Tupi* in Rio de Janeiro; *Record, Cruzeiro do Sul, Cosmos, Cultura,* and *Tupi* in São Paulo; *Farroupilha* in Porto Alegre; *Rádio Club de Pernambuco* in Recife; and *Pampulha* in Belo Horizonte. In *Hora do Brasil*—one hour of official Brazilian government broadcasting, mandatory for all radio stations across the country—five minutes were yielded to the OCIAA, which transmitted from New York. On the normal airwaves, Brazilians also heard daily commentaries from Júlio Barata, who spent a short period in the United States, or Raimundo Magalhães, a high-ranking DIP employee who had been on loan to the Office of the Coordinator of Inter-American Affairs.

On Saturday afternoons, the *Magazine no Ar* presented a "variety program with the participation of celebrities, great orchestras, activities for women, interviews with Hollywood stars, news updates." It included a hit parade, military bands, and the Harry James orchestra.[37] Brazilian listeners also tuned in to programs such as *The United Nations Speaks, We Are at War,* or *The Americas at War, The March of Time,* and *Believe It or Not,* by Bob Ripley. In large part, the programs emphasized the potential of Americans to resist the advance of the Axis, both materially and morally. Other programs took it on themselves to disseminate among Latin Americans the American way of life, relying most on music and film. The scripts were produced by CBS, NBC, and other companies subcontracted for this project, but the authorization to air a program still remained with the Office of the Coordinator.[38]

The programs produced in the United States were sent to Brazil in different ways: direct transmissions via powerful stations located in the United States could be heard by listeners with adequate devices; retransmissions by local stations affiliated with CBS or NBC; delivery of scripts from the office's production centers to be used by Brazilian stations; programs produced locally under the office's supervision.

One of the important functions of the Radio Division was the transmission of news at regular intervals. A section of journalists in the Press and Publication Division handled the news production, utilizing announcers who spoke Spanish and Portuguese. The contracts between the two big radio networks and the OCIAA allowed the stations to adapt the scripts.

The relationship between the companies and the office was not free of friction. There was the fear of state interference curtailing freedom of information. If the office was directly involved in the production of programming to be sent to Latin America, the same did not occur with the work to be developed in the United States. In order not to collide with the principles of liberalism, Rockefeller would only make suggestions about the topics to be covered. The commercial broadcasting companies were in charge of developing the programming.[39]

The principles of the Good Neighbor Policy had been adapted to the commercial programming of the big American broadcasting companies. A symbolic union between Rudy Vallee, the American showman on NBC, and the Brazilian performer Carmen Miranda, who "got married" in a humorous sketch, was aired in May 1941. The performance ended with both of them saying: "Our two countries could have better relations after our marriage." The show was called the *Royal Gelatin Program*.

Continental Integration: Transportation, Education, Culture, Raw Materials

The communications concept was so tied to the market that it was not restricted to the media. Transportation by air, railroad, river, sea, and road had been analyzed by the OCIAA's specialists, who had concluded that, for the continental war effort, the Brazilian transportation system was extremely precarious. Different studies and proposals resulted from these analyses. Some of these studies seemed excessively ambitious for the standards of nonindustrialized nations. This was the case of a proposal for a waterway that would link Manaus to Montevideo.

When Nelson Rockefeller was in Brazil in September 1942, the agenda of the visit included, evidently, a meeting with Vargas.[40] In this meeting, he discussed with the president, among other things, the possibility of the construction of a system of canals to link the Amazon with the coasts of Colombia and Venezuela that would bypass the sea. According to Rockefeller, the project was necessary to prevent German submarines from sinking ships carrying products being exported or imported by Brazil. The skillful

American undersecretary, Sumner Welles, suggested that Rockefeller abandon the project because it did not serve the emerging U.S. interests in the war. It became apparent that the project would serve mainly Creole, the Venezuelan petroleum company, a subsidiary of Standard Oil. The plan was abandoned as the Atlantic became free of German submarines.

For strategic reasons, it was aviation that worried the OCIAA men the most. A symbolic manifestation of this was the formation of the Inter-American Squadron. On March 5, 1941, a squadron of different types of planes left Washington for various Latin American capitals. The U.S. pilots were received as winged gods. Their leather jackets and Ray-Bans exerted a powerful fascination. They seemed to have stepped out of movie screens, which were already showing some war films. Poet Mauro Mota in a poem, "Boletim sentimental da guerra no Recife,"[41] very well describes this fascination with certain gadgets used by the pilots:

E os presentes? Os presentes eram nossa tentação	And the gifts? The gifts were our temptation
. . .	. . .
verdes óculos Ray-Ban.	green Ray-Ban sunglasses.

Some people from the Latin American countries visited were chosen to be sent to the United States for technical training. This was the case of Dr. Paulo Sampaio, who spent a year in the United States, accompanied by his wife. On his return to Brazil, he became the president of Panair of Brazil, a subsidiary of Pan American. It is known that VARIG, VASP (both associated with Condor, a subsidiary of Lufthansa, a powerful German government company), and LATI (Linee Aeree Transcontinentali Italiane) dominated a big part of Brazilian air transportation. The control of Brazilian air routes, until Brazil entered the war, was an important issue in the battle between the Americans and the Axis.[42] Thanks to the performance of the information services of the OCIAA, the State Department, Pan American, and the Brazilian government itself, the two companies linked to the Axis (Condor and LATI) were eliminated, and Brazil's skies were liberated for U.S. airlines.

The integration would have to be complemented in the technical-scientific area. Prof. Robert Caldwell, director of the College of Humanities of the Massachusetts Institute of Technology, was put in charge of the Culture Division, or Science and Education Division. In close participation with the State Department, there were many exchanges of students and professors. For example, on October 23, 1941, Nelson Rockefeller announced today the establishment of the Inter-American Trade Scholarship program under which qualified young men from the other American republics will be brought to the United States for vocational training.

Trainees brought to this country under the plan will be assigned to representative United States concerns engaged in technical, engineering, scientific, economic, commercial, industrial or agricultural pursuits. They must be citizens of the American republics, at least 18 and not over 28 years of age, should have a technical background or special aptitude in the fields they intend to study and a working knowledge of the English language. Scholarships will be awarded on a merit basis, and selection will be made with regard to vacancies or opportunities for training in particular concerns in the United States.[43]

In September of the following year, the Science and Education Division asked for $350,000 to be allocated to a vocational training program in Latin America. Of this total, more than a third was allocated to young Brazilians who would go to the United States and be trained in naval construction and manufacture of steel, armaments, and planes.[44]

Expeditions of archaeologists and the founding of English schools were part of the educational program. By expanding the teaching of English, especially by making it part of the official curriculum, the main intention was to fight the strong Italian and, above all, German presence in the southern states. The União Cultural Brasil–Estados Unidos (Brazil–United States Cultural Union), created in 1938 in cooperation with the office, played an important role in activities related to cultural exchange between the two countries.

However, there was a broader interest related to the interchange of technicians between Brazil and the United States. When geologists arrived in Brazil, they were to examine the soil and evaluate the potential of Brazil's natural resources. Strategic materials were vital to feed American industry. In September 1941, the OCIAA, together with the Board of Economic Warfare (BEW), the organism that coordinated the war economy, under the vice president, completed an important project: mapping the possible sources of materials considered vital for U.S. and continental security. The project was called the Agricultural and Mineral Technical Advisory Service.

When the United States entered the war in December 1941, seventeen of the twenty technicians who were working in the agriculture sector specialized in rubber. The Amazon area was the main target of this "army" of specialists: fourteen mineral technicians came to Brazil. Anthropologists, among them Charles Wagley, studied the indigenous population.

At the end of 1941, a group of specialists was sent to the Amazon basin in cooperation with the Brazilian government to analyze the health conditions

THE SEDUCTION OF BRAZIL

of the *caboclos*, that is, the hinterlands' population, and to determine the best way to fight tropical diseases and malnutrition. The mission of the other members of the group was to begin prospecting for strategic minerals. The extracted natural rubber of *seringueiras*, that is, rubber plants, one of the most essential raw materials for the war—the "sinew of the war"— was found in the Amazon rain forest. The importance of rubber was such that a specific entity, the Rubber Development Corporation, substituted for the BEW. Its objective was "to concentrate all activities of the Rubber Program."[45] Rockefeller ended up being removed from the rubber program because of his aggressiveness in negotiations with the Brazilians.

In reality, it was not only in reference to rubber that the eager young millionaire had problems. The complicated Roosevelt administration, replete with agencies created to act in the most diverse areas, was characterized by internal disagreement. The Rockefeller office had become known as one of the central areas of conflict, which almost always needed to be resolved by the president's personal intervention.

Trimming the Edges: Conflicts Provoked by the Rockefeller Office

Rockefeller had been in conflict with the Department of State since the creation of the OCIAA. I have already mentioned the resistance of Sumner Welles to the OCIAA's creation. Welles exerted strong pressure to make Rockefeller break the contract with the research companies linked to Gallup. From the diplomat's point of view, the objectives of the research were excessively commercial. Therefore, until the dissolution of the OCIAA, special sections were created for analysis and propaganda, which published daily bulletins such as the *Daily Information Bulletin,* and secret documents for the army, navy, FBI, and State Department intelligence services.

Rockefeller acted with great independence. Often, he did not consult with the State Department. Cordell Hull, the secretary of state, felt disrespected, which, by the way, also marked the relationship between Roosevelt and Hull, as the president did not value the secretary's proposals.[46] Rockefeller's boldness and his initiatives aggravated the Hull situation. The section of the National Archives in Washington that holds the papers of the OCIAA and the Rockefeller Archives in Pocantico Hills, New York, contain many letters between Hull and Rockefeller in which they are trying to minimize their mutual antagonism. The areas where the State Department traditionally acted were "invaded" by Rockefeller's "boys."

This was exactly what happened when John Hay Whitney, head of the office's Motion Picture Division, visited Brazil. In correspondence sent to the United States, he declared that Berent Friele was without a doubt "the most important American in Brazil."[47] And who was Berent Friele? He was a Norwegian American, an expert on Brazil, fluent in Portuguese. He had worked in Brazil since 1917 buying coffee for a U.S. chain of supermarkets. He had close access to key people in Brazil, especially Oswaldo Aranha. Friele was chosen by Rockefeller to be the director of the Brazilian division of the OCIAA. Whitney's statement, in a certain way, meant that the American ambassador in Rio de Janeiro did not have much autonomy of action.

From then on, there was friction between Amb. Jefferson Caffery and the staff of the OCIAA, in particular, with Rockefeller himself when the latter visited Brazil in 1942. During a luncheon given by the embassy for politicians and Brazilian businessmen, Caffery, the "ambassador of revolutions,"[48] prevented Rockefeller from mentioning his Amazon project because it collided directly with Brazilian interests. Rockefeller initiated efforts to get Caffery out of his way, which indeed happened two years later.

Rockefeller confronted other agencies that tried to diminish part of his office's authority. This occurred, for example, with film. The importance that Roosevelt gave to film as a propaganda weapon can be confirmed by the creation of the Office of Coordinator of Film some days after the Japanese attack on Pearl Harbor. With enormous effort, the OCIAA was able to keep a friendly rapport with this new governmental agency, which coordinated film production related to the war effort. However, this did not occur in relation to the Office of War Information, the information and propaganda agency created in June 1942. When OWI moved to act in the south of the continent in the distribution of noncommercial 16-millimeter films, Rockefeller's office reacted immediately. It was already working on the production and distribution of this material, and the young millionaire and Roosevelt administration bureaucrat did not intend to relinquish this valuable slice of his "ideology factory." After hard political battles, and thanks to the interference of Vice Pres. Henry Wallace,[49] film stayed under the jurisdiction of Nelson Rockefeller.

Almost simultaneously with the conflict with OWI, Rockefeller was involved in a more difficult battle to maintain the autonomy of his office. He confronted the director of the OSS, the future CIA, in a dispute over radio broadcasting. The plans to expand a radio service with clear propagandistic objectives found a strong obstacle: the complicated Roosevelt bureaucracy. Rockefeller came up against a bureaucrat and man of action who was as conscious as Rockefeller himself of his importance to the policies of the Roosevelt government: Col. William J. Donovan.

With the intention of unifying all the information services, Roosevelt created the Office of Strategic Services, the U.S. intelligence service that was active during World War II. This espionage system was made official on July 11, 1941, under the name of Coordinator of Information (COI). Its direction was given to the retired Col. Bill Donovan. When President Roosevelt published the decree, he made it clear that COI "should not supersede the activities of other sectors of the intelligence services of other departments and agencies, or duplicate them or get involved with them."[50]

Despite the recommendations contained in the presidential document, the collision with the intrepid "Wild" Bill—as the head of U.S. espionage was known—was inevitable. Donovan had fought against Pancho Villa in the Mexican Revolution, fought in World War I, and returned as a hero. He was also a defeated Republican candidate for governor of New York in 1932. Thus "Wild" Bill had a combative résumé and a tough image in tune with the culture of the Wild West disseminated by the "shoot 'em up" cowboy Westerns.

The creation of new divisions and departments in the Rockefeller office proved its increasing influence. The Press and Radio divisions had started to "invade" Latin America with various publications and radio programs. For Donovan, this was propaganda, and propaganda was his, not Rockefeller's, domain.

Besides detecting actions of the German Secret Services in Brazil, the COI also was charged with organizing a propaganda system for the radio to oppose the programs broadcast by the Nazis. The German interest in Brazil was not new. By 1916, Otto R. Tannemberg had written *Gross Deutschland die Arbeit des XX Jahrhunderts* (Greater Germany, the work of the twentieth century). In this work he proposed the formation of a German territory in the southern part of Brazil and Latin America. In this "new" Germany, the Portuguese language would have to be eradicated.[51] In the 1930s, Hermann Rauschning, an important member of the National-Socialist Party, made a similar proposal: "We shall create a new Germany there. We will find everything we need there . . . and we will transform a corrupt mestizo state into a German domain . . . we shall not land troops . . . and gain Brazil by the strength of arms. . . . Our weapons are not visible."[52]

The American Secret Service planned to fight Germanism with aggressive propaganda, and if this was not enough, the use of force would be an option. In the eyes of Rockefeller's OCIAA, the work of Donovan of the COI, at least in reference to Latin America, did not have the necessary subtlety or the refinement of Whitney's proposals, of Rockefeller's, or of the diplomatic actions of Caffery. The divergences between Rockefeller's office and Donovan's agency became increasingly evident.

In spite of these divergences, the OSS/COI, as well as the OCIAA, tried to understand Brazil in the best possible way in order to keep the country on the U.S. side in case the war crossed the ocean. The OSS, as an espionage service, was more preoccupied with developing analyses of a strictly military nature, which did not coincide with Rockefeller's plan of action. In any case, the espionage service produced various documents on the situation in southern Brazil, where there was a large population of German descent.

A document dated August 11, 1942, for example, has the following heading: "Strategic survey of South Brazil—Copy n. 23—Latin American Section."[53] The OSS study contains a brief historical survey, from the eighteenth-century Portuguese (Azores) settlements in the southern region, to the specific situation of the twentieth century. The topics of race, prejudice, behavior, and customs deserved attention, with special emphasis on the interrelationship and the "coexistence" of the different ethnic groups that formed the Brazilian population.

The perspective of the document was purely strategic-military. Hypotheses such as the invasion of the south of Brazil were considered. In the whole text, however, there was an underlying question that seemed to disturb the analyst bureaucrats of the agency, which was the precursor of the famous American CIA: How did the Brazilians manage to survive in a society with poorly defined limits on the roles of each racial group? Even though it is subtle and not easy to detect, an excerpt from the document demonstrates a certain concern with the Brazilian racial mix: "The few blacks who had been brought to this region and the Indians who had escaped slavery had been absorbed by means of inter-racial marriages. Others had relocated to regions further west."[54]

The main objective, however, was to study the formation of European immigration centers between the nineteenth and twentieth centuries. A demographic density map created at the time analyzes the arrival of German immigrants based on statistical data. In Rio Grande do Sul, there were approximately 550,000 Germans or their descendants; in Santa Catarina, about 275,000; and in Paraná, another 120,000—almost one million Germans, with strong reasons to support the Nazi idea of a great Germanic Fatherland that would extend throughout Latin America.

This was a frightening prospect. The United States had to take into consideration the different strategic proposals to prevent the dissemination of Nazism in the region, which was considered the beachhead for the occupation of the South Atlantic by Germany. Among the various possibilities suggested by the Secret Service commanded by "Wild" Bill Donovan was the invasion of Rio Grande do Sul. But pragmatic U.S. racism got the OSS to formulate a curious hypothesis: What if the invasion of the south of Brazil by the United States was carried out by a troop of black soldiers? In this case, it would be necessary to take certain precautions, because it was a region where there was a certain racial prejudice, that is, "uneasiness in the relationship between colonies of German origin and the descendants of

Portuguese," which was a result of the "superior attitude of the Germans." In spite of this, the American army should be concerned with the Brazilian pride in being a country without racial prejudice.[55]

The reflections of the OSS have a deep meaning. The Americans were visibly worried about the possibility of their "racist laws" not being accepted by the local populations in the case of an invasion. Compared with the proposals of Rauschning ("We shall not land troops") to conquer the *Volksdeutsche* (Germans born in foreign countries), the hypotheses of the American espionage service were not very sophisticated. In spite of their barbarism, in some cases, the Germans insisted that it was better to conquer the "hearts" of a people before using conventional weapons, which, by the way, had been recommended by Josef Goebbels at the Nazi Party Congress in September 1934.[56] Some Donovan agents—such as Edmund Taylor, who worked in the propaganda section of the Foreign Information Service—had even thought about "borrowing" Goebbels's methods.[57]

In summary, it can be said that the vision of Donovan and the OSS was closer to the "gunboat diplomacy" of the first Roosevelt than to the Good Neighbor Policy of the second. Therefore, Donovan was a strong adversary. He sent a letter to Rockefeller on October 9, 1941, that left no doubt about the jurisdiction of the OSS, at least in respect to international broadcasting:

Under date of July 14th, 1941 the President directed me to assume responsibility in respect of international broadcast relating to the achievement of morale objectives abroad.

It seemed to me then, and it is clearer now, that in the interest of the national welfare the entire job be done by a united front of all the various governmental agencies involved.

When I undertook this task I told you that although this responsibility rested solely with me, I would want to work out an arrangement with you that would make for your fullest satisfaction in meeting your obligations to Latin America. . . .

This can be effectively and efficiently done by only one agency. As a matter of practical operation, only one agency can deal with the broadcasting companies . . . in the transmission of news and in the matter of program schedules, direction of beams, and all the mechanical matters pertaining to transmission and re-transmission.[58]

Nelson Rockefeller met with Donovan and protested the interference in his area of activity. Facing the young millionaire, who was furious at seeing his authority questioned, Donovan impassively reaffirmed his position.[59] Donovan, however, could not count on friends with the clout of

Adolf Berle, or the heavy weight of J. Edgar Hoover, the famous head of the FBI, or of John Hay Whitney, the great Hollywood producer, or of Anna Rosenberg. The Roosevelt family friend and special consultant Berle, by the way, had already suggested that the FBI create a special division for Latin America, weakening Donovan's position. Rockefeller set in motion this powerful influence network to work in his favor.

One autumn afternoon in 1941, Rockefeller asked Anna Rosenberg to speak with the president. The same evening, John Whitney was invited to dinner with Roosevelt. When the refined Whitneys arrived at the White House, they were astonished to meet Bill Donovan, Rockefeller's enemy. Rockefeller's name was not even mentioned during the dinner. But the following day, Bill Donovan received the official information that he would remain excluded from the Latin America information services.

On October 15, 1941, Roosevelt wrote to Donovan:

> It appears that some question has been raised as to the feuds of responsibility of your work and that of Nelson Rockefeller's organization.
>
> I continue to believe that the requirements of our program in the Hemisphere are quite different from those of our programs to Europe and the Far East. In order that information, news and inspirational matter going to the other American republics, whether by radio or other media may be carefully adapted to the demands of the Hemisphere, it should be handled exclusively by the Coordinator of Inter-American Affairs in cooperation with the Department of State.[60]

Therefore, the OSS kept the whole world, without Latin America, whose jurisdiction was under the sophisticated machine to conquer hearts and minds directed by Nelson Aldrich Rockefeller.

The Consolidation of the Rockefeller Office

On July 30, 1941, while Nazi troops were invading the Soviet Union, the office directed by Rockefeller changed its name to Coordinator of Inter-American Affairs. The wider scope of the office was owing to the urgency triggered by the Nazi advance during the second half of that year.

The office's structure became much more complex, with new divisions and an increased number of employees. In reality, the office's organizational structure changed constantly, depending on the situation. In documents, there is no consistency in the names of the units within the office. Sometimes a division was named a section, at other times, a division, and at still other times, a department. In any case, the organization commanded by Nelson Rockefeller was being transformed into a complex structure of subdivisions, with headquarters in the main cities of the United States and in most Latin American countries. The OCIAA was considered one of the American agencies that was best prepared for war.

Most of the employees were people trusted by the coordinator. Rockefeller used executives of big companies, people who could apply their knowledge to prepare the Americas for war and the acceptance of U.S. hegemony. This was the case of James W. Young, the first director of the Department or Division of Communications, a director of Thompson, the well-known public relations company, with headquarters in New York. Don Francisco, director of the prestigious Radio Division, was an executive at Lord & Thomas,[61] another powerful public relations company, who also relied on the contribution of J. W. G. Ogilvie, vice president of International Telephone and Telegraph. Karl August Bikel, who also worked in the Division of Communications, was head of United Press, known as UP. As already mentioned, Rovensky, assistant for commerce and finances, was vice president of the Rockefeller family bank.

Andrew V. Corry, a mining engineer, was invited to be part of the OCIAA's group of experts, as he was a distinguished strategic minerals expert. The modern phase of the exploration of natural resources in the Latin American countries started then. Without a doubt, there was an effort to fight Axis expansion, but also the bases for systematic economic exploration had been launched in a peaceful world. Signals of change in the worldwide situation were already noticeable in 1943. Nazi troops had lost the initiative after the defeats at Stalingrad and Kursk. North Africa was reconquered. Italy was already out of the conflict, even though Nazi forces resisted in the region until 1945. This transformation in the international picture encouraged a change in U.S. policy toward Latin America. Rockefeller knew how to adapt the objectives of his office to this new reality.

Rockefeller was proposed for the position of assistant to the secretary of state for Latin American affairs in 1944. The official title, the Office of the Coordinator of Inter-American Affairs, lost the word "Coordinator" and turned into the Office of Inter-American Affairs. The exclusion of the figure of the coordinator removed the political character from the Rockefeller office. A friend of Rockefeller's took it over. From then on, U.S. foreign policy underwent significant changes. Good Neighbor diplomacy started to agonize.

1. President Vargas and President Roosevelt's first meeting in Rio de Janeiro, November 1936. At this meeting FDR said: "The New Deal had two creators. I'm one of them, and the other is President Vargas of Brazil."

2. *The 1939 New York World's Fair was planned by U.S. businessmen. This poster represents their optimism.*

3. and 4. *Futurama, the General Motors pavilion at the 1939 fair. Visitors could "see" the future in a simulated flight into the year 1960.*

5. *The Brazilian Pavilion at the New York World's Fair was designed by Lúcio Costa and Oscar Niemeyer, creators of the futuristic city of Brasília, the new Brazilian capital.*

ENDEREÇO TELEGRÁFICO "HOBALCOP"
TELEPHONE 27-0020

Avenida Atlântica
Rio de Janeiro

See Proper reply [handwritten]

ak 6/26/40 [handwritten]

June 15,1940.

President Franklin D. Roosevelt,
The White House,
Washington, D.C.

Dear Mr. President:

I thought you might be interested in this copy of a radio address which I made last night at the invitation of the Brazilian Government over the "Hora do Brazil" hookup.

This broadcast followed an interview I had in the afternoon with President Getulio Vargas, and I hope coincides with your ideas of Pan-American unity and friendship.

I trust you are enjoying the best of health, and with kindest regards to Mrs. Roosevelt and yourself, I remain,

Cordially yours,

Errol Flynn

c/o Warner Bros,

x 87
x 11-A

6. Errol Flynn wrote this letter to President Franklin Roosevelt just after a meeting with President Vargas in the Catete palace. Flynn was convinced that Vargas was favorable to the ideas of unity and Pan-American friendship.

7. President Vargas playing golf in 1941. Is this a sign of his Americanization?

8. *Vargas greeting Douglas Fairbanks, Jr., the Hollywood star. Mr. Fairbanks's real mission was to get information on Nazi activities in Brazil.*

9. *Heitor Villa-Lobos, the famous Brazilian composer, and Walt Disney, the magician of cartoons, chatting: They have more things in common than we can imagine.*

10. The imaginary Disney alliance: Donald–U.S., Joe Carioca–Brazil, and Panchito–Mexico.

11. Walt Disney watching a small Afro-Brazilian sambista *with admiration. Despite this admiration, he did not include black people in his Brazilian movies (*Aquarela do Brasil *and* Você Já foi à Bahia?*).*

12. *President Vargas, his wife, Darcy, and Nelson Rockefeller in the Rio de Janeiro Jockey Club, 1942. They appear to be truly good friends.*

13. *Orson Welles between Oswaldo Aranha, Brazilian Foreign Minister, and Lourival Fontes, head of the Department of Press and Propaganda. Welles was a kind of Pan-Americanist ambassador.*

14. President Vargas and the quasi-socialist American writer Waldo Frank. Vargas was an open-minded person.

15. The great American movie director John Ford with President Vargas. He was in Brazil to shoot a documentary on the Brazilian war effort.

16. *At a large luncheon meeting, Bill Paley, the CBS president (second from right), agreed to transmit shortwave radio to Brazil.*

17. Jefferson Caffery, U.S. ambassador in Brazil. A real southern gentleman, he knew how to make a peaceful agreement with Brazil.

18. Ambassador Caffery checking Brazilian coffee with President Vargas. Notice the V for victory with Brazilian and American flags on the coffee bag.

2. Brazil for the Americans

The United States of Brazil in the United States of America

Got any coffee on you?   MAYOR FIORELLO LA GUARDIA WELCOMING
CARMEN MIRANDA AT THE PORT OF NEW YORK (IN *The Gang's All Here,* 1943)

Brazil in American Radio Broadcasting and the New York World's Fair

As we have seen, the Office of the Coordinator of Inter-American Affairs, headed by Nelson Rockefeller, had two important objectives: to foster in the United States a positive image of Latin America and especially Brazil; and to convince Brazilians that the United States had always been their friend. During the 1940s, these tasks were undertaken by the mass media.

The importance of radio as a modern medium had already been a topic of diplomatic discourse between Rio and Washington. Evidently, North Americans were far more used to the medium. The communications revolution was already "old" in the northern nation. Thus, the Good Neighbor Policy was in large part propagated by radio.

By 1939, Brazil's foreign minister, Oswaldo Aranha, had already envisioned radio's ability to affect public opinion as a propaganda tool that could be used both by the "forces that enslave" humankind and by those that would free it. But implementation proved more difficult than theory. Transmission of shortwave programs to Brazil required technology, money, know-how, and agreements not imagined by the Brazilian minister. This was especially the case in negotiations between Rio and the gigantic NBC and CBS networks.

As already seen, the OCIAA did not intervene directly in the production of radio programs aimed at the U.S. audience; this was the networks' exclusive territory. Such interference would have been considered an attack on the First Amendment's freedom of expression, dear to U.S. constitutional tradition. Thus, the networks retained exclusive control over the content of U.S.-aimed programming related to Latin America.

This was not the case with programs intended for the "other American republics." Here, Rockefeller's staff created the programs. The experimental laboratory for this radio project was the 1939 New York World's Fair. Thus, in a certain way, it can be said that the World's Fair contributed to the Americanization of Brazil.

The World's Fair opened its doors in 1939 in the midst of the Great Depression. An immense showcase of sophisticated gadgets was displayed to visitors from all over the world. Brazilians who visited or read about the fair could hardly contain their admiration. They were astonished at the sight of the shaving devices, washing machines, primitive television sets, and robots. The gadgets fascinated them so much that they returned with the idea that Brazilian modernization must follow the American model. But in the two-way street of this exchange, Americans who visited the fair also gained a better understanding of their neighbor to the south.

The fair was planned by U.S. businessmen. Its objective was to create an optimistic image of the future and new possibilities for material progress. Between April 1939 and early 1940, many visited, for example, Futurama, the General Motors pavilion. Visitors boarded an airplane and, in simulated flight, traveled across the United States in the future of 1960. In this "Land of the Future," the fair's slogan was "The World of Tomorrow." The voyager traveled on superhighways with suspension bridges controlled by radio. At the trip's end, the visitor received a button reading, "I have seen the future." The Westinghouse pavilion exhibited a parade of electric marvels for the home. Dishwashers promised an end to the housewife's exhausting drudgery. A robot, Electro, foretold the extinction of housewifery.

On April 30, 1939, RCA-NBC televised the fair's opening. The broadcast showed FDR visiting the Westinghouse pavilion.[1] A closed-circuit television broadcast enabled visitors to witness this "miracle." Radio had already made Americans familiar with Roosevelt's voice. But this was the first time the word "telegenic" was used to refer to his physical attractiveness.

The fair was the place "where dreams come true," said fair president, Grover Whalen. One could dream of the future, but the exposition marketed the present. If big exhibitors were capable of showing such imagination and the will to produce those wonderful things, the fair's promoters hoped that people would buy the gadgets they exhibited.

Brazil was one of several other countries that participated in the fair. The Brazilian pavilion was designed by Lúcio Costa and Oscar Niemeyer.[2] When the building's cornerstone was laid on April 16, Dr. Waldemar Falcão, minister of industry, commerce, and work, spoke to the American public in a shortwave broadcast sent by Brazil's Department of Press and Propaganda.[3] Speaking from New York's Radio City Music Hall, the announcer directed listeners to Rio de Janeiro, where he "handed off" his announcing duties to a Brazilian counterpart. In good but accented English, Americans heard: "This is Brazil . . . under the Department of Press and Propaganda we hear the Brazilian anthem." Falcão followed with a speech applauding the Good Neighbor Policy, "so praised by Presidents Roosevelt and Getúlio Vargas." In the minister's view, participation in the World's Fair would serve to cement friendship and peace between the "two powerful democracies of America." Falcão's phrase demanded a certain semantic-ideological juggling, for "democracy" for U.S. citizens was something very different from the regime established in Brazil after November 10, 1937.[i] After the speech, Rio's Municipal Orchestra played "Descobrimento do Brasil" (Discovery of Brazil), composed and conducted by Heitor Villa-Lobos.

With the World's Fair, U.S. media began to disseminate news and images from Brazil more frequently. Moreover, the fair introduced singer and performer Carmen Miranda to the American public.

On September 7, 1939, at an inaugural luncheon, Dr. Armando Vidal, Brazil's general commissioner, officially opened the Brazil pavilion. In a photo Vidal included in his report,[4] three gentlemen appear to be tasting different types of high-quality coffee. It was important to guarantee that the huge U.S. market would remain loyal to Brazilian products—especially coffee.[ii] In another photo, blonde women and children look at Brazilian mineral ores. In another, the painter Cândido Portinari appears. He had taken twenty-five of his works to display. Later, he was commissioned to paint murals in the Library of Congress. Accompanied by his wife, Dr. Vidal appears next to Eleanor Roosevelt, who is savoring a steaming *cafezinho* (espresso). In another, Dr. Vidal and his family are seen entering the Ford pavilion. The Brazilians were fascinated by "American ingenuity."

The Brazil pavilion's gardens possessed specimens of forty-one rare birds from the Amazon. The building's furniture was made of jacarandá, a Brazilian hardwood, with armchairs upholstered with hand-tooled leather. The carpet was from São Paulo's Santa Helena factory, and silk curtains came from Petrópolis's Weber factory. A bookcase featured volumes from the Brazilian collection of Editora Nacional: the collected works of Machado de Assis; *Nova política do Brasil* (New Brazilian politics) by Getúlio Vargas; a guide to Ouro Preto by Manoel Bandeira, a modernist poet; works by Gilberto Freyre, the well-known sociologist, and historian Rocha Pombo. On the second floor was an Hildegardo Leão Veloso bust of President Vargas.

Brazil's products were presented: textile fibers, vegetable resins, all variety of hardwoods (*ipê-amarelo, copaíba, ingazeira, angico-preto, maçaranduba, jenipapo-manso*), mineral ores (compact hematite, marmoso chalk), rubber (raw, crude, washed), goatskin manufactured by Rio's Franco-Brazilian

Tannery, canned corned beef, guava paste, hearts of palm, clothes manufactured by indigenous people, cotton, *babaçu* (palm tree), *oiticica* (wood for canoes), soy, sisal, Brazil nuts, and cashews. The Americans showcased the future, Brazil, its present, without any inferiority complex. The World's Fair was a great show where Brazil not only displayed its worldly goods but also showed a rich creative spirit. Brazil's potential was richly revealed in intellectual production, especially music.

Brazilian Image and Music:
From the World's Fair to the Rest of the United States

The biggest attraction of the Brazilian pavilion could be found in its restaurant, where live performances of national music were featured. Visiting Americans were able to "see" and "feel" Brazil through the music of its composers. This was also true at the Museum of Modern Art and at Town Hall. The pavilion's musical program included works interpreted by Romeu Silva and his orchestra. Having recorded with Josephine Baker in the 1920s, he had international touring experience.

In September 1939, American and Brazilian radio stations broadcast a shortwave program transmitted by NBC and distributed to Brazil by the DIP. "We are here again at the Brazilian restaurant in the World's Fair of New York," the announcer began. "We are going to hear a march by Andrés Filho, 'Cidade maravilhosa' [Wonderful city]." A men's chorus sang music that symbolized Rio, the storied capital.[iii] Several songs were interpreted by Romeu Silva's orchestra, including compositions by Ernesto Nazareth. Walter Burle Marx, another Brazilian maestro who participated in the New York World's Fair, explains Nazareth's importance: "This man was . . . the creator of the Brazilian tango, which, despite the name, does not have anything in common with the Argentine tango. With this tango, Nazareth introduced the contrapuntual, a division that enriches stylization techniques."[5]

In October 1940, New York's Museum of Modern Art presented the Festival of Brazilian Music. The five-day program mobilized a large number of artists, materials, and instruments. The festival was broadcast by NBC Radio to the American audience,[6] transmitted to Brazil by WCBX, and retransmitted by DIP. The chairman of MoMA's Music Committee spoke to the Brazilians in Portuguese. In addition to Romeu Silva, Maestro Walter Burle Marx, and soprano Elsie Houston, the festival also attracted the participation of important Brazilian and American conductors and composers.

The content of the program varied from classical to folkloric to popular. The New York press gave the festival careful coverage. Pianist Arthur

Rubinstein was featured, playing a piece by Villa-Lobos. The American newspapers called the Brazilian composer the "Wolf of the Village." In an interview, Burle Marx was conscious of the necessity to clarify aspects of Brazilian musical culture: "Popular Brazilian music comes from two main sources: the Portuguese and the African. The Portuguese contribution is limited to the sphere of melody, linguistics, and cultural development, while the African contributes with a primitive rhythm. To all of this we must add the contribution of the natives."[7]

According to Armando Vidal, some newspapers attributed to Carnaval a political function: the prevention of revolutions.[8] By 1938, Americans had been exposed to the Carnaval Carioca via radio. Considering what they had heard, the newspaper's assumption was correct. Speaking in correct but accented English, a Brazilian announcer explained to NBC listeners the meaning of Carnaval. In the background, a rhythm marked by a drum mixed with automobile horns, male and female voices singing:

Seu condutor	Mr. conductor
dim, dim . . .	dim, dim . . .
Yes, nós temos bananas	Yes, we have bananas
bananas para dar e vender.	bananas to give and to sell.

The announcer emphasized that in this *festa* there was no distinction between social classes. All Brazilians became brothers during Carnaval. The "carnivalesque" democracy prevented revolutions. And closing the program: "This is the way Cariocas amuse themselves. . . . Special transmission from NBC/RCA."[9]

In 1940, a more elaborated propaganda apparatus explained the participation of Brazilian (of American heritage) soprano Elsie Houston in strengthening ties between the countries.[10] There was a touch of refinement in this image of Brazil. As we will see, it was different from Carmen Miranda's image. In a sense, the singers' images complemented each other. Miranda represented the popular stereotype of the sensual Latin woman. Elsie Houston, in a way, can be interpreted as having a more erudite sensuality. By being born in Brazil, Elsie Houston possessed a set of qualities that could be measured by her statements on the country's music. Houston's physical appearance resembled a "more Latin" type of American. The myth of racial democracy became stronger with the arguments of a Brazilian of U.S. origin.[iv] The daughter of Americans, she had absorbed Brazilian culture to such an extent that she declared Brazil to be more advanced than the United States in musical and social terms: "We [Brazilians] were open to any form of influence. The absolute absence of color prejudice made the assimilation of black/African and Indian influences easy. Who here [in the United States], except George Gershwin, has shown in his work sensitivity for a real music? I am convinced that Brazilian music is contributing a great deal to music everywhere by mixing the classic tradition with the structure of the primitive rhythms of old Africa and Indian ritual."[11]

Those who could not take a subway to MoMA or to Town Hall could "visit" Brazil through the music played on the radio. Ary Barroso was already well known. Rio was typically associated with this composer. "Rio de Janeiro is indeed a city of rare charm and beauty" rhapsodized a CBS announcer. Rio "is truly one of the great capitals of the world." He also spoke of the beauty of the architecture, of Monroe Palace, inaugurated in homage to the nineteenth-century U.S. president and Tiradentes, a Brazilian national hero.[v] But his discourse did not have the same impact as the music "Aquarela do Brazil," or simply "Brazil," which played after the announcer had concluded his speech.[12]

On the April 18, 1942, *Major Bowes' Amateur Hour*, sponsored by Chrysler Motors,[13] the samba was heard. NBC's announcer explained that the company's sponsorship was owed to its desire to support the U.S. war effort. Featured artists included a trio of harmonica players. The leader of the group, a soldier about to leave for the front, asked Major Bowes: "Do you like samba, Major?"

"Yes."

"We'll play 'Brazil' for you."

Without skipping a beat, Bowes commented: "This is a Good Neighbor offer."

The leader of the group continued: "Will this be the first time that you [Major] will present a samba?"

Despite these performers' virtuosity, in reality, the samba was a kind of military march. Consequently, Brazil was formed in the imagination of the Americans as a mixture of samba and military and Carnaval marches. Barroso became almost as popular in the United States as in Brazil.[14] This occurred mainly after "Aquarela do Brasil" was included in the Walt Disney film *Saludos Amigos*. In early 1944, Barroso was able to experience this popularity personally when he traveled to Hollywood. In letters sent to relatives, he mentions that, in different bars and nightclubs he visited, he was recognized and asked to play "Aquarela do Brasil."[15]

In February 1942, Francisco Mignone arrived in the United States. In a press release the State Department affirmed that the music of Mignone was inspired by "São Paulo country folk of European ancestry."[16] Mignone was accompanied by a group of Brazilian musicians; among them was the legendary Bidu Sayão, a star of the Metropolitan Opera House; the pianist

Arnaldo Estrella, who played with the New York Philharmonic, conducted by Bruno Walter; and the composer/conductor Camargo Guarnieri.[17]

On December 16, 1943, NBC broadcast *Music of the New World: Music of Brazil.*[18] The announcer gave a brief lesson in Brazilian history, from discovery to the Republic. He referred to Rio as one of the world's most beautiful cities and related the samba, *choro*, and *maxixe* (Brazilian tango) to the city's cultural formation. To illustrate this point, he cited "Choro Number 1," by Villa-Lobos, which was played for listeners.

The announcer compared the history of Brazil with that of the United States: "While Americans no longer have the frontier, Brazilians still have the *sertão*, the hinterlands."[vi] Solos of horn and strings in staccato and another piece by Villa-Lobos reminded the listener of streams of water and rivers. The music would evoke an image of the Brazilian sertão in the American listener, who compared it with the image of the frontier.

In an American tour the same year, soprano Olga Coelho included in her repertoire some lesser-known pieces of Brazilian music: a *candomblé* (music used in Afro-Brazilian religion) called "Star from Heaven Sprayed with Gold" and several *modinhas* (sentimental songs) that, according to the announcer, could be traced to the eighteenth-century Portuguese sentimental genre from Vila Rica (Ouro Preto), the old baroque city in the Minas Gerais mountains. She also sang, in very fast style, an *embolada* (declamatory song—a duel in improvised verse—from the Northeast accompanied by tambourine), another popular genre:

Olha o sapo	Look at the frog
tá na toca	It's in the hole
tá na loca	It's crazy/willing
tá danado pra brigá	It's eager to fight

The announcer explained that the embolada, a very difficult word to pronounce, was similar to an American folk song.

According to *Pan-American Radio* magazine, Coelho's Brazilian roots were responsible for her colorful soprano and sweet contralto voice. In a photograph of the singer standing before a CBS microphone, one sees a pretty and smiling girl holding a guitar. She performed on several radio stations because, according to the magazine, "the Brazilian government . . . recognized in Olga Coelho the greatest interpreter, duly authorized, of the beautiful folkloric songs of her country."

By 1943, several Latin American artists in addition to Olga Coelho and Elsie Houston were known to the American public. Among them were Mexicans like Carmen Redondo (soprano) and Eva Garza (popular singer), the

Hispanic Americanized Margarita Carmen Casino—aka Rita Hayworth—and Dolores Del Río. Eva Garza was on the cover of *Pan-American Radio* as a brunette wearing a sombrero and a serape (the poncho popularized by American movies), an embroidered vest, and a belt with a holster and a pearl-handled Colt revolver. The "Cancionera del Norte," as the Mexican singer was known, has her right hand on the gun, as if she is ready to draw the Colt. Her left hand touches the sombrero. She is smiling at the camera, her bright teeth surrounded by a beautiful tanned face with black eyes and thick eyebrows. Latin America is identified by adjectives such as "attractive, melodic." Garza "sings the songs of the southern countries" before a microphone with CBS's "eye" logo. Underneath is the inscription "C de las A" (Cadena de las Américas, i.e., the radio network of Pan-Americanism).

According to the same publication, when compared with Garza, the Brazilian Coelho had different qualities that heightened Latin America's exoticism: "Since her birth, in Manaus—a city of the interior, on the banks of the powerful Amazon—she has already covered a long distance on the route to fame. Her Indian wet nurse lulled her to sleep with the legend of 'Uirapuru,' the fabulous bird of the Amazon rain forest, whose first notes provoke the silent admiration of all the other feathered inhabitants of the forest."[19] The author's clear intent was to entrance the reader with the mystery and intrigue of this voice of the Amazon rain forest.

The program on which Coelho performed was part of a series known as the *University of the Air*. The average American could "attend a course" at a university without leaving the house and learn everything about Brazil (and other Latin American countries). To complete the course, the listener sent 25 cents to receive an attractive catalogue of the "Music of the New World."

Before presenting Brazilian music, the program *Salute to Brazil*,[20] transmitted on September 7, 1942, explained to the American listener who Dom Pedro I was and what his importance was for Brazilian independence.[vii] It also demonstrated that Carlos Gomes and Alberto Nepomuceno were composers as important as Villa-Lobos.

By invitation of Rockefeller's OCIAA, in November 1944, it was Heitor Villa-Lobos's turn to visit the United States. During his stay, Villa-Lobos gave several recitals. In February of the following year, he conducted the Boston Symphony Orchestra, which performed only his compositions. In New York, he shared the baton with Leopold Stokowski in a performance with the city's symphony orchestra. Villa-Lobos also gave several performances at the CBS studios. In addition to Rockefeller, those attending his farewell luncheon included Stokowski, Benny Goodman, Duke Ellington, Cole Porter, Arturo Toscanini, Yehudi Menuhin, and Eugene Ormandy.[21]

In addition to music, New York museums' exhibitions of Brazilian painting and photography showed another face of the country's high culture. Portinari, whose pictures had been displayed at MoMA, showed a side of Brazil unknown to many Americans. A photo essay in the newspaper *O Estado de São Paulo* recorded the opening of Portinari's exhibition.[22] In late 1940, the painter himself appeared at the vernissage. Before that, John Jay Whitney, Rockefeller's good friend and collaborator, hosted a dinner at the former speakeasy and sumptuous 21 Club, attended by Portinari, Armando Vidal, and American celebrities. Portinari, celebrated in the land of Uncle Sam, came back to the United States in mid-1941.[23]

Painter Lasar Segall also exhibited in New York, showing, mainly, his pictures of Brazilian laborers. But the piece that attracted the most attention was *Mãe preta* (black mother), depicting a young black woman with slanted eyes cradling a child. This was a different face of Brazil from what Americans had seen before.[24]

In 1943, Genevieve Naylor, an American photographer known for her work for the Associated Press, *Fortune*, and *Harper's Bazaar*,[25] mounted an exhibit at MoMA, "Faces and Places in Brazil." She had gone to Brazil under Rockefeller's auspices and traveled extensively. What was striking in Naylor's photos was the attractiveness of Brazilians in the same way as shown by Orson Welles. Her photos must have surprised MoMA visitors. One photo depicted white and black children playing with musical instruments on the sidewalk of Copacabana; another showed black and white women seated under a poster announcing the 1941 Rio Carnaval; a third, a white and a black child preparing for a procession in Congonhas do Campo, Minas Gerais.

Beyond the melting pot, the races coexisted. There was no trace of the color line or Jim Crow.[26] This was the image absorbed by the American elite, who, besides viewing the MoMA exhibit, attended concerts, read books by Waldo Frank, the utopian Pan-American socialist, and listened to radio news reports.

News from Brazil and the World

Interested in increasing its coffee sales to the United States, the Brazilian government used the Good Neighbor Policy's atmosphere of U.S.-Brazilian amity. Rio sought to disseminate via radio and newspapers ideas that fostered a positive image of Brazil.

In the second half of 1940, for example, NBC Radio began broadcasting a program sponsored by the Brazilian government. *News of the World,* by Drew Pearson and Bob Allen,[27] offered fifteen minutes of political analysis. The two journalists were well known to U.S. listeners. Their column, "Washington Merry-Go-Round," appeared in "over 600 American newspapers." The journalists broadcast daily, always in the same way: "This is Drew Pearson and this is Bob Allen, speaking from Washington." The news was highly diversified. To the standard reporting on national and world events, they added expanded and sympathetically tinged coverage of Latin America.

Brazil appeared with more prominence in the news reports. President Roosevelt himself sent a cheerful message to the "largest neighbor that is standing shoulder to shoulder with the United States."[viii] The importance of Brazil and its products for the United States was always emphasized. The news explained, for example, the need for Brazilian manganese in steel manufacture; for quartz crystal in the electronic communication industry; for chromium, diamonds, and other indispensable Brazilian products. Significantly, all of these exports were needed by the United States in its effort to rearm prior to its entry into World War II. Another distinction: as journalists explained, Brazil had the biggest iron reserves in the world; Hitler's plans for economic and territorial expansion included transfer of the factories then located in occupied Czechoslovakia to Brazil's Itabira, Minas Gerais, mining region.

This was the type of argument that Nelson Rockefeller—by the way, Drew Pearson's friend—needed to convince U.S. isolationists, who opposed the formation of an exclusive government office for Latin American issues. While FDR tried to cloak the step in the most persuasive arguments, Rockefeller tended to prefer the alarmist approach.

According to Pearson, if the United States needed Brazilian raw materials, Brazil urgently required U.S. manufactured goods. The journalist attempted to convince his listeners that cooperation was essential to safeguard the Western Hemisphere from the Nazi threat. In a simulated Socratic dialogue, the newsmen proved the point: "You know, Drew, Singapore is threatened by Japan."

"Yes, Bob, I realized that."

Then the program went to a politically tinged commercial message that urged listeners to "buy" the Good Neighbor Policy by purchasing Brazilian coffee. On January 11, 1940, the newspaper *Diário de São Paulo* reproduced a survey conducted in the United States during the previous year concerning the acceptance of the Good Neighbor Policy. The sole question posed to respondents was "Should the United States help Brazil if it is threatened by an external superpower?" In 1939, 27.1 percent of those interviewed said yes; 53.7 percent said no. One year later, 36.3 percent said yes, and 40 percent said no. Therefore, a considerable number of Americans preferred to embrace the Good Neighbor Policy just by buying coffee.

Between news reports such as one on Nelson Rockefeller's secretly hiring a journalist from the Associated Press for a "public relations" mission in Latin America, and another about the needs of the U.S. Navy and Air Force for South American bases, there was always a message from the Brazilian government. In one of the commercials, which resembled a news report, Pearson and Allen interviewed a U.S. Army officer. This officer was responsible for purchasing Brazilian coffee for American soldiers, and he revealed that each American soldier consumed about forty-five pounds of coffee annually. The journalists asked him why the government bought so much. Because, the officer said, coffee kept the soldiers ready to fight.

In addition to radio, Brazil used newspapers as a vehicle to promote coffee; in the same package went its allegiance to the Good Neighbor Policy. On January 3, 1943, the *New York Times* published an ad featuring the U.S. and Brazilian flags together with a column of marching infantry.[28] "Brazil: home of the world famous Brazilian coffee, extends season's greetings to the American People." The soldiers were marching, and in perspective the line of men disappeared into the horizon. Above the soldiers were representations of the Statue of Liberty and a cup of steaming coffee with the swirling steam spelling the word "coffee." Beneath this was written: "[It] is the greatest stimulating beverage for the soldiers fighting to preserve democracy and liberty." Below was a highly revealing statistical datum: "Brazil furnishes 58.49 percent of the coffee consumed in the United States—National Coffee Department of Brazil."

In the October 20, 1940, edition of *News of the World*, Pearson and Allen presented a long strategic analysis of the world situation. In their view, the importance of the South Atlantic as the key element for U.S. security had recently expanded. Now that region loomed as important as the Pacific, where Japan challenged U.S. interests. A few months later, Vichy France proved unable to prevent the occupation of Indochina by Japan. The remedy "was to arm our southern good neighbors." In Pearson's view, arming Latin America was more important even than equipping the United States. The logic went as follows: first, arm Latin America, for that region was more vulnerable and would therefore become a target for Nazi expansionism. This step would "buy time" for the United States, which would gain in preparedness with time and could later face the Axis. If the Axis attacked a well-armed Latin America, the United States would have more time, and would require less work, to help its good neighbors.[ix]

In the program's final minutes, listeners were encouraged to visit Brazil. With a simple telephone call they would receive a free forty-page booklet explaining everything about the country. Now the announcer urged: "Drink an extra coffee to help the friendship between Brazil and the United States." In thickly accented Portuguese, Pearson followed with: "'Boa noite e muitas felicidades' which means in English: Good Night and Good Luck.'" It was noteworthy that the announcers referred to "the United States of Brazil" instead of simply Brazil, which suggested a greater affinity between the countries in their shared federal constitutions.[x]

BY JULY 1942, the United States having entered the war and Brazil having broken relations with the Axis, Rio had become a close American ally. Within the State Department and the Pentagon, policy makers formed a lobbying group to improve overall relations with Brazil and to pave the way for a full-fledged military alliance. Their employees needed to familiarize themselves with Brazilian culture. In July 1942, the Office of Strategic Services issued the "Short Guide to Brazil—Report No. 60—Restricted."[29] There were instructions on the correct use and pronunciation of Portuguese. Americans traveling to Brazil should always say that they adored the country and that the United States was not shown accurately in Hollywood movies: U.S. society also had poor people, not only the wealthy and the upper middle class.

Regarding morality, there was an item worth mentioning: "Prostitution exists in Brazil, as in any other place . . . but it is a very serious insult to mistake any woman for a prostitute. When in doubt, assume that she is not a prostitute."[30]

From analysis of this document and others, it is clear that, while the Office of Strategic Services and the OCIAA were both concerned about Latin America, primary responsibility for the area continued to reside in Rockefeller's agency. As we have seen, the special status of the OCIAA was ordered by the chief executive at Rockefeller's request.

During 1941, NBC Radio's programming continued the effort to project a positive image of Brazil. Bob Ripley, the creator of the program *Believe It or Not!*, announced that he would create a program in collaboration with the Coordinator of the Office of Inter-American Affairs.[31] In common with all of Ripley's programs, it was presented in radio theater format. The show spoke about the positive qualities of South Americans; in particular, they were friendly and affectionate. Believe it or not, Ripley guaranteed that even the Brooklyn Dodgers were indebted to Brazil: the baseballs were made from Amazonian rubber. The program had a soundtrack with rumbas accompanied by maracas and other Caribbean instruments. It was clearly made for an American audience.

From the program, Americans learned that Dom Pedro II had been emperor of Brazil in the nineteenth century, and that Dr. Getúlio Vargas was the leader of the great Brazilian democracy in the twentieth century.[xi] The American listener also was informed that Dom Pedro II helped

THE SEDUCTION OF BRAZIL

Alexander Graham Bell develop the telephone: he became the world's first telephone subscriber. According to Ripley, this event happened on June 25, 1876, in Philadelphia. Dom Pedro II was visiting an exhibit of technological innovation at the Century of Progress World's Fair, commemorating the centennial of U.S. independence. The monarch was so fascinated with Bell's invention that he signed up on the spot for service. As we will see in the next chapter, Ripley's programs were also broadcast to Brazil.

NBC Radio made these broadcasts, together with reports from the London blitz. Bombs could be heard whistling through the air as the announcer described in detail aerial combat between Spitfires and Messerschmitts. Therefore, American audiences were exposed to a wide variety of programming focused on the war. NBC's programming contained a not-so-subtle subtext: the unity of the Americas was essential to prevent the war from arriving on this continent. And later, after the United States had become a belligerent, the broadcasts emphasized that a joint effort of all the Americas was essential for Allied victory.

Carmen Miranda, Radio, and the Movies: Samba Is Not Rumba

Carmen Miranda, the Brazilian Bombshell, as she was known in the United States, and her band, Bando da Lua, "arrived in New York on May 17, 1939, just in time to attend the opening of the Brazilian restaurant at the World's Fair."[32] On the twenty-ninth· they made an acclaimed first performance in Boston. Their first Broadway performance took place in the second week of June,[33] with the show *Streets of Paris*. At the same time, she participated in the *Rudy Vallee Show*, or *Royal Gelatin Program*—one of the most popular American radio shows, broadcast weekly between 8:00 P.M. and 9:00 P.M. from New York's Radio City Music Hall.[34]

In this variety show, Rudy Vallee acted as showman and bandleader. He sang and participated in scenes from different Broadway musicals. On June 29, 1939,[35] the announcer introduced "the first radio appearance of Carmen Miranda" in the United States.

The "Latin spirit" was already present in radio programs and in some American music. Rudy Vallee sang Cole Porter's "Begin the Beguine": "When they begin the beguine / It brings back the sound of music so tender / It brings back a night of tropical splendor." An announcer said that the popular American composer had been inspired by a case of Latin American love when he composed the well-known song.

A guitar accompanied by a tambourine hinted at a tropical and exotic number. The announcer introduced Miranda: "Where does she come from?

From Brazil. I don't speak any Portuguese and 'Señorita' Miranda doesn't speak any English. But that doesn't matter because . . ." Carmen sang "O que é que a baiana tem?" (What does the woman from Bahia have):

O que é que a baiana tem?	What does the Bahian have?
Tem torso de couro? Tem	Does she have a leather torso? She has.
Tem brinco de ouro? Tem	Does she have a gold earring? She has
Sandália enfeitada? Teeeem	Does she have decorated sandals? She haaaas

Miranda asked the question and the Bando da Lua answered in chorus. Later it was the band's turn to ask, and Miranda's to answer with "hum . . . hummm," in a mischievous manner. They were warmly applauded. The announcer asked: "Do you understand now?"

The very rapid singing characteristic of Miranda's interpretations pleased the American public. An animated Miranda launched into "The South American Way." The "th" so difficult to pronounce for those who are not native English speakers was said in an amusing way. It sounded like "ssse," with a slight hissing sound. The audience laughed.

Starting with her first U.S. radio appearance, Miranda stamped her image with a good-humored sensuality. "I would like to take a cruise to South America. All women look like you, Señorita Miranda?" Rudy Vallee asked.

Carmen continued performing on the Vallee show until mid-1940, when she went back to Brazil. On her return to the United States in October of the same year, she returned to the program. Always singing the same songs, she gained the acceptance of the American public. The lyrics were repetitive and the compositions rather simple, almost all of them from the Brazilian Carnaval repertoire. "Pirulito que bate-bate" (Lollipop that beats) was one of these songs; "Mamãe eu quero" (I want my mama) became well known; "Tico-tico no fubá" (Tico-tico bird in the cornmeal) was sung also, for GIs at the front. In the show *Command Performance*, presented on August 15, 1945, in honor of the American Armed Forces, Carmen sang "Tico-tico" and was warmly applauded. To this day, in the subway stations of New York City, Jamaican musicians using steel drums fill the distracted ears of commuters with "Tico-tico no fubá."

On another *Rudy Vallee Show*, in May 1941, Miranda added more eroticism to the mythical Latin image. She had already improved her English and was speaking with much more confidence and boldness. At one point she says to the showman: "You are a dream man, Rudy . . . Would you like to make love with me?" This effusive manifestation of sensuality coming from a woman was not unique. In 1945, Sarah Vaughan sang "Lover Man" by Roger

"Ram" Ramirez, Jimmy Davis, and James Sherman, which has a similar verse: "I go to bed / with the prayer / that you'll make love to me." But there was a certain intimate mood in the lyrics of the song, and Vaughan, accompanied by Dizzy Gillespie and Charlie "Bird" Parker, sang in small clubs.

Early bebop was not for everybody. Radio had stiffer morality norms, and performers had to pass muster with Federal Communications Commission censors. Therefore, Miranda's "proposal" caused a certain stir in the audience. However, the permissive attitude could be accepted within the spirit of the Good Neighbor Policy, especially coming from a woman from the tropics. Even so, Vallee quickly changed the subject: "Good evening, good evening, good neighbors. A tour of good will. Now we will fly to Rio de Janeiro."

This sequence was part of a humorous sketch with the scenery of Rio de Janeiro as the background, but the scriptwriters confused some Portuguese words with Spanish. As seen in the previous chapter, a symbolic union between Vallee and Miranda, who "got married" in a small humorous sketch, was aired in May 1941. The performance ended with both of them saying: "Our two countries could have better relations after our marriage." What mattered was the message of a happy ending, associated with the Good Neighbor Policy. Carmen sang:

Rebola, rebola	Shimmy, shimmy, shake
você diz que dá na bola	You say you are the man
na bola você não dá	But you are just a fake

At the same time that she was becoming famous on the radio and, later, in the movies, Miranda made commercials for lipstick and beer, opened nightclubs such as New York's Copacabana, and increased her participation in the dissemination of the Good Neighbor Policy. She was present at the serious Pan-American Congress of Chess in 1945, swaying her hips and wearing a fezlike hat that made her resemble a Turk more than a Bahian.[36]

Miranda's presence in the United States and her importance have been discussed a great deal elsewhere. Critics tried to understand the reasons for the artist's enormous success, especially on Broadway. Henry F. Pringle, for example, concluded: "In this day of strip acts, it should be noted that Miss Miranda does not remove a single garment and that her only appeal to the baser emotions is a slight, slight swaying of her hips It should also be recorded that the only portion of her more intimate anatomy visible is an inch or two of tummy between her skirt and her blouse."[37]

Between 1939 and 1945, the Brazilian Bombshell appeared in several successful 20th Century Fox films. She assumed the mantle of ambassador of Brazilian popular music culture in the United States. In July 1940, in connection with her participation in the film *Down Argentine Way*, she declared that the film showed for the first time in Hollywood "an authentic manifestation of the popular soul of Brazil as it is in reality."[38] Miranda sang the film's title song and other better known songs such as "Mamãe eu quero" and "Touradas de Madri" (Madrid bullfight). But the melodious treatment she gave to the songs was hardly an authentic representation of Brazil's popular culture. The film's seemingly random mixture of Brazilian music with Cuba's habanera and rumba, the Afro-Caribbean samba-*jongo*, Argentina's tango, the march, and other genres was more appropriate to the musically untutored ear of the American public.

Her only film that has Brazil as a backdrop—but was entirely shot in Hollywood—is 1941's *That Night in Rio*, directed by Irving Cummings. Between madcap misadventures typical of the era's "screwball comedies," Miranda sings, accompanied by the Bando da Lua, in nightclubs and in millionaires' mansions. Like the previous one, this film contains little of the "authentic manifestation of the popular soul of Brazil." Hollywood had transformed her into a crude stereotype of the Latin American woman.

According to Vinícius de Moraes,[39] Carmen Miranda was everything but Brazilian. Her outfit was exaggerated; her gestures were frenetic and snake-like; her turban resembled that of a Hindu snake charmer. His critique came from the Brazilian point of view as he analyzed a Brazilian performer who had lost her nationality's characteristics.[40] However, for the image makers of the Good Neighbor Policy, the authenticity of the culture of the other Americas disseminated by the U.S. mass media was of little importance. What did matter was securing Brazil's alliance in the U.S. war effort.

Hollywood made many films promoting the spirit of the Good Neighbor. One of them, *Charlie Chan in Rio*, shows the legendary Hawaiian-Sino-American detective coming to Brazil to solve a mysterious crime. Joined by his son as assistant, he launches his investigation in a stereotypical nightclub. The plot unfolds in a series of misadventures. Imitations of Carmen Miranda are included as well as stereotyped choreographies.

In the film *Now Voyager*, Bette Davis cures her depression in Paul Henreid's arms while on a cruise to Rio. On their arrival, they gaze at a glistening Sugar Loaf. But Rio's famous landmark sits on the opposite side of its real position in the famous landscape.[41] After disembarking, the two spend the night in a mountain shack, amid pine trees and frosty weather: not a very tropical climate! Later, they are seen in a small restaurant, very similar to those found in the interior of France or Italy. The "Brazilian" taxi driver's name is "Josepi," and he speaks a mixture of Portuguese, Spanish, and

Italian. Most of the films set in Brazil had young women dancing samba-rumba, Christ the Redeemer, Sugar Loaf . . . and many people speaking a language similar to an Italianized Gallego. To please the American public and show that the United States' Latin neighbors were likeable—that was all that was needed.

And it was undoubtedly this image of Brazil, of happy people who liked to dance, that Orson Welles conveyed to the American audience in a radio broadcast in April 1942.

From the Urca Casino to North America

American radio listeners could tune into NBC's Blue Network on April 18, 1942, and hear a shortwave rebroadcast of an homage to President Vargas for his birthday. Broadcast from Rio's Urca Casino, the party was sponsored by U.S. Ambassador Jefferson Caffery. The master-of-ceremonies was Orson Welles, who had arrived in Rio de Janeiro in February. Clad in a white tuxedo, he opened the show in theatrical English:

> This is Orson Welles, speaking from South America, from Rio de Janeiro, in the United States of Brazil. This is a special broadcast commemorating a special occasion. This is a birthday party in behalf of the president of the United States of America, tonight's birthday party is in honor of the president of Brazil, Mr. Roosevelt's great and good friend, Dr. Getúlio Vargas. This radio show is for all his friends. From Maine to Manaus, from São Paulo to Chicago, from São Salvador to San Francisco. This is being transmitted over most of the stations in Brazil and over a hundred stations in North America. . . . Many of those friends who were able to come to the same party and join us here in Rio are sending to Brazil's president heartiest congratulation from all Americans.[42]

This was not the first time that President Vargas was referred to as a "great and good friend" of President Roosevelt. FDR had used the same expression in November 1936, when he visited Rio en route to Buenos Aires. Welles emphasized that all Americans wished Vargas happiness from the bottom of their hearts. In the background, the orchestra played a slow fox-trot. "I can see people from most of our twenty and two Republics from where I'm standing right now," Welles continued, in an obvious effort to evoke the Good Neighbor spirit.

In the universe of Realpolitik, the attainment of hemispheric unity under U.S. leadership proved to be more complicated than Washington envisaged. At the January 1942 Rio de Janeiro Pan-American Conference, the United States was forced to swallow a watered-down version of its call for mandatory breaking off of relations with the Axis. Pressed by still-neutral Chile and Argentina, the foreign ministers instead adopted a resolution merely recommending the step.[43]

Welles's speech was about ideals and what was ideal for U.S. interests. Projecting his voice, he said that the Urca Casino affair was not official: "I am not speaking for the government." But, if he was not speaking for the U.S. government, for whom was he speaking? In an interview with Peter Bogdanovich, Welles admitted that he came to Brazil for political reasons, that is, to help Rockefeller's office promote inter-American relations.[44] During one of FDR's electoral campaigns, he declared that Welles and he were the best American actors.

Welles's presentation grew more animated. The Urca Casino, he concluded, was the last truly happy place on earth. The show in Vargas's honor, presented as the *Symphony of Brazil*, included artists such as Grande Otelo, Jararaca and Ratinho, and Brazilian acrobats with Americanized names, Vic and Joe. The nationalistic touch was given by a group of "girls" from the ballet Grande Siderúrgica, an obvious allusion to President Vargas's efforts to create a steel industry in Brazil. Welles also announced to the auditorium that "the best South American stars are going to perform, accompanied by three orchestras, for your entertainment." The march "Cidade Maravilhosa," interpreted by the Carlos Machado orchestra, was announced with great enthusiasm by the American actor-director. The march was changed into a fox-trot, with emphasis on the brass instruments. It was a Brazilian big band. Welles, evidently, was not speaking to a Brazilian audience; the target audience was the American public. Therefore, it made sense to explain that one of the most important characteristics of the Brazilian people was their love of dance.

French maestro Ray Ventura's orchestra took the place of Carlos Machado's. Ventura greeted the audience in Portuguese, English, and French and announced the song "Tudo é Brasil," a fox-trot composed by Vicente Paiva. Amid the static of the shortwave broadcast, a choir singing in Portuguese with a French accent could be heard.

Welles translated the song's title: "Tudo é Brazil. That means All Is Brazil." With an emotional voice, he continued: "Oh! my Brazil." The Shakespearean actor almost made his American listeners believe that he, too, was Brazilian. In an interview given on his arrival in Brazil, he declared that he had been conceived in Rio de Janeiro during his parents' honeymoon. Had it not been for the urgency of their return, he would have been born in Brazil. His role at the party in the Urca Casino was to transmit a positive image of Brazil and its people. This led him to exaggerate somewhat by stating that Brazil was the biggest country in the Western Hemisphere: "The United States could fit inside Brazil and there would still be space for Uruguay, Chile, and Costa Rica."[45]

When Ventura's orchestra finished playing "Tudo é Brasil," Welles continued his emcee role, describing didactically to the American listener how samba was created. "If you mix two words, 'music' and 'Brazil,' and stir well, you will get samba. And if you mix in some Brazilians, you will get the samba dance."

In the sequence, Carlos Machado's orchestra played the samba "Dolores," by Alberto Ribeiro, Mariano Pinto, and Arlindo Marques Júnior. The singer was Emilinha Borba. After the musical piece, Welles continued his explanation. Samba was not a form of jazz, he said. It was "100 percent Brazilian."

Carlos Machado and orchestra returned and presented "Ai, que saudade da Amélia" [Ah, I miss Amélia], by Ataulfo Alves and Mário Lago, in fox-trot rhythm. Welles then alerted the American listeners: the orchestra was going to change pace and play a real samba, and Welles guaranteed that it would be the first time that the other side of the equator was going to hear this song. He explained the meaning of the lyrics: "Amélia was a beautiful woman who was not worried about anything beyond the love for her man."

There followed applause and more of Welles's explanations about the samba: "Samba is the soul of Brazil. Is that right?" And in Portuguese: "Alô! Linda, como vai? [Hello, Linda, how are you?] This voice you are hearing . . . is of one of the most important singers of the Urca Casino: Linda Batista."

Batista, speaking English with great self-confidence, promoted Brazil: "It's a big, big country." Welles agreed. She said enthusiastically: "I like Brazil very, very much. Every Brazilian likes Brazil very much." Welles, with a certain irony, answered that he had already noticed that. Batista laughed. Speaking of Brazilian greatness, Welles asked her why the Brazilians loved Brazil. "Two reasons: this is Brazil. . . . And Brazilians are Brazilians. Correct?" said Batista. A little later, the actor announced that Batista would sing "Sabemos lutar" (We know how to fight), a patriotic march by Nássara, Frazão, R. Magalhães Jr., and P. Frischauer, composed in the previous year. Welles said the title of the march in Portuguese, and Batista translated it for the American listener. This was a very remarkable performance and characterized the Good Neighbor Policy: the American spoke in Portuguese, while the Brazilian spoke in English.

Welles explained the lyrics before Batista started to sing. He spoke of the importance of love for your country, of the duty of all citizens to fight for their country, etc. Batista, accompanied by the orchestra, sang:

Na gueeeerra! Se eu tiver que combater . . .	In waaaaar! If I have to fight . . .
Nós mostraremos que sabemos lutar	We will prove that we know how to fight

After the music and applause, Welles passed the microphone to Jefferson Caffery. The ambassador said that the Americans congratulated President Vargas on his birthday and thanked Brazil for its cooperation with the United States. Long applause followed.

Welles also wished Vargas happiness. Without waiting for the emcee's conclusion, Batista repeated the march: "In waaaaar! If I have to fight." The audience was enraptured with the moment. "Good night from Rio" concluded the broadcast. Another speaker announced: "This is the Blue Network from Rio de Janeiro, in celebration of the birthday of Dr. Getúlio Vargas, the president of Brazil."

The patriotic enthusiasm of Linda Batista and the Urca audience pleased the American ambassador very much. It was a demonstration that the United States could count on from a people who "knew how to fight."

Three years later, the world situation had changed. Nazi Germany was no longer a threat. The same was true for Japan. FDR, Vargas's "great and good friend," was dead. Rockefeller was no longer in the State Department. Brazil, as the big raw materials supplier, was no longer indispensable. Brazil—even after sending its Força Expedicionária Brasileira to fight in the campaign to liberate Italy, even after becoming a raw materials and air base provider for the Allies—had lost its strategic importance in South Atlantic defense. Ambassador Caffery, who managed to bring tears to Vargas's eyes at his farewell,[46] had been reassigned to France, a much more important ally.[xii]

With his increasingly nationalistic position, Vargas was now an inconvenient partner. To free themselves of this partnership was suitable not only for the new American administration, but also for the officers of the Brazilian Armed Forces, the same ones who had helped to install the Estado Novo.[47] Ironically, these officers had once been regarded by American intelligence as dangerous and sympathetic to Nazi Germany. The new ambassador, Adolf Berle, began a policy of increasing antagonism toward the Vargas government.

Even so, the Good Neighbor Policy seemed to have survived Roosevelt, but only on the rhetorical level. Newly inaugurated president Harry Truman had, for example, signed an agreement with Mexico on the use of rivers common to both countries. Truman declared on that occasion that the agreement symbolized the continuity of the Good Neighbor Policy. In reality, it was the end of the Rooseveltian policy for Latin America.[48]

Vargas's foreign policy, now without the guidance of Oswaldo Aranha, continued to give credit to the Good Neighbor Policy. In September 1945, on the anniversary of Brazil's independence, President Vargas made a speech, broadcast to the United States by shortwave by NBC and CBS: "Brazil's Bureau of Information by shortwave . . . presented . . . the speech made by President Vargas."[49] Fifty-two days after the broadcast of the program "in commemoration of Brazilian Independence Day," Vargas was overthrown. No U.S. radio station considered this news significant.

But United News, one of the well-known newsreels of the time, showed that Franklin D. Roosevelt had become the name of an aircraft carrier and that Pres. Getúlio Vargas had resigned. A strange resignation, since tanks and soldiers could be seen in the streets. José Linhares, president of the Federal Supreme Court, was installed in Vargas's place by Gen. Aurélio Góes Monteiro.

Thus ended the Good Neighbor Policy, the United States' forced affection toward Latin America and its exotic culture. In the same year, Noël Coward, the English equivalent of Cole Porter, wrote "Sigh No More." The lyrics are emblematic:

I've seen too many movies,
And all they prove is
Too idiotic.
They all insist that South America's exotic
Whereas it couldn't be more boring if it tried.

She said with most refreshing candor
That Carmen Miranda was subversive propaganda
and she should rapidly be shot.
She didn't care a jot
Whether people quoted her or not.[50]

19. An advertisement alerting people in cities like São Paulo and Rio de Janeiro that it was very dangerous to leave the lights on because they could become targets for German bombers. It was time for a blackout.

20. Jordan Young, the future Brazilianist, worked in 1942 at Serviço Especial de Saúde Publica, sponsored by the Office of the Coordinator of Inter-American Affairs. Fighting malaria was part of the war effort.

21. O Estado de São Paulo *newspaper published a special magazine showing the Brazilian painter Candido Portinari on a goodwill trip to the U.S., where he worked on a mural at the Library of Congress.*

EM GUARDA
ANO 1 · Para a defesa das Américas · N. 12

EM GUARDA
ANO 1 · Para a defesa das Américas · N. 11

ENFERMEIRA VISITADORA

EM GUARDA
ANO 1 · Para a defesa das Américas · N. 9
O COMANDANTE DE UM DESTRUIDOR DE TANQUES PREPARA-SE PARA ENTRAR EM COMBATE

22., 23., and 24. Three samples of the Em Guarda *magazine cover. The magazine was published in English, Portuguese, and Spanish. The Americans could win the war—this was the message of the magazine.*

25. Olga Coelho, the beautiful Brazilian singer, conquered a more educated American audience.

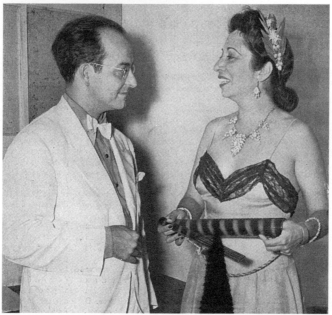

26. Conductor Burle Marx and Brazilian/American singer Elsie Houston captivated a more educated American audience, as well.

27. *The American photographer Genevieve Naylor showed Americans the young and poor people of Brazil.*

PROGRAMAS DE ONDAS CURTAS *em português* **DOS EE.UU. PARA O BRASIL**

Transmitindo simultaneamente das seguintes estações:

WCBX - 17.83 Mgcs. (Faixa de 16 ms.) das 18.00 às 20.45 ★
" - 9.49 " (Faixa de 31 ") das 21.00 às 24.30
WRCA - 15.15 " (Faixa de 19 ") das 18.00 às 24.30
WGEA - 11.85 " (Faixa de 25 ") das 18.30 às 24.30 ★

Hora do Rio — Quinta
18:00 Resumo dos Programas e Notícias
18:15 O Clube do Swing
18:30 Música Norte Americana
19:00 Notícias
19:15 Orquestra "Pops" de Boston
20:00 Rádio Jornal
20:15 Enoch Light e sua Orquestra
20:45 Fred Waring e sua Orquestra
21:00 Resenha dos Programas
21:02 Notícias
21:15 Orquestra de Raymond Scott
21:30 Notícias Culturais por Gaspar Coelho
21:45 A América do Norte Canta
22:00 Notícias
22:15 Olga Coelho, Trio Charro Gil e a Orquestra Panamericana
23:00 Notícias
23:15 Trio Charro Gil
23:30 Banda da Marinha dos EE. UU.
00:00 Resumo das Notícias
00:15 Devaneio Musical
00:30 Encerramento

Hora do Rio — Terça
18:00 Resumo dos Programas e Notícias
18:15 Canções das Nações Unidas
18:45 Resenha Literária
19:00 Notícias
19:15 Chopiniana
19:30 Conheça Nova York
20:00 Rádio Jornal
20:15 Enoch Light e sua Orquestra
20:45 Fred Waring e sua Orquestra
21:00 Resenha dos Programas
21:02 Notícias
21:15 Orquestra de Raymond Scott
21:30 Notícias Desportivas
21:45 Música por Tucci
22:00 Notícias
22:05 André Kostelanetz e sua Orquestra
22:30 Eva Garza e Orquestra Panamericana
23:00 Notícias
23:15 Trio Charro Gil
23:30 A Opera Municipal de St. Louis
00:00 Resumo das Notícias
00:15 Orquestra Panamericana
00:30 Encerramento

Hora do Rio — Domingo
18:00 Sinfonia da NBC
19:00 O Mundo Hoje
19:10 Resumo dos Programas
19:15 Melodias de Broadway
19:30 A Vida em Hollywood
19:45 Seleções de Opereta
20:00 Rádio Jornal
20:15 Salão de Concerto
20:45 Música Semi-Clássica
21:00 Resenha dos Programas
21:02 Notícias
21:15 Música da América
21:45 Bandas Militares
22:00 Notícias
22:15 Olga Coelho e Trio Charro Gil
22:30 Reinaldo Henriquez e a Orquestra Panamericana
23:00 Notícias
23:15 Orquestra Filarmônica de Nova York
00:00 Resumo das Notícias
00:15 Devaneio Musical
00:30 Encerramento

Hora do Rio — Sexta
18:00 Resumo dos Programas e Notícias
18:15 Momento Musical
18:45 Revista Cultural
19:00 Notícias
19:15 Música do Novo Mundo
19:45 Música de Dansa
20:00 Rádio Jornal
20:15 A Página Feminina
20:45 Música Semi-Clássica
21:00 Resenha dos Programas
21:02 Notícias
21:15 Orquestra de Walter Gross
21:30 Cartas em Revistas
21:45 Alma de Minha Pátria
22:00 Notícias
22:05 Pelos Sendeiros da Música
22:30 Comentário
22:35 R. Henriquez e Orq. Panamer.
23:00 Notícias
23:15 Trio Charro Gil
23:30 Orq. de Concertos CBS e Solistas
00:00 Resumo das Notícias
00:15 Orquestra de Paul Barron
00:30 Encerramento

Hora do Rio — Segunda
18:00 Resumo dos Programas e Notícias
18:15 Magia Tropical
18:30 A Semana em Revista
18:45 Divirtam-se Conosco
19:00 Notícias
19:15 Tesouro Musical das Américas
19:45 Música de Dansa
20:00 Rádio Jornal
20:15 Sammy Kaye e sua Orquestra
20:45 Música Semi-Clássica
21:00 Resenha dos Programas
21:02 Notícias
21:15 Orquestra de Walter Gross
21:30 Música de Manhattan
22:00 Notícias
22:15 Eva Garza e Trio Charro Gil
22:30 O Desfile das Américas
23:00 Notícias
23:15 Trio Charro Gil
23:30 Convite à Música
00:00 Resumo das Notícias
00:15 Orquestra de Raymond Scott
00:30 Encerramento

Hora do Rio — Quarta
18:00 Resumo dos Programas e Notícias
18:15 Valsas Famosas
18:45 Serenata Tropical
19:00 Notícias
19:15 Seleções de Opera
19:45 Dinah Shore – canções
20:00 Rádio Jornal
20:15 Contrastes Musicais
20:30 Aviação Americana
20:45 Música Semi-Clássica
21:00 Resenha dos Programas
21:02 Notícias
21:15 Orquestra de Walter Gross
21:30 Notícias de Hollywood
21:45 Concertos de Jazz
22:00 Notícias
22:15 Eileen Farrell e a Orq. da CBS
22:30 Reinaldo Henriquez e Orquestra Panamericana
23:00 Notícias
23:15 Eva Garza e Orquestra Panamericana
23:30 Música de Manhattan
00:00 Resumo das Notícias
00:15 Quarteto Golden Gate
00:30 Encerramento

Hora do Rio — Sabado
18:00 Resumo dos Programas e Notícias
18:15 Orq. de Alfred Wallenstein
18:45 Bolet. Latino-Americano
19:00 Notícias
19:15 Chopiniana
19:30 Música Popular
20:00 Rádio Jornal
20:15 Caravana Tropical
20:45 Fred Waring y sua Orquestra
21:00 Resenha dos Programas
21:02 Notícias
21:15 Orquestra de Raymond Scott
21:45 Bandas Militares
22:00 Notícias ou Comentário
22:15 A Hit Parade
22:45 R. Henriquez e Orquestra Panamericana
23:00 Notícias
23:15 Orquestras de Variedades
23:30 Música de Hoje e Ontem
00:00 Resumo das Notícias
00:15 Orquestra de Harry James
00:30 Encerramento

TRANSMISSÕES EM "ONDAS DIRIGIDAS" PARA O BRASIL.

28. The schedule of shortwave American stations. Brazilians could listen to war news, jazz, American big bands, singers, and lessons on Pan-Americanism.

29. *President Roosevelt's second visit to Brazil, to the Natal base, painted by Raymond Neilson.*

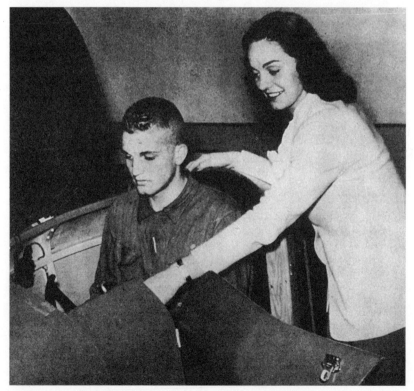

30. *For training Brazilian pilots, Americans used their expertise and charm.*

31. Eleanor Roosevelt on a goodwill trip to Brazil autographs a Brazilian snakeskin.

32. Brazilian soldiers returning home after the war in Europe. Note that there were no color barriers among them.

33. American officers of the 5th U.S. Army being greeted by President Getúlio Vargas.

34. *American canned juice ad to win over Brazilian consumers.*

Down Argentine Way
(20th Century-Fox, 1940)
Costume designer: Travis Banton

*35. Carmen Miranda
for kids: she conquered
American hearts and
minds.*

Two costumes from
That Night in Rio
(20th Century-Fox, 1941)
Costume designer: Travis Banton

36. *The Smoking Snake was the FEB (Força Expedicionária Brasileira) symbol.*

3. The Boogie-Woogie in the Favela, or the Brazilian Attraction to the American Standard of Living

Since I was a kid I have imagined myself on board a great transatlantic ship going to the country of skyscrapers. The movies only increased this desire.

ALINE CARACCIOLO

Americanization via the Movies

The U.S. government made a tremendous effort to transform the Latin American image into something more palatable to the American public. This effort needed to be reciprocated by the change in the image of the United States South of the Rio Grande.

The task of Rockefeller's emissaries in Brazil was in a way made easier by the strength of the American economy, the American standard of living, the fetish for gadgets, and Hollywood films; they all acted as vanguard troops in advance of an "invasion." Before the creation of the Office of the Coordinator of Inter-American Affairs, a cultural interchange between the United States and Brazil was already in place. Officially, this policy of closer relations was handled by the Cultural Division of the State Department. Privately, it was carried out by the big movie studios. Starting in the mid-1940s, the studios themselves had looked for close contact with Latin America to compensate for the loss of the European market, which was closed to the American movie industry because of Nazi expansion.

Hollywood artists who came to Brazil to promote their studios often cooperated with the U.S. government in the task of carrying out the policy of developing closer relations with Brazil. In general, they gathered information to guide the actions of the State Department in order to win over Brazilian public opinion to the American cause: the defense of the Americas under U.S. leadership.

This happened on the afternoon of June 14, 1940, when Errol Flynn was received by President Vargas in the Catete Palace.[1] The star of *Sea Hawk*, a film that would be shown in Brazilian movie theaters, wrote to Pres.

Franklin Delano Roosevelt the following day describing what had happened. From the conversation with Vargas, Flynn assumed that Vargas was favorable to the ideas of unity and Pan-American friendship proposed by Roosevelt. At 8:45 P.M., after the meeting with Vargas, the American actor made a statement in English for *Hora do Brazil* on national radio hookup. He greeted the Brazilians with a "Good evening," in Portuguese. He said that he had very much liked the reception that the Brazilian people had given to a "stranger" and was grateful for the honor granted by DIP. He wanted to speak about a subject that was not related to his films. He expected that his visit would help to strengthen the relations between South America and North America. The actor excused himself for speaking in English and for mentioning a very serious topic. He did, however, say farewell in Portuguese: "Terei saudade," which means I will miss you.[2]

Some days before Flynn's visit, minor friction occurred in diplomatic relations between Brazil and the United States. It was provoked by a Vargas speech on June 11, 1940, which was interpreted as favorable to the Axis. Two weeks later, on June 26, after the speech had been "parsed" by U.S. undersecretary of state Sumner Welles, who assured U.S. officials that Vargas's comments related to domestic political issues and should not be construed as admiration for fascism, that concern subsided.[i] Roosevelt sent a telegram to Vargas speaking of cooperation between Brazil and the United States.[3]

The political opinions of artists were rarely noted by Brazil's newspapers, which were more concerned with informing readers about Hollywood gossip and publishing film reviews. Stories about the artists helped to sell papers, and the papers promoted their films; it was a win-win situation. The public was interested in the most trivial things: Henry Fonda, who had visited Brazil at the same time, was described by a São Paulo newspaper as "inelegant, wearing old and very crumpled clothes." This differed from what was said about Errol Flynn, whom the papers described as "very elegant."[4] On February 3, a thousand people went to the São Paulo airport to greet Westerns hero George O'Brien.[5]

The Brazilian market was increasing in importance for American movie companies. In March 1940, the Paramount International Convention took place. It was presided over by Adolph Zukor himself, the president of the studio.[6] In October, Columbia Pictures made a move to expand its presence in Brazil.[7]

There was rapid growth in the exhibition of American films in Brazilian cinemas. In São Paulo in mid-1940, fourteen of the sixteen movie theaters were showing at least one American film. By the end of the year, all of them were showing American films. The prominent feature film in July in the view of critics was MGM's *Broadway Melody*, with Fred Astaire and Eleanor

Powell. The movie section of *O Diário de São Paulo* published various commentaries on the private lives of Bing Crosby, Gloria Jean, Laraine Day, Marlene Dietrich, and Billie Burke.[8] Two years later, films were approved by Brazilian censors as follows: "American: 2164 long features and 1410 short features; 604 Brazilian, 102 English, 16 Argentine, 11 French."[9]

The repetitive action of the films imprinted on the Brazilian imagination the image of American heroes. The process of Americanization via film was accomplished in the market. In goods advertised in the press, it was possible to identify a perfect relationship between the concrete notion of the item itself and its representation: Americanism in the significant and in the significance. Ads or news articles often seemed to reproduce scenes from films, in the illustrations as well as in the text itself; for example, the dishwasher represents not only the object but also the housewife's comfort and the image of the American way of life.

Some American films also taught Brazilians to organize charity institutions:

Everywhere the influence of the Metro-Goldwyn-Mayer film *Boys Town* [1938] has been enormous on the establishment of charity homes to shelter abandoned minors, like the ones that exist in the United States. Recently we heard that . . . the honorable wife of President Vargas, Mrs. Darcy Vargas, would soon found a similar institution, meant to receive young women and girls, along the basic model of the home founded and run by the famous Father Flanagan. . . . Brazil is the fifth country to be inspired by the Metro-Goldwyn-Mayer film to solve the problem of poor and abandoned children.[10]

In August 1940, Brazilian writer Érico Veríssimo returned from a trip to the United States sponsored by the Cultural Division of the State Department. The author from Rio Grande do Sul describes this trip in *Gato preto em campo de neve* (Black cat in a field of snow). However, what impressed him most was the ability of the cinema to disseminate culture: "North America is in fact a nation of extraordinary importance, but the American cinema makes it seem a supernatural thing, unique, and with no equal."[11]

Veríssimo understood the power of film and foresaw U.S. supremacy, thanks to its invention of a tradition. This tradition was unique and unprecedented; Brazilians, trying to create their "own cinema," reenacted, in some cases, the American heroes: "In the city of Jundiaí [interior of São Paulo State] local amateur actors began the shooting of a film in Western style . . . the film will last approximately two hours, presenting, in addition to carefully chosen panoramic angles, all the typical scenes of cowboy movies, such as fights, bad guys, horsemen, bar fights, roundups, shoot-outs, cow-boys, and cowgirls."[12]

Disney cartoons were famous before the creator of Mickey Mouse arrived in Brazil as one of the Good Neighbor Policy's ambassadors. In 1940, the film *Fantasia* could be seen in various movie theaters in Brazilian cities. Donald Duck appeared sometimes in the newsreels. Also familiar to Brazilians were Disney characters such as Snow White, Pinocchio, and Bambi.

There was already a link between cinema and the press. In August 1940, Walt Disney, in association with *O Diário da Noite*'s children's supplement *Gury*, among others things brought one hundred Disney prizes from New York on the ship *Argentina* (part of the Good Neighbor Policy fleet). These prizes included ten bicycles, two automobiles, tricycles, and scooters, which would be distributed in a promotional competition at the launching of Pinocchio in *Gury*. On March 7, 1942, Donald Duck appeared for the first time in the Brazilian children's magazine *O Globo Juvenil*. Matarazzo Industries also issued a collection of trading cards with the Disney characters. All that was left to be done was to ask "your mom and your dad to save the cards they find in the Matarazzo products."[13] In a newsreel in the same year, children danced a Carnaval hit wearing costumes with papier-mâché masks representing Pinocchio, Popeye, and the ubiquitous Donald Duck and Mickey.[14]

Thus, the expansion of Hollywood companies into the Brazilian market propagated the popularization of American culture in the country. This surely facilitated the Americanization of Brazil project that had Rockefeller's office as one of its main engines. The conditions became favorable for the success of Roosevelt's Good Neighbor Policy, and the physical presence of mythical film figures strengthened the "Hollywood dream," as mentioned by Aline Caracciolo in the epigraph of this chapter.

Orson Welles contributed to the dissemination of the American illusion among young Brazilian women. For a while, young Cariocas had been dreaming of becoming movie stars, not in Brazil, but in Hollywood. An ad in April 1942 announced a search for "young women between 18 and 25 years for an Orson Welles film." Good wages "of 70$000 to 100$000 per day" were offered,[15] and chosen candidates would not be "mere extras."[16] This meant that the young women chosen would be prominent characters in Welles's film, which meant a preliminary step toward work at RKO in Hollywood. It is not known whether any of the women went to the United States.

IT WAS NOT JUST SIMPLE dressmakers or young Cariocas of the lower classes who were fascinated by Hollywood; the imperialism of the time tried to seduce the heart of President Vargas as well. Berent Friele, a friend of Nelson Rockefeller's and director of the Brazilian Division of OCIAA, personally took the first copy of *Saludos Amigos* to the Guanabara Palace. Disney had developed the idea for this film during his trip to Brazil the previous year. It introduces the character Zé Carioca (Joe Carioca), who was presented to Vargas and his family: "Dr. Figueiredo [from the Division of Motion Pictures of DIP, who was the person in charge of showing the film to the president], was very enthusiastic and guaranteed that the film was a great success among the president, his family members, and a group of friends who had attended the private screening."[17]

Success was not limited to the Vargas family—which viewed the film several times during a long weekend that lasted from Friday to Tuesday—but was repeated in the entire city of Rio de Janeiro and, later, in all Brazilian cities. The totemized Disney animals confirmed and strengthened the glorification of the American way of life.[18]

Zé Carioca appears only in the last of the four episodes of the film, guiding a talkative Donald Duck through Rio de Janeiro, aka the Wonderful City, which guaranteed two weeks of absolute success in the Carioca cinemas. "The Walt Disney film in Rio de Janeiro is now in its second week. It has been receiving consistent good reviews from critics and is growing in popularity on the famous Vital cinemas circuit in five different movie houses."[19]

Disney's Puritanism placed a certain subtle sensuality in the part of the film that relates to Brazil. *Saludos Amigos* is a film that mixes real documentary scenes with animation. In the film, an airplane leaves the United States carrying designers, musicians, and photographers with the mission of looking for new characters for the world of Disney, preferably, to find Latin friends for the Americans Mickey Mouse and Donald Duck. After a three-day journey, the airplane lands in Rio de Janeiro for mechanical reasons. Its destination was Lake Titicaca, in the Andes. However, llamas and other animals receive little exposure in the film. Perhaps they did not have a great interest in the Good Neighbor Policy. The most that Donald accomplished was to make one llama do the fox-trot.

One small airplane is the central character of the segment on Chile. It is part of the airmail fleet and fulfills its duty under poor atmospheric conditions. In Argentina, the pace picks up a little more. The American representative is now Goofy, who swaps his cowboy clothes for the decorated outfit of an Argentine gaucho. Adventures and mix-ups abound in controlling a horse and in handling the *boleaderas*.[ii] When night falls, the solitude weighs on Goofy, and he begins to dance with the horse. Women are rare in Disney films, and when they appear they are asexual, like the ones that Sarmiento, the clever intellectual politician and Argentine diplomat, observed on his trip to the United States about a century earlier. The few women who appear in the three first chapters of *Saludos Amigos* do not reveal characteristics of their gender.

Things change in the last episode of the film. Disney's employees land at Santos Dumont Airport. They take a walk on the mosaic sidewalk of Copacabana and watch Carnaval. Everybody is singing. Sensuality surfaces, mainly in the women; Carnaval does not allow Disney to conceal it. At this point, the cartoon really begins. The opening scene is in the form of an opera libretto: *Aquarela do Brasil*, with music by Ary Barroso and the voice of Aloysio de Oliveira. The voice of José de Oliveira, Zezinho of Carmen Miranda's Bando da Lua, is that of Zé Carioca. Brushes create color and life. A fruit turns into a colorful bird that flies in the direction of a banana tree, where a cluster transforms into various colorful toucans, and so on . . . until the symbol of the Carioca jokes appears: the parrot. Dressed as a *malandro*, he transforms himself into Zé Carioca, the only Latin American character in Disney's Pan-American adventure who survives, at least in Brazil. Donald, who observes the creation of Zé, is in a certain way the godfather of the parrot. The serious secret agent, Mickey, does not have the wit to deal with the Carioca ambience. Disney was successful in creating the malandro of the Good Neighbor Policy.

Zé hands Donald a business card. Donald reciprocates, and Zé immediately recognizes the Hollywood star. The address printed on the card is simply "Hollywood." A friendly hug from the "Brazilian" Zé Carioca conquers Donald. Zé is a fast talker, which is characteristic of a malandro. Donald does not understand. Zé summarizes in good English: "Let's go see the town." And they're off, the two new friends.

Samba is the first lesson: "Tico Tico no fubá," by Zequinha de Abreu, was already well known to the American public in the voice of Carmen Miranda. Its notes emerge from Zé's umbrella, which functions as a flute. In a bar, Donald tastes the incomparable *cachaça,* strong liquor made of sugarcane. From the bar they pretend to go to a kind of Urca Casino. The show in the casino is presented using a common technique from Disney films: the spectator sees only the shadows of the scenes. Obviously, it does not lack a swaying Bahiana.

It is not my goal to discuss the Puritanism of a "society without progenitors," as proposed by Dorfman and Mattelart.[20] Nevertheless, according to them, parents are absent from Disney's society because they would be reminders of the sexual relations necessary for reproduction. Temporarily, however, what Disney concealed in the United States seems to have been compensated for by the swaying of the Bahian. Sensuality was allowed on behalf of a greater cause: the fight against fascism. Disney suggests that his characters liberate their libido south of the Equator. Donald Duck is allowed this treat, which is repeated with much more intensity, when Zé Carioca takes Donald to Bahia in the 1943 film *The Three Caballeros*. Donald barely manages to control his excitement when he sees the Bahian Aurora Miranda.

However, the subtlety of Disney's imperialism did not go so far as to include a black woman or a mulatta in Donald's temporarily sexualized world. When Donald returned to the ascetic arms of his perpetual fiancée, Daisy, he must have dreamed of the curves of the swaying Brazilian women. In Disney's Rio de Janeiro, as in his Bahia, there are neither blacks nor mulattoes. Perhaps the absence of blacks and mulattoes in Disney's films on Brazil pleased the Brazilian elite, victims of the complex of belonging to a country of blacks and mestizos.[21]

In October 1943, São Paulo's children saw a Pluto cartoon. Pluto is, of course, Mickey Mouse's silly dog, but he never appeared alongside Zé Carioca. Unlike Donald, who was guided by Zé and got to know the Brazilian semiunderworld in Rio de Janeiro and Bahia, Mickey Mouse seemed to be too much of a WASP for this. As stated in a review in *O Estado de São Paulo*, Mickey did not go to Brazil, but he sent his "civilized" dog to share the scene with a Latin armadillo: "Armadillo fooled around and conquered an old friend, the civilized dog that traveled in an airplane to these areas of the continent. Is this a likeable, clever parody of the Good Neighbor Policy? It is possible."[22]

Disney's name had already become so important that he was involved in the creation of the famous "smoking snake," the symbol of the FEB.[iii] Sgt. Ewaldo Meyer, stationed in Italy, suggested that the smoking snake he had sketched be adopted as a symbol of the GIs, known in Brazil as *pracinhas*.[23] His sketch landed in Disney's hands and returned more elaborated to Italy. Although wearing a combat helmet, Disney's snake had the appearance of a cowboy from a Western. There was even a certain similarity to the famous General Patton, who was known during World War II for his independence and aggressiveness and for always wearing Colt revolvers with mother-of-pearl handles. Compared with Disney's snake, the symbol that prevailed was a natural snake, neither aggressive nor tame. It was simply a snake in a near-primitive style, with a pipe in its mouth, to differentiate it from other serpents.

AMERICAN ACTORS who were well known to the Brazilian public also appeared in the newsreels. In a 1942 newsreel by United News Reel,[24] Brazilians became aware that Clark Gable had interrupted his acting career to serve in the army. The star of *Gone with the Wind* boarding an airplane in a khaki uniform was the image of American solidarity personified in the fight against fascism. In the same newsreel, a Brazilian convoy appeared patrolling the Atlantic. Brazil's coasts were guarded by the Brazilian navy under the supervision of the Americans.[iv] Thus, the Hollywood actor was identified as a soldier of Pan-Americanism in the fight against the common enemy.

Pan-Americanism also had the support of the fighting power of such commanders as John Ford and Greg Toland, who had arrived in Brazil to film the war effort in the country. President Vargas received Ford and listened to the well-known American director's plans. In May 1944, one of Ford's films about industrial São Paulo was presented to the audience of the Brazilian Press Association and was also shown in the United States.[25]

These films were made thanks to cooperation among the OCIAA Motion Picture Division, the OSS, and several Hollywood studios. More than fifteen weeks of filming in Brazil were necessary for Ford's team to photograph some aspects of the war effort. They filmed the cooperation of the Brazilian and American navies, the patrolling of the South Atlantic, and the production of essential war matériel, such as quartz, rubber, mica, and manganese.

Projects like these were feasible thanks to the presence of more than 215 film specialists among the U.S. Marines, Air Force, Navy, and Army.[26] This fascinating relationship between the motion picture industry and the war industry exerted a cosmic force on Brazilians such as Carlos Ferraro, a native of the Brás neighborhood in the city of São Paulo. On November 10, 1942, the Cultural Division of the U.S. State Department registered the receipt of a letter addressed to President Roosevelt. The stamp of the Division of European Affairs indicated that the lowest bureaucratic level did not have the necessary knowledge to identify the origin of the letter. Only when the letter arrived at the Motion Picture Division was it duly taken care of and, evidently, filed. It was written by Carlos Ferraro on lined paper, in good handwriting with some errors in the Portuguese. "The writer, a poor Brazilian youth, wishes to produce a great film depicting the history and progress of Brazil from the time of discovery until now. He requests the President to finance the undertaking with federal funds, or to arrange for his employment by 20th Century Fox."[27]

Hollywood dreams combined with aspirations of the great United States filled the heads of Brazilians. The paradigm was the United States, but Vargas's accomplishments were as great as those of the American nation's president. Ferraro cannot be considered a "modest Brazilian," but naïve and, therefore, not modest. The Brazilians who wanted to contact Hollywood film studios could find addresses published in newspapers of the time. Carlos Ferraro preferred to write directly to the president of the great American nation, imagining that he would be treated like the director-commander John Ford. Americanized, Carlos Ferraro could "fly" from Brás in São Paulo to Sunset Boulevard in Hollywood. Ferraro's letter is a synthesis of the objectives of this Americanization project.

In Weberian terms, Carlos could be seen as the representative of the ideal type of Americanization longed for by the OCIAA. He did not stop loving Brazil, but he was seduced by Hollywood and by the American standard of living. He was an ideal nationalist, because he was not opposed to the expansion of American capitalism. On the contrary, he promised profits to the film industry. In addition, he had other films in mind that would also be lucrative for 20th Century Fox. Work was the foundation for his projects, in agreement with the Protestant work ethic. Finally, he could be a soldier of democracy, ready to die for the ideal of freedom that was being threatened in the Pacific, the Atlantic, and North Africa.

While young people like Carlos Ferraro dreamed of Hollywood, American students who arrived in Brazil to work on projects for the OCIAA unconsciously reiterated a cinematographic image of their experience in Brazil. In late 1941, Brazilian newspapers announced the arrival of a delegation of American students. Stanley Stein, later an eminent scholar of Brazilian history, and Jordan Young, also a future Brazilianist, were part of the group.[v] Many of them traveled all over Brazil, as the news article reported. After hearing the news of the attack on Pearl Harbor, Young tried to return to the United States, but was prevented by the war.

Consequently, Young traveled extensively through Brazil's hinterlands in the service of the Office of the Coordinator of Inter-American Affairs, which was involved in a joint project with the Public Health Special Service (Serviço Especial de Saúde Pública, SESP) of the Brazilian government:

> In few days there I was in the state of Minas Gerais [Itabira do Mato Dentro]. It was very pretty . . . that landscape enchanted me. But most important was my work with the people who came down from the mountains to work in the iron mines . . . It was incredible . . . people who came from the rustic world to produce for advanced capitalism! . . . my task was to help people adapt to the use of bathrooms, to utilize backyards to plant, and even to teach basic arithmetic, to facilitate the urban life of these men.[28]

From Minas Gerais Young went to the Amazon rain forest. He planned to stay in Brazil for a year but remained for two more years. There is a picture of him on a boat on the Amazon that he took himself. He is dressed in the best style of white civilized explorers in the wilderness. He has kept his necktie on, a souvenir of urban culture, but wears a cinematographic hunter's hat. Since he could not defend the Americas against the Axis on the battlefields of Europe, Africa, and the East, he was working in the rain forest for their future. It was a different way of fighting for the same cause. Latin America would be able to defeat the enemy only if it adopted the fundamentals of hygiene and agricultural techniques that had allowed the United States to accumulate enough wealth to have a prominent place on the global scene.

In another photo he is holding a 12-gauge shotgun. Jordan Young has said that he felt like Humphrey Bogart in the middle of Africa, hunting elephants or lions. In this photo he appears to be content with some alligators.[29] Cinema was the reference even for Young, who seemed to search for the local reality in the fantasy produced by the Hollywood studios. Sometimes, the movie stars themselves looked for experiences that were more real than those they portrayed on screen, as in the case of "Errol Flynn, [who went to] Mato Grosso to hunt jaguars."[30]

Americanization via Radio

As we have seen, the path of the radio project of the OCIAA was prepared by American emissaries. Three months after the creation of Rockefeller's office, William S. Paley, the president of CBS, was asked to travel to Latin America to investigate the possibilities of organizing more consistent programming in South America. In late 1940, Lourival Fontes, director of DIP, received the CBS president in Rio with the highest honors.[31]

Why did William S. Paley go to Brazil? He appeared with Fontes in a photo in *Fortune* magazine taken as they discussed details of the shortwave broadcast of U.S. radio programs in Brazil. In addition to a banquet at the Jockey Club, the meeting included a night out at the Urca Casino. Paley appreciated the quality of the shows and even considered broadcasting some in the United States.

Júlio Barata, the head of the DIP's Radio Division, served as Paley's tour guide. In May 1941, Barata was in New York to organize the Brazilian sector of the radio broadcasts. The future minister of the military government in the 1970s marked his arrival in Manhattan with grandeur by giving a cocktail party in the Basildon Room of the Waldorf Astoria Hotel, with guests such as John Hay Whitney.[32]

Paley's visit made radio relations between Brazil and the United States official. The broadcast of radio programs from one country to another materialized thanks to the agreements signed by Paley and Lourival Fontes.

If Americanism was based on the general idea of technical and material progress, the war offered a chance to show the potential of U.S. industry. It had to be made known to Latin Americans that the United States alone could defeat the Axis. It was not difficult for OCIAA employees working in New York radio studios to "manufacture" a great number of programs with this idea.

A good example is a radio program, *Ouçamos* (Let us hear), produced for the OCIAA in the General Sound Corporation studios, broadcast in Portuguese in Brazil in 1943: "The Ameeericaaas aaat waaaaarrrrr. . . . The whistles of the factories dedicated to the war effort, in all U.S. cities." The announcer continued: "Today they call to work millions of women, because without the valuable cooperation of millions of them on our production and combat fronts, we cannot win this war."[33]

In the same year, the American audience saw in movie theaters a very remarkable cartoon, *The Spirit of 1943*, produced by the Disney Studios. Here Donald Duck behaves as an exemplary American citizen asking for all Americans to fight shoulder to shoulder against Nazi Fascism. The radio program produced for the OCIAA was similar to the Disney cartoon. It was transmitted from New York via shortwave by the big American stations and retransmitted to Brazilian radios via DIP. In the listener's imagination, the dynamism of the factories was conveyed with the help of the soundtrack: whistles calling workers to handle noisy machines. The listener was involved in the war effort, admiring the solidarity of the people, especially the women,[34] who took on an increasingly important role in American society during the war.

Although Brazil began its role as a World War II combatant nation in 1944, according to the programs, it seemed as if the country had been involved in the fighting much longer. In 1943, Brazil was engaged in the war effort (i.e., it was already playing an important role as a supplier of war matériel to the Allies), but the statement sounded strange: "[We] *could not* win the war." It sounded strange because it emphasized the plural, "we," as if Brazil already had a more important and official role in the war—such as sending troops to fight against the Axis. How could it be "our" victory if there was no "us," only the "U.S."? Also, the war did not end until two years later, but that was of no importance.

Confidence in democracy's industrial machine allowed the forecast of victory. The form of disseminating this belief was reminiscent of soap operas or soccer games transmitted by Brazilian radio from São Paulo, which evoked curiosity, emotion, and adventure. Emotion and adventure were experienced in the war films seen by Brazilians: *All Quiet on the Western Front*, *Sergeant York*, *Gung Ho*. We were at war. On the radio and in the movie theaters the war was *ours*, as Americans, and *ours*, as Brazilians.

The masculine voice was replaced by a feminine one announcing the well-known Bob Ripley slogan: "Believe it or not!" Again the masculine voice of the announcer: "This is another of the seeerieeeees . . . *The Americas at War*: the true story of our war production, which is constantly increasing in rhythm to take the United Nations [Allies] to victory and to keep America free forever." The narration was continued by another announcer: "This gigantic production, the biggest ever registered in the history of the world, is a promise of lasting peace. This program is of essential importance for all of us, wherever we live in the free territory of the Americas at war."

Americanize the Americas "wherever we live." This presupposes that everyone who lived in America, in any part of it, would have to recognize the United States as the guardian of a *lasting peace*.

A march, with emphasis on the brass, introduced Bob Ripley himself, who announced in his heavily accented Portuguese the already well-known *Believe It or Not!* A Brazilian announcer continued: "We present . . . *the American woman and the war effort*." Ripley was already a star of radio, newspapers, and cinema who earned hundreds of thousands of dollars. The programs he produced for Brazil were part of the war effort and were not lucrative.

The radio theater carried the listener to a scene of war. An artilleryman of the Flying Fortress in Japan has sent a letter to his mother. An emotional, trembling female voice reads the letter. A masculine voice overlaps and continues reading the letter in a more emphatic tone, narrating the adventures of his struggle against seven Japanese Zero fighter planes. In the background the noise of failing engines and the voice of a pilot: "Emergency landing . . . no fuel."

The narration continues. The members of the crew and, mainly, Bob (this was the name of the presumed author of the letter) escape with their lives, thanks to the lifeboats. The feminine voice, surprised: "But I build lifeboats! . . . And the number of the lifeboat that saved my son's life is the same as the one I built!" A metallic sound is heard: *taaaa . . . tare tarararaaaaaa!* The announcer takes over the narrative: "This is an emotional truth. A laborer working in a factory in the United States made the lifeboat that saved her son's life. Why do women work? They work because their children, their brothers, their husbands are at war. . . . They work so there is never a lack of lifejackets or medicine."

The energetic spirit, a constant in the idea of American progress, appeared in its totality in these programs. From lifeboats to Flying Fortresses, the goods produced in the factories, in addition to being of high quality, were assumed to be simple, resistant, and powerful. They were the result of collective and solidarity-improving actions. Solidarity and collectivity, together with destiny itself, allowed that mother and son to connect in the distant Pacific Ocean.

After this, the program concentrated on working conditions in modern U.S. factories. The companies established day-care centers, rest days to alleviate the tension provoked by the noise and the monotony, and "even music" (here light music played). The announcer continues the narration: "It seems incredible, but it is true. Music increased the production of war armaments in the factories where females worked."[35]

Taylorism and Fordism. The rising Brazilian modern entrepreneur was interested in information on the rationalization of American industry. The idea was not new among Brazilian entrepreneurs, especially in São Paulo. On July 23, 1931, Armando de Salles Oliveira had established the Instituto de Organização Racional do Trabalho (Institute for the Rational Organization of Work, IDORT), hoping to create mechanisms that would help industry in a crisis situation. This would happen thanks to automation and standardization. The word was "Brazilianized," but the method—the standard—was American; that is, it alienated the worker.

Another program, also in the series *Believe It or Not!*[36] that must have impressed Brazilian listeners was the government-supported "Liberty ship" program. Liberty ships were U.S.-flagged merchant ships that could be built in only three days in a "no-frills," scientifically managed manufacturing process. Like the other programs, this one also was in the style of a radio soap opera—sound track with machine noises, voices, whistles, and shouts. The factories, in the state of Washington, belonged to the conglomerate Kaiser Corporation, with headquarters in California. Kaiser's method of building a ship was the same used to build a Jeep.

This dexterity and so-called American ingenuity captured not only the admiration of many Brazilians, but also the will to participate in this "futuristic" process. During the 1950s, Oswaldo Aranha, Brazil's "Americanophile" former foreign minister (1938–1944), became associated with Quartim Barbosa and established Willis Overland of Brazil, in partnership with the Kaiser Corporation.[37]

However, in the first half of the 1940s, cars were no longer being produced in Detroit, which was busy manufacturing tanks, trucks, and weapons for the war. The machines introduced at the New York World's Fair were for a better future. The advent of the easy and enriched life provided by the production of goods benefiting the affluent members of society was delayed during the war.

Radio and films, however, disseminated an image of the great technical advances of the war machines produced in the United States. "There are always secrets during war, gossip, rumors. . . . There are secrets the existence of which the majority has no idea. Yesterday one of them was revealed. . . . Only the result is known, . . . and some details were extremely interesting. . . . Japan was bombed again. We knew that already."[38]

This was narrated in a suspenseful manner and prepared the listener to penetrate the secrets of the U.S. Army Air Force. At this time, the acronym USAAF and its symbol—a circle on a blue background with a five-pointed star overlapped by a rectangle, printed on the airplane's fuselage—were already familiar to Brazilians and Americans.

The Brazilian listener's imagination was captured, admiring the force of U.S. industry. The announcer continued:

> and . . . was bombed by a Flying Super Fortress—the B-29—an enormous airplane, super-strengthened, in all aspects. Not much more is known about this. This, however, as little as it is by itself, is sensational. The engines of these airplanes are twice as powerful as the biggest known bombers. The Flying Fortress, with its four engines, has 4800 horsepower. The B-29 reaches more than 9,000 [horsepower]. . . . It can be assumed that these airplanes approach their targets at an altitude of more than 10,000 meters [about 33,200 feet], and at a speed of 500 kilometers per hour [about 310 mph] and carry the biggest load of explosives ever lifted by an airplane. Its weaponry is the most perfect in existence.

Although they played a large role in the war, Super Fortress bombers were not well known. They were deployed in the Pacific war and used only in mid-1944. More than three thousand of these models were produced, which demonstrates the incredible production capacity of the U.S. aircraft industry, led by Boeing. The program continued, describing the absolute superiority of the airplanes. It was useless for Japan to continue resisting.

There were a series of programs in this format.[39] Listening to the *March of Time*, for example, listeners were informed about schools for submarine crew members, food production in wartime, the situation of Catholics in Germany, the war in the desert, the work of American nurses, and American victories in the Pacific.

A series with broad themes, the *Radio Theater of the Americas*, covered Brazil's role in the war, techniques for handling blood in the laboratory, and the like. The series *Spirit of Victory* provided information on the role of the resistance in countries occupied by the Nazis. The series *Winged Words* supplied information about modern communication techniques.

These programs dealt with subjects related to technical advances in the United States. These advances were often presented as true heroic facts about the people and the nation, but, at the same time, as the natural result of the American lifestyle.

In addition to theatrical programs, there were news reports and chronicles. A program of the latter type attracted attention by commenting on typical U.S. cultural manifestations. On October 31, 1944, journalist Alfredo Pessoa explained to Brazilian listeners the meaning of Halloween, on the Network of the Americas (part of the Columbia Broadcasting System).[40] From Washington, the announcer described, with details, the characteristics of the typical American party. The program concluded with a message of peace: "Rumor has it that at this time there is always a full moon, like the one I am seeing, to fill generations of children with hope. I wish for it to fill the heart of men with hope and peace."

The theme of adventure, typical of films and some radio programs, was emphasized in a series entitled *History in Action!!!*[41] Martial music played as the announcer began the broadcast: "We present dramatic moments of current facts, based on information gathered by North American correspondents on all war fronts. Today *History in Action* focuses on the life of a North American town in these afflicted days. The story is called "The War Arrives at Red Oak."

The announcer's care in pronouncing the words in English disclosed familiarity with American language and culture. "Red Oak is typically American." The music was staccato, reminiscent of bucolic scenes and already registered in the minds of Brazilian listeners as a Western-type film from Hollywood. The listener learned that the town was located in a region of small farming communities. Such information was necessary to "transport" the listener and convey the atmosphere of the small "cinematogenic" city.

"The war takes over the hearts of those people," says an emotional female voice in the farewell scene. Many voices give the impression of a crowd. Farewells, a train whistle, and a mother crying for the children who are going to war.

On a training field in Washington, the youngsters talk about patriotism and the fight that they will have to face against the Axis forces. At the same time, they comment, with homesickness, on the lives they led in Red Oak:

"Hey, you, Darrell, why are you daydreaming?"
"Who, me? Nothing, I was only resting . . ."
"I know! You're homesick, missing Mary. Right, Darrell?"
"Well, it's true. It was thinking about Red Oak, those spring nights with a full moon, flowers, oh! my God . . ."
"It's true. After a good ice cream at old Jenks' . . . one game of pool, and . . ."

"Rides in the convertible with the top down with Mary, the radio play-ing, and she's looking at me with those deep blue eyes . . . yes, that was the life."

The message became more emphatic as *History in Action* continued. In the next scene, the group of youngsters from Red Oak is in North Africa. As is commonplace in war films, neighbors meet on the front, where the true character of each will reveal itself more clearly. The listeners are anxious to know the end of the story, which is now much more exciting. Airplanes are attacking, bombs are falling, there are bursts of machine-gun fire—a story with a good soundtrack, revealing the drama of hard combat. All the youngsters from Red Oak die. The listeners become aware of this when the scene changes to the American town and someone reads to the mothers the official telegram announcing their deaths. A voice is heard over the moth-ers' crying: "The mothers are the true heroes of this war."

The narrative created an expectation in the listener, a desire to know the destiny of these youngsters. What would they face in the war? Would they survive? Would they be able to see their relatives again? Would they return to their beloved hometown? As in a soap opera, the listener is overtaken by emotional anxiety.

All the stereotypes of the U.S. way of life, consecrated by the cinema, seemed even closer aurally, in the imagination of Brazilians. The convert-ible—*barata* in the Brazilian version of that time—a radio playing roman-tic music, moonlit nights, ice cream parlors, blue eyes, and games of pool.

Without a doubt, the automobile was a strong and captivating symbol of the U.S. way of life. Happiness, success, charm, freedom, also sexuality— the American dream itself seemed impossible without this true modern-day object of desire. Americanism was becoming a paradigm for Brazilians. Stereotypes of the American lifestyle had been propagated via movies and radio since the previous decade. General Motors, Ford Motor Company, the Thompson Company,[42] all these American companies had been in Brazil and were using modern commercials. But the programs of this earlier time were not quantitatively and qualitatively comparable to the ones produced in the 1940s, which reached more people and in a much more sophisticated way.

A more earthbound aspect of Americanism reached Brazilians who had listened to programs such as the *University of the Air*,[43] which often pre-sented "lessons" in radio theater form. For example, in 1943, the listener followed a young Brazilian on a trip around Mississippi. One could hear the youngster, on board a steamboat, the "same" as the one seen in *Gone with the Wind*, reading the letter that he was writing to his parents in Bra-zil: "Dear Mom and Dad, I am in the company of Professor Richmann, from Bloomington, on a boat traveling the Mississippi. It is a steamboat, similar to the ones we see in movies." As the alleged student continues his narration, one can hear in the background a typical boatman's song of the region. "Tomorrow," the Brazilian continues, "we will be in New Orleans, at the beginning of Mardi Gras, similar to our Carnaval."

The United States represented progress. In the urban-middle-class listeners' imagination, the Mississippi, even though it had been compared with the Amazon, was more navigable and more dynamic than Brazil's biggest river. Beyond the radio theaters, radio news programs reached a large audience at the time. Several Brazilian announcers transmitted news of the war directly from New York, via DIP with many daily editions. On June 12, 1944, at 8:00 A.M. the following was broadcast:

> Special news program to inform our listeners, at the earliest possible moment, about breaking news . . . daily at 8 A.M. and at 1:00 P.M., sponsored by the DIP network of Brazilian stations.
>
> The Allied Expeditionary Forces, operating in northern France, have made new advances during recent hours. The official notice arrived this morning from the headquarters of General Eisenhower.
>
> Of about 7,000 Allied airplanes operating in the battle zone, 24 were lost. Since the beginning of the invasion of France six days ago, for the first time we have access to news from the front . . . but they did not disclose details of the attack, because the radios are keeping a customary silence. . . .
>
> Here ends, dear listeners, this special bulletin on war news, presented jointly by the stations of the National Broadcasting Company, the Pan-American Network, and Columbia Broadcasting System, the Network of the Americas, from their studios in New York.[44]

The Allies invaded France on June 6, 1944. Other news reports emphasized the FEB's performance in the fight against the Nazis in Italy, the combat of Soviet armies in the region of Leningrad, and the action of the powerful U.S. Navy force in the Pacific, which advanced on the islands of Taipei and Guam.

At the same time, the Radio Club from Rio de Janeiro broadcast a humorous show concerning a metalinguistic satirical radio station called PRK-30. One of its most famous sketches was a "pretend" radio news show that transmitted information about the worldwide situation through its war "correspondent," who gave names of people, places, and battles that were impossible to identify. The comedians played with words, and listeners could find relief from the tense climate of war.

The humorists, inspired by the programming that came from the United States, produced their "news report." Even though it was a parody, the journalistic model was idealized in the studios headed by the OCIAA. Also at this time, and since 1941, serious Brazilian radio journalism was aware of *Repórter Esso*, which was distributed initially by National Radio of Rio de Janeiro and by Record of São Paulo, and later by Farroupilha of Porto Alegre, Inconfidência of Belo Horizonte, and the Radio Club of Pernambuco.

WHEN THE WAR ENDED, there was a memorable show in the United States: the *Performance for Victory*, which aired on August 15, 1945, with Bing Crosby, Carmen Miranda, Dinah Shore, and the boxer Joe Louis. Very little of this program arrived in Brazil. But a few days earlier, a musical program carried the Brazilian listener to Broadway and Hollywood, already free of the shadow of the Nazis: "Jointly with the Department of Press and Propaganda of Brazil"—but in reality, DIP no longer existed. In March, Vargas had dissolved it and created the Departamento Nacional de Informação (National Department of Information)—"the Columbia Broadcasting System presents one more program in the series of interchanges between the United States and Brazil. Today we will begin a series of programs under the heading of 'Favorites of the North American people.'"[45]

The great CBS orchestra played with piano, brass, and strings. The voice of the announcer overlapped the music: "If we look into the hearts of the North American people, we see that they beat to the musical rhythm that lives in the feelings of the people, and that's why it's a favorite. On the first page of the album *Favorites of the North American People* we found a song . . . by Irving Berlin entitled 'Always.'" The announcer translated the title—"Always," "Sempre"—anticipating that the Brazilian listeners would understand at least something of the meaning of the lyrics. But the melody was enough to imagine a movie star meeting her leading man in a bucolic scene on the West Coast or the New York skyline in the background:

> I'll be loving you always
> with a love that's true, always . . .
> I will understand always, always.
> Days may not be fair always
> That's when I'll be there always.

The speaker continues: "We will now hear a song with the joy that is manifested when we take a sip of alcohol, that does not harm anyone. . . . As a special guest we have with us today Vera Holly, star of the program *Viva América*, broadcast weekly in the United States and by shortwave in Latin

THE SEDUCTION OF BRAZIL

America. Her first number will be a romantic one by Carmichael, entitled "Stardust":

> Sometimes I wonder
> why I spent the lonely nights . . .
> The melody haunts my reverie . . .
> The nightingale tells his fairy tale
> Of paradise where roses grew . . .
> My stardust melody
> The memory of love's refrain.

Did music have the same potential as the cinema to be a tool of Americanism? As we have seen, Elsie Houston, the Brazilian American singer, had declared in New York in 1939 that,[46] at least in musical terms, Brazil was ahead of the United States. A survey by the Instituto Brasileiro de Opinião Pública e Estatística (Brazilian Institute of Public Opinion and Statistics, IBOPE) in July 1944 confirmed that Brazilian music was heard more than American music.[47] An example: Bing Crosby was heard by 0.5 percent of those interviewed, while Carlos Galhardo was heard by 26.7 percent.[48] Thus, music was a good vehicle for Americanism, but not the best. It might seem obvious, but as Brazilians saw more American movies and bought more American goods, one might assume that the same would happen with popular music.

Waldo Frank, the "Unquiet" American, and the Crusade for the Integration of the Americas

Beyond the cinema and radio, Rockefeller used intellectuals who had a critical vision of American society ideologically in tune with the generation of the 1920s. The utopian and humanitarian project of these intellectuals was aimed at more honest relations between the United States and Latin America. Rockefeller did not share the critical proposals of these intellectuals, but used some aspects of their point of view in his concept of relations with Latin America.

One of the outstanding examples of this was Waldo Frank. Although his trip to Latin America was subsidized by the State Department, Frank was one of these independent intellectuals, who made his contribution without ever officially being part of the OCIAA. A New York intellectual, Waldo Frank arrived in Brazil in April 1942, two months after Orson Welles. His humanist education was that of a rational socialist, which was the reason for his critical attitude toward U.S. society. In New Mexico,

Frank became fascinated with the Pueblo Indians of the region, who, in his view, lived in harmony with the environment. This attitude, according to him, was not an inheritance of the Pueblo Indians alone, but also of Iberian colonization.[49]

When Frank was flying over the Amazon rain forest in 1942, he was already known for his novels, essays, and books of poetry. In *Casa-grande e senzala*, Gilberto Freyre mentions an article written by Frank. This was not the first time that he crossed the equator and visited Brazil, but he had never been in the Amazon area. As the Catalina hydroplane was starting to descend in Belém, Frank was fascinated with the dark red color of the Amazon: "It was the continent bleeding," as he describes it in *South American Journey*.

This telluric vision was in tune with the thought of the post–World War I generation of outsider intellectuals, for example, Gertrude Stein, Anaïs Nin, Ezra Pound, and Ernest Hemingway. By means of public performance, novels, poetry, articles, and studies regarding inter-American relations, they hoped to stop, metaphorically, the continental bleeding caused by the "greed" of U.S. capitalism.

Frank had been captivated by the Amazon rain forest, which, according to him, was the gateway to Brazil. In the streets of Belém, under leafy trees (in particular, mangos), his sharp ear caught the sounds of a samba coming from a loudspeaker. The samba—a product of the Carioca urban culture of the radio age—was also present in the Amazon. According to the perceptive interpretation of Valter Krausche, Brazil already had been "embraced" from North to South by the "radio singers" of Lamartine Babo in the 1940s.[50] The national culture was being superimposed on the regional one.

Frank's gaze on Brazilian women and their racial mixture was that of the uneasy American. The result of the mixture of Africans, Indians, and Portuguese, their beauty was, in his words, "with long hair, skin of honey, and melancholic looks, prettier than in any part of the world."[51] The Jewish New Yorker of refined education, a socialist, moving between mysticism and rationalism, was taken aback by the Brazilian melting pot. All the rejection of the white aristocracy did not prevent Brazilian *mestiçagem*. Waldo realized what Oliveira Vianna and Gilberto Freyre, each in his own way, were investigating at the same time. As formulated in the intellectual world of the U.S. East Coast, the myth of the melting pot had been put into practice in the tropics.

Aside from the beauty of the women, Frank also noticed Brazil's wounds: poverty. This was reflected in clothing and housing but not in food. Frank concluded that Brazilians, although poor, did not starve, at least not in the Amazon area. Fish, bananas, and, especially, the cassava, the "queen of Brazil," as Luís da Câmara Cascudo called it,[52] kept hunger at bay.

Frank came to realize that there was also a color line in Brazil, but he had the sensitivity to notice the difference: the separation was more economic than racial.[53] There was a socioeconomic "glass ceiling," some sort of a "dollar line."

While observing Brazilian women, Frank compared them with American women: "Free they are, all, in their deep acceptance of their sex; and in this, different from our women."[54] Monteiro Lobato had also been intrigued by the odd gender relations in the United States during the 1920s. Lobato believed that American men had exaggerated respect for women and did not agree with Frank that they feared them. He felt that respect was really a type of fear, which caused frustration for American women: "Between respect and love, she prefers love. The exaggerated respect with which the American male deals with her is a protective astuteness. Placing the naked sword of Puritanism between himself and her, the man protects himself against temptation. . . . This business giant during the day, where he engages in business ventures with the entire world, is too tired at night—and love is nocturnal. Since he is tired, he runs away from the woman under the protective excuse of respect."[55]

Americans had always been intrigued by Brazilian women. Fifteen years after Frank's visit to Brazil, Pres. Juscelino Kubitschek (1955–1961) visited the United States. In an interview given to the American press at the National Press Club in Washington, one of the journalists asked Kubitschek: "Why are Brazilian women so attractive?" Kubitschek answered: "Brazilian women are attractive mainly because we, Brazilian men, treat them well."[56]

In Belo Horizonte, Frank confirmed in a more concrete way his vision of Brazilian women. In a bar he met a leftist Brazilian dentist-journalist. They talked about Brazilian politics and Vargas, whom Frank found very enigmatic. The dentist, who already had been jailed because of his ideas, emphasized that Vargas was a great politician who cared about human beings. He compared him with Lincoln. Frank was seemingly more confused. The dialogue continued, but Frank's attention switched to Ifigênia, the waitress who was serving the next table:

> She is not our waitress, another girl brings us our drinks. But the one in my eyes seems, across the noise of the large room, to hear me. She turns and smiles. Of course, she has not heard; my message reached her by another channel.
>
> She is a girl of eighteen. . . . a mulatto with some Indian blood heightening her skin to a luminous honey. Her heavy hair is black; her features strong and perfect; her lips not too heavy. The whole face, gay with vitality and beauty, is matriced in sadness.

When at last I reach my hotel for dinner, I am full of the revelation of this girl. . . . After coffee, with Dr. Teixeira and a journalist, we go to the café. . . . The girl is still there; busy at the end of the smoke-filled room. She feels our entrance, and smiles.

And now, a strange event: where but in Brazil could it happen? The whole café seems to know my interest, and to take part in it: indulgent, affectionate part. The girl knows, too. She comes and sits with us, at our table. She tells me her name: Ifigenia Silva. She lives alone with her mother. And do I know Robert Taylor? She smiles, and I smile.[57]

Frank ended up going to bed with the simple Ifigênia, who wanted to know if he knew the film star Robert Taylor. According to Fredrick Pike, it was not a simple physical relationship. To Frank, the Brazilian mulatta was an archetype of Latin America and her body, a representation of Brazil itself. Their encounter represented a fusion of the two cultures.

From a naïve perspective, Frank seems to incarnate the spirit of Simón Bolívar and foreshadows that of the Mercosur South American trading bloc. According to him, the united Americas could have a common market to facilitate intercontinental commerce. On the political and institutional level, the result would be one continent strong enough to defend its independence in a dangerous world. This concern made sense at the time when Frank wrote it, because both Germany and Japan were at the height of their expansionism. And Brazil, as we have seen, was not left out of the plans of the racists of the Wilhelmstrasse. A united America could concentrate its energies and national powers to ensure wealth and harmony on the continent. This would be cemented by democracy, the common destiny of the Americas.

Frank's utopian vision conflicted with Latin America's political reality. At that moment, most of the region had fallen under the sway of authoritarian governments. There clearly existed different concepts of democracy. In the case of Brazil, Vargas claimed to espouse an "illiberal democracy." He criticized monopolies at the same time that he advocated a strong state that guaranteed the essential rights of the people. It is necessary to remember that Vargas did not get to power by means of direct elections, as is customary in liberal environments.[vi] For Frank, political authoritarianism and democracy were mutually exclusive.

Frank's mysticism turned into a utopian vision of America. A City of Men would be built here, similar to the City of the Sun of the Renaissance writer Tommaso Campanella. America would be the utopian island where people would find peace and prosperity. A believer in the American concept of democracy, Frank invoked Jefferson and Franklin to unite Hispanic America, which included Brazil.

This inclusion stirred bitter controversy during a luncheon given by Minister Oswaldo Aranha at the Rio Jockey Club. In 1931, Frank had published *Hispanic America*, a book of essays on Latin American culture and society. Frank's inclusion of Brazil in Hispanic America in this book was sharply questioned by Oswaldo Aranha, who was supported by Herbert Moses, Afrânio Mello Franco, Paulo Bittencourt, and Assis Chateaubriand. All criticized Frank's "error" in employing the term "Hispanic America" to agglomerate Lusitanian Brazil with its linguistically and culturally Hispanic neighbors. Frank defended his position and cited the Portuguese writer Camões; even so, his listeners continued to criticize his incorrect usage. They demanded a new edition, which would reserve a special place for Brazil. The Jeffersonian paradigms and those of other founding fathers were not criticized directly, but the disagreement was certainly inherent in Eduardo Prado's arguments, as discussed in the Introduction.

A united and democratic America was but an illusion. Was it not Jefferson himself who had declined to support the *inconfidentes* [the first Brazilian independence movement] at the end of the eighteenth century? Did not Washington reject the credentials of the emissary from rebellious Pernambuco—who had gone to the American nation to ask for help for the 1817 insurrection against the repressive Portuguese?[58] Although these arguments were not raised during the luncheon at the Jockey Club, they must have existed in the imagination of the Brazilian government at the time.[vii]

But Frank did not give up. The basic points of his program for American unification were as follows: (a) natural resources—mines and oil wells—should be returned to Latin American hands, and U.S. companies should facilitate the purchase of these companies by Latin Americans; (b) no recognition of dictatorial governments; (c) Americans would have to realize that U.S. democracy was lacking in an important aspect: race relations.

Frank believed that the United States could not obtain the confidence of the other republics while harsh discrimination and racism existed within its borders. American children should be taught subjects that compared existing American cultures. African and Amerindian cultures should be part of the core curriculum. The history of Portugal and Spain should receive the same emphasis as that of France and England. He expressed all these arguments later when he returned to his country at the end of 1942.

When Frank arrived in Rio, he did not expect an official reception. When he landed at Santos Dumont Airport, he had hoped only to meet the Chilean writer Gabriela Mistral. But there were journalists and a group led by Graça Aranha, Vargas's cultural affairs representative.

Frank had the good luck to arrive on April 23, the feast day of Saint George, "the greatest of all the saints in the heart of the Cariocas, the people of Rio de Janeiro."⁵⁹ Now the unquiet American faced one more demonstration of Brazilian democracy: Saint George did not make distinctions of social class, race, sex, or age; all venerated the saint. "By nightfall, the streets leading to the Place of the Republic are crowded with a mass of men, women, children, mothers with babes in arms, who (without benefit of police to preserve order) line up and patiently wait their turn to enter the Church."⁶⁰ People of various social classes and races who kissed the ribbon of Saint George confirmed the democratic character of the saint.

In certain passages in his *South American Journey*, Frank uses the royal "we" to introduce his guides: Vinícius de Moraes and friends. Moraes gave the American some explanations and took him to another democratic space: the "Mangue," Rio's poor red-light district. Frank demonstrated a certain familiarity with this topic and risked what seemed to be a Freudian interpretation: "Prostitution for men who work is more, far more, the seeking of a mother than a sexual delight."⁶¹

Frank's official program was intense. There were improvised conferences and interviews. He was interviewed by Samuel Wainer, director of *Diretrizes*, a left-wing magazine that enjoyed freedom of expression in the repressive Estado Novo government.ᵛⁱⁱⁱ The interview was followed by a dinner in Copacabana. There he was almost convinced that the Vargas dictatorship could not be analyzed according to known models.

Frank accepted a dinner invitation to Jorge de Lima's home, which allowed for some moments of tranquillity and reflection. Jorge de Lima, a native of Alagoas, was a physician known for his contributions to both public health and literature. His poems "O acendedor de lampiões" (The lamplighter) and "Mulher proletária" (Proletarian woman) were well known, but his dissertation, "O romance de Proust" (Proust's novel), earned him an academic chair in literature.

Frank enhanced the idea of communitarian America in the home of this black, Catholic, and respected Brazilian intellectual. It could shelter "brothers" from Franklin Delano Roosevelt to Frank himself, Jorge de Lima, Lourival Fontes, and even Getúlio Vargas. The black intellectual Jorge de Lima captured Frank's attention. The American seemed to be in tune with the feeling of peace that emanated from the traditional culture of the Alagoan's home state, where family relations seemed to confirm the Brazilian concept of "racial democracy." Lima's wife and two children were as white as the New York intellectual. "The different-colored skins, to all seeming, harmonize, as in a home of ours, different-colored eyes or hair. Nothing unnatural in this happy, Christian family—unless thinking make it so."⁶² Without a doubt, this was an important issue in the humanist reasoning of the American outsider: to try to apprehend and utilize as alternative paradigms Ibero-American formulas to purge the existing gender and race conflicts in American culture. Paradoxically, Brazil had become a paradigm for this kind of intellectual.

However, important sectors of the Brazilian ruling class turned their backs on what was genuinely Brazilian. Their paradigm was either European culture or modernizing American materialism. They wavered. At that moment, the Nazi and Japanese war machines still had not been deterred. The Americans had barely pulled themselves together from the shock of Pearl Harbor and were still shaken from defeats in the Philippines. Although Lt. Col. Jimmy Doolittle's B-25s had bombed Tokyo, the Japanese still seemed invincible. The same could be said about the Germans. German generals Manstein and Kleist approached the Caucasus. The fighting in Stalingrad had begun, and Leningrad shook under the thousand-day German siege. In spite of this, the Brazilian elite (and especially its Paulista branch) still cherished the liberal constitutional spirit shaped by American federalism. The creation of the University of São Paulo (USP) was the gaúcho's consolation prize for the Paulista rebels after the defeat of their uprising, in the so-called Constitutionalist Revolution of 1932. And it would be from USP—which sheltered intellectual representatives of European thought—that concepts of liberal or social democracy emanated, both with antiauthoritarian tendencies, but mainly anti-Vargas ones.[ix]

Frank seemed to direct the attention of the intellectual Brazilian elite to the fact that Brazil did not need paradigms. On the contrary, it *was* the paradigm, at least regarding race and gender relations.

Frank was also shaken by his meeting with Oswald de Andrade. Andrade arrived from São Paulo projecting an effusive, extremely welcoming attitude. He said that he came to Rio especially to see Waldo Frank. The American did not believe one word of the Brazilian Communist dandy. Frank found it odd that Andrade called himself a Communist but was not in prison like Luís Carlos Prestes.[x] He also found it very strange when Andrade told him that he was married to the sister of his son's wife, that is, his daughter-in-law's sister. An "exaggerated" demonstration of gender democracy.

As mentioned earlier, Vinícius de Moraes was Frank's guide in Rio de Janeiro and introduced him to Carioca culture, but Moraes also discovered the rest of Brazil, led by the American. Vinícius de Moraes had been assigned by the Brazilian government to travel with Frank through the North and Northeast. For the first time, the Brazilian poet observed the *mocambos* (a community of runaway slaves) of Recife and attended a *capoeira* (an Afro-Brazilian martial arts dance) show in Salvador.[63]

Waldo Frank's anti-Hollywood attitude helped to bond the friendship with Vinícius de Moraes:

I don't remember if it was José Lins do Rego or Octávio Tarquínio de Souza [two Brazilian writers] who asked him [Frank] if he already had any of his books turned into films, in connection with the U.S. film version of Melville's *Moby Dick*. The talk continued with Frank's expression of his contempt for Hollywood. He felt that the filmmakers were both incompetent and corrupt. "I have never let them [make a film of any of my books]. . . . Hollywood is corrupt to the soul. I know very well what they would do with a book of mine. It would not be difficult to make money this way, but as a writer it is not what I want." I immediately understood that we had the same vision of the relations between culture and politics.[64]

In Rio, Frank was invited by Orson Welles to visit the location where Welles was filming part of his quasi-documentary, *It's All True*. There he saw Cariocas singing and dancing as he had never seen them before. Sunset in April was the backdrop of the spectacle he witnessed. The American was fascinated, and he had reason to be:

I could listen to Brazilian folk music forever. It is unfathomably beautiful and unfathomably profound. Upon its surfaces, it is honey-sweet, petal-soft, caressing the skin like the touch and scent of flowers. Within its depth, it is complex like organic life; and dark as tragedy. Beside it (I speak of the plentiful best) our popular music (jazz, swing, torch-song, chant of cowboy, ranger, pioneer) is repulsive with its skin-nervous intricacies bristling about emptiness and inorganic softness. Beside it, even our best Negro spirituals reveal the false simplifying and diluting process of an alien culture upon the Negro. Brazilian folk music is not African or Negro; it is Brazilian. Its components, African, Indian and Portuguese, are organically fused like the elements in a living body.[65]

It is unknown whether Frank read "On the Fetish Character in Music and the Regression of Listening" (Über Fetischcharakter in der Musik und die Regression des Hörens) by Adorno, but his analysis is very similar to the conclusions of the philosopher of the Frankfurt School. The "nervousness" of American music had already been noted by Adorno in 1938, in a famous study: "The phenomenon presents convulsive features, which remind us of the illness called Saint Vitus's dance, or the reflexes of mutilated animals. The passion itself seems to be caused by specific functional imperfections. The ritual of ecstasy is revealed as pseudo-activity through the mimical moment."[66]

Frank's and Adorno's positions, in reality, converge through the idea that the market diminishes the creativity of popular music. At the time when Frank was falling in love with Brazilian music, the widespread appropriation of folk and popular music by commercial studios did not yet exist in Brazil, but, according to Adorno, was already common in the United States.

Brazilian music was one of the cultural manifestations that was most resistant to Americanization. The reference to elements of American culture in the lyrics of Brazilian songs of the 1940s does not mean that Brazilian music had absorbed the "nervousness in the skin, the tension" of the American music.

Boogie-Woogie in the Slums

Americanization was the theme of many songs of the 1930s and 1940s.[67] Some of them had nationalistic messages in defense of Brazilian culture. It was almost an anti-imperialist movement in Brazilian popular music. Some songs satirized Americanization as a way of overcoming Brazilian "backwardness." The list is long, but a few examples include "Boogie-Woogie do rato," by Denis Brean; "Oh! Boy," by Haroldo Lobo and Ciro de Souza; "Cowboy do amor," by Wilson Batista and Roberto Martins; "Dança do boogie-woogie," by Carlos Armando; "Samba da casaca," by Pedro Caetano and Walfrido Silva; "Gosto mais do swing," by Lauro Maia; "O samba agora vai," by Pedro Caetano; and the classic "Yes, nós temos bananas," by Alberto Ribeiro and João de Barro.

Assis Valente, one of the greatest samba composers from Bahia, wrote in 1940—during the highpoint of the Good Neighbor Policy—the emblematic song "Brasil pandeiro." Seven years earlier, Carmen Miranda had recorded the gracious melody "Good bye! Boy," also by Assis, at the same time Noel had composed "Não tem tradução" (There is no translation). "Good bye! Boy" is part of a phase in Brazilian music that could be called nationalist—or "anti-imperialist," to differentiate it from patriotic:

Good bye, good bye boy,	Good-bye, good-bye, boy,
deixa a mania do inglês	quit the craze for English
Fica tão feio pra você	It does not look good for you,
moreno frajola.	an elegant mulatto.

The "anti-imperialist" sambas such as "Good bye! Boy" were a thing of the past in the 1940s. Noel died in 1937; Carmen Miranda was already on Broadway, even though she had recorded a type of mea culpa, "Disseram

que voltei americanizada" (They say I returned Americanized), and Assis
had composed "Brasil pandeiro":

Chegou a hora dessa	It's time for this
gente bronzeada	(bronzed) suntanned people
mostrar seu valor! . . .	to show their value! . . .
Na Casa Branca	In the White House
já dançou a batucada.	he already danced the batucada.

The value Assis refers to is the value of the *sambista*. Originally, the "sun-
tanned people" were restricted to the favelas of the Saúde area and the hills
of Rio de Janeiro. Now, however, it was their turn. They had to seize their
moment to prove their importance in a cosmopolitan context. They needed
to leave the hillside favelas of Vintém and Pindura-Saia to international-
ize themselves. The samba could be known worldwide only with the help
of Uncle Sam. Uncle Sam playing the tambourine for the world to dance
the samba. Anthropophagically,[68] Assis suggested a swallowing up: different
sambas, different countries, and different people. The world will dance the
samba according to Uncle Sam's music but from the Brazilian perspective.
Was Brazil not the "United States" of South America? Was Brazil not similar in a certain way? In a musical sense, Brazil and the United States could
also have a partnership. Fox-trot or swing could adapt to the samba, and
American music could be kept in rhythm by the Brazilian tambourine.

Nelson Rockefeller was the incarnation of Uncle Sam. Roosevelt had
given him carte blanche to play this role. And, as seen earlier, he did a lot
to prevent Brazilians from switching from the easy fox-trot to a Wagnerian
aria. He would even have been capable of learning Brazil's batucada, and
he would teach Brazil the swing, fox-trot, and boogie-woogie. The tasteless
hot dog was better with Bahian molho.

Assis had composed this samba for his declared passion, Carmen
Miranda, after she had danced and dressed more conservatively in order to
perform for Eleanor and President Roosevelt. Therefore, the White House
had danced Ioiô and Iaiá, the mythical names of the *umbanda* places and
the samba circles.

A newspaper article reported on Carmen Miranda's success in Washington in 1940. The "Bahian" Miranda described with emotion her visit
to the White House. She mentioned that she sang for the Roosevelts. The
president, who already had seen her show in the Urca Casino in November 1936, was not as surprised as his wife. Carmen was the representation, the epitome, of samba. In the dressing room she received greetings
from famous Hollywood performers. She also stated that there was a

great interest in Brazilian popular music in the United States, and that her outfit was the determining factor in her victory. Brazil was acknowledged in Carmen Miranda in both a political sense and in mass culture.

If Brazilians expected that Uncle Sam would dance the samba and use Brazilian seasonings in 1940, the slums' inhabitants were dancing boogie-woogie in 1945. Denis Brean composed and Ciro Monteiro recorded the great hit "Boogie-woogie na favela":

Chegou o samba minha gente	The samba arrived, people
Lá da terra do Tio Sam . . .	From the land of Uncle Sam . . .
Que faz parte da Política	That is part of the Good Neighbor
da Boa Vizinhança.	Policy.

The cosmopolitan from São Paulo, Denis Brean, understood the "new samba." While Brazilian music had been exported to the United States and presented by Carmen Miranda with Romeu Silva and others—now it had returned influenced by boogie-woogie, a genre with its roots in blues. Although the Good Neighbor Policy was drawing its last breath, Brazilian samba conformed to the new dance that emerged. This time the Brazilians were dancing. No longer in partnership with Uncle Sam, as Assis had envisioned, nice Brazilian women wholeheartedly adopted the music that was part of the Good Neighbor Policy. If earlier the samba could be a partner in the Good Neighbor Policy, now it would have to dance according to the music coming from the land of Uncle Sam. The boogie-woogie moves were less demanding than the samba as danced four years earlier by the black girl Disney saw on Portela Hill. The great embrace with which Lamartine Babo's "Radio Singers" united the south and north of Brazil was confirmed with the inclusion of the Amazon, the great São Paulo, and the great Rio, which joined the new dance that had emerged.

As demonstrated by pollsters from IBOPE, Brazilians still preferred their music. Although Brazilians had incorporated elements of American music in some Carnavals, it did not mean—as Frank had noticed—that a simple imitation had occurred. At the time, it was an Americanization with conditions.

Conclusion

Americanization Was Not Imitation

THE GOOD NEIGHBOR POLICY was a U.S. government initiative under the administration of Franklin Delano Roosevelt. During the administration of Republican Herbert Hoover, Roosevelt's predecessor, there was an earlier effort to improve U.S.–Latin American relations. As has been mentioned, the expression itself—Good Neighbor Policy—was coined by Hoover, but it was Roosevelt who, through his words and actions, expressed the clear meaning of the new policy for Latin America. Soon after his inauguration, he declared: "I would dedicate this Nation to the policy of the good neighbor—the neighbor who resolutely respects himself and, because he does so, respects the rights of others—the neighbor who respects his obligations and respects the sanctity of his agreements in and with a world of neighbors."[1] During the Seventh Pan-American Conference, which took place in Montevideo in 1933, Cordell Hull, then secretary of state, said: "Not a single state has the right to intervene in the internal and external affairs of another nation."[2]

Despite the secretary's and the president's declarations, there were secret unarmed interventions. The most obvious example is the case of Cuba. The formidable pressure exerted by the United States prepared the way for the dictatorship of Fulgencio Batista. However, this small demonstration of force in Roosevelt's foreign policy made those brutal interventions at the beginning of the century look like things of the past that would never again be repeated.

The change in direction in American policies was confirmed by Roosevelt's visit to Brazil in November 1936. It was in Rio de Janeiro that the policies for Latin America acquired a better-defined outline on the representational level. President Roosevelt was received with all pomp. "A huge crowd welcomed Mr. Roosevelt at the port quay. The ship in which the North American president arrived crossed the bay shielded by civil and military airplanes and protected by fortresses," wrote a Brazilian newspaper at the time.[3] Pres. Getúlio Vargas held a banquet for President Roosevelt. Roosevelt's thank-you speech on this occasion may be considered an important oratorical representation of the new and seductive American diplomacy.

At the beginning of the speech, the U.S. president recalled having his first contact with Brazil in Paris. In the French capital, the young Roosevelt was pleased to be introduced to the exiled Brazilian emperor, Dom Pedro II. Brazil's national icon, who in the nineteenth century diplomatically confronted the arrogant England, was recognized by the representative of the now major continental power. That was just the beginning of the speech.

Then Roosevelt tried to demonstrate the successes and mistakes of the actions of the United States. He suggested that Brazil should avoid those mistakes. He also recognized that the Americans did not help Brazil in the same way the Brazilians helped the Americans: "You have done much to help us in the United States in many ways in the past. We, I think, have done a little to help you, and may I suggest that you, with this great domain of many millions of square miles, of which such a large proportion is still open to human occupation, can learn much from the mistakes we have made in the United States."[4]

However, the American president left the most remarkable part of the speech for the conclusion: "I am leaving you tonight with great regret. There is one thing, however, that I shall remember, and that is that it was two people who invented the New Deal—the president of Brazil and the president of the United States. . . . So I am going to ask you to rise with me and drink to the health of my good friend President Vargas and to the great Republic of Brazil, our sister nation."[5] This signified that the idea of a strong state equipped to reorganize society was common to both countries.

In a way, it wasn't just rhetoric. Roosevelt was partially right, because the 1930 revolution in Brazil preceded programmatically by a few years his administration. On November 27, 1936, Vargas wrote in his diary:

> The man arrived. Everything went according to plan as described in the newspapers. But the impression left by the man was truly profound and pleasant: exuding kindness, with sincere pacifist idealism, his handicap, which makes him physically sick, improves his moral qualities and increases the interest in him. He is a clear speaker, plain and full of imagination, but free of criollas' hyperbole. He showed great interest in assisting Brazil to solve its military defense and economic problems. He promised that Sumner Welles, on his way back from Argentina, would remain here a few days to discuss several related issues.[6]

In 1936, Roosevelt's speech was a notable gesture that improved relations between the United States and Brazil. The Rockefeller project was inspired

THE SEDUCTION OF BRAZIL

by the themes proposed in the president's speech, which was made in Brazil four years prior to the foundation of the OCIAA. Using the United States as a model was one of the central points of Rockefeller's philosophy and that of his administration. Radio broadcasts, film, sanitation, and health projects, as well as economic programs, had a paradigmatic feel to them; in other words, the United States possessed the secret to progress, and, most important, it was willing to share it with Brazil.

If the OCIAA was preoccupied with constructing an image of the United States as a model, this was not done in a despotic manner. On the contrary, the office was concerned about toning down the victorious image by using the mediating influence of artists, musicians, and intellectuals. To make this project successful and to guarantee Brazil's support in the war effort, Rockefeller was forced on many occasions to confront partisans of more violent methods.

We have seen that the formulation of the Office of Strategic Services, headed by Bill Donovan, brought in, subtextually, an Americanism that emphasized the superiority of the white race, of Protestantism, and of passionate imperialism. The documentation I analyzed indicates that Donovan, among others, was a partisan of military intervention in certain regions of Brazil.[7] The OCIAA, headed by Rockefeller, also was a vehicle for Americanism, not in its traditionalist definition, but more closely allied with progressive values. For this very reason, demonstrations of arrogance were unnecessary.

Rockefeller's strategic victory was significant: the victory of the "conquest of the hearts and minds" of the Brazilian people approach, instead of military submission. In truth, it was a double victory for the OCIAA. On one side, it was a victory over sectors of the U.S. government whose philosophy was Americanization by force; on the other side, it was a victory over the Nazi proposals to Germanize the region ("We should create a new Germany," suggested the Nazi Hermann Rauschning), based on the Aryan racial project. It was a double victory, because the proposals of Donovan's OSS and of the Special Intelligence Service of Hoover's FBI—created on June 3, 1940, to guard the Latin American coast—recommended the use of force and espionage. Americans as well as Germans viewed the Latin American yokel or peasant with an air of racial superiority. In Rauschning's interpretation, Brazil, being of mixed race, would not offer resistance to the implantation of a new Germany in America. The analysis of the OSS was no less racist, because it used expressions like "half-caste" to designate those of mixed race in a document titled "Preliminary Report on the Dossier of Insecurity in Brazil," dated October 13, 1941.[8]

The problem of race and its implications was always present in the analyses of the intelligence organizations of the time and in the "nice" inter-pretations of the OCIAA, which, after all, was an information agency. It suffices to recall Walt Disney's Bahia and Rio without black people.

Even with all the efforts that were put into forging a more likeable American image, manifestations of arrogance were sometimes inevitable. But this was compensated for by careful dedication to creating an image that Americans were a hospitable, educated, and considerate people. One of these initiatives was the Department of Hospitality,[9] created by Rock-efeller. This small department received Latin American visitors arriving in the United States, provided lodging and guidance, and organized activities for the new guests.

Another form of maintaining a favorable U.S. image was oversight of commercial films exhibited in Rio de Janeiro by functionaries of the OCIAA's Brazilian Division. In a memo dated May 19, 1942,[10] the Brazil-ian Division analyzed *You Can't Get Rich*, a film from Columbia Pictures directed by Sidney Lanfield, with Fred Astaire and Rita Hayworth. The writer of the memo was worried:

A film which should have been barred from receiving an export license in the U.S. before being allowed to be shipped to Brazil. It is another case of using a military background to show soldiers in a ridiculous manner and while Americans would understand and enjoy the antics of the principal players, Brazilians are just the reverse because their military training is compulsory and therefore a very serious proposition giving them a high respect for the army and all it stands for while from this film our war effort gives an impression that is just the contrary.[11]

The office's analysts who worked in Brazil were also preoccupied with the manner in which Brazilian artists who worked in the United States were treated by the Hollywood studios. Brazilian dancer Eros Volúsia had worked with Abbott and Costello in *Rio Rita*, a film that had some suc-cess in Brazil. Volúsia was dissatisfied with MGM, which did not honor the contract signed with the artist. Furthermore, Volúsia complained that food prices in the United States were too high. Not all artists from Bra-zil received millionaire salaries, as did Carmen Miranda. In any case, the attention dispensed by functionaries of the Rio de Janeiro section of the office in the case of Volúsia, a "girl [who] has a lot of talent, to whom the film gave a grand opportunity,"[12] confirms their efforts to maintain a posi-tive image of the Americans.

Nonetheless, the preoccupation with Latin America shown by this policy was losing ground by the fourth year of the war. The Allied victory in North

Africa and the invasion of Sicily demonstrated the tension that existed in the United States in connection with the vulnerability of the southern flank of its area of influence. There was no longer any danger of an invasion of the American subcontinent. After these new developments, the interests of the OCIAA in Latin America gradually returned to the arena of economics, with the objective of overcoming the state of poverty in Brazil, which was considered a focal point of instability.

Simultaneous with the change in direction on the front, a gradual transformation occurred in American policies toward Latin America. The constant conflict between Secretary of State Cordell Hull and Undersecretary of State Sumner Welles ended with Welles's dismissal in September 1943. Adolf Berle, assistant secretary of state for Latin American affairs, lost a large part of his power and was later removed from the position. Nelson Rockefeller could no longer count on the support of these two important allies. Brazilian foreign relations felt the consequences of this change: Oswaldo Aranha lost his confidant and friend Sumner Welles.

Hull's actions demonstrated the loss of importance of the United States' neighbors on the continent. In August 1944, at the Dumbarton Oaks conference concerning the founding of the United Nations, there was no room for any American country except, evidently, the United States of America. Many Latin American representatives blamed Hull for the indifference to the countries that had given all of their support to the United States during the war.[13] At the time of the conference, Brazilian soldiers were in Italy, preparing to fight the formidable German forces.

Argentina, which still had not declared war on the Axis, continued to be a problem for Hull's diplomatic efforts. Rockefeller tried to pressure Argentina to search for a solution, but the secretary of state did not accept the interference of the OCIAA boss. Skillfully, Rockefeller helped President Roosevelt make the decision to dismiss Cordell Hull, in November 1944. Edward R. Stettinius, Jr., top administrator of the United States Steel Corporation, was invited to take Hull's place.

In a sequence of carefully considered actions, Stettinius appointed Rockefeller his assistant secretary for Latin American affairs, and the latter appointed Adolf Berle as ambassador to Brazil in place of the experienced Jefferson Caffery. President Roosevelt ratified all these appointments. These actions diminished the function of OCIAA.

Rockefeller dominated U.S. Latin American policy. It was as assistant secretary that he participated in the Chapultepec Conference in Mexico City in January 1945. The objective of this congress of American countries, marked by anticommunism, was to plan the future of relations among the American countries after the war. Rockefeller's reasoning incorporated the fears of big American capital. Latin America presented many risk factors: nationalism, fascism, socialism, and communism. These ideologies represented obstacles to the expansion of Anglo-American liberalism.

Even Rockefeller's more skillful advisors, from their Calvinist-capitalist perspective, failed to distinguish between communism and nationalism in the Latin American context of the postwar era. They were not able to, and they did not want to. For the nationalists, as well as the Left, foreign greed, especially that of American companies, sucked the wealth from the region. It suffices to recall how Rockefeller, the American government, and Wall Street were all caught by surprise when Lázaro Cárdenas, president of Mexico, nationalized his country's oil industry. Retaliation—defended even by Rockefeller—was evaded only through the interference of the American ambassador, Josephus Daniels, who, although he was against the expropriation, preferred resolution via negotiation.

Latin America transformed itself into an experimental laboratory for the world's most powerful nation. With the Good Neighbor Policy, the United States had hoped to promote and improve the quality of life in Latin America, especially in Brazil. Therefore, at the Chapultepec Conference Rockefeller defended the increase in foreign investment in the region, but in the spirit of defense of the free market.[14] The market was the best weapon to combat state nationalism and the dissemination of Communist ideals. With this, the architects of the modern relationship between Anglo-America and Ibero-America hoped to combat the economic and social underdevelopment of Latin American countries.

In order to develop this periphery, it was necessary to combat nationalism and socialism by inserting the periphery into the market. The preoccupation with the Good Neighbor Policy manifested by Rockefeller, Vice President Henry Wallace, and other influential Americans indicated that the project was more than just rhetorical. James Reston, the well-known *New York Times* journalist, confirmed in 1941 that the OCIAA's objective was

> to persuade the Latin Americas to take joint defensive action with
> us against the German menace which many of them do not admit
> exists . . . [to] persuade them that in the end the planes that are now
> only on our planning boards will conquer German bombers that have
> struck down eight countries in twenty-two months . . . [to] convince
> them that we know the answer to the economic as well as the military
> defense of the hemisphere . . . [to] convince them that somehow we
> will help them get rid of the same agricultural surplus we have not
> been able to get rid of ourselves, and . . . above all things [to] convince
> them, all of them, that the "Good Neighbor" policy is not a temporary

expedient designed to get us out of a tough spot, but a sincere and permanent reversal of our nineteenth century policy of "dollar diplomacy" and "manifest destiny."[15]

Two years later, Wallace expressed his worry over the gradual deflation of the Good Neighbor Policy. This occurred as the Axis forces were being beaten on the battlefield. Wallace was thinking in December 1943 that it was "a rather disturbing thought that we the United States can maintain a deep interest in Latin America only so long as we think we have something to gain by it. I hope . . . during the next few years that Latin America will feel that we are really her friend and not merely a friend for expedient purpose in time of great need."[16]

Wallace was a sincere Pan-Americanist whose vision was close to that of Waldo Frank. Consequently, he displayed a naïve hope that Latin America would perceive in subsequent years that the United States was really an ally from which the region could expect disinterested help. In this respect, Rockefeller's position was similar to Wallace's. In January 1945, Rockefeller stated that, only with the expansion of industry, agriculture, and educational interchange, could they "have hope of reaching economic, social, and political stability among the nations of the hemisphere. Without this, we will never realize the true American union."[17] The difference between Rockefeller and Wallace was that the former was a businessman with his eye on the market, and the latter was a utopian Pan-Americanist.

The market-based integration of the American countries proposed by men like Rockefeller and the prominent American industrialist Henry J. Kaiser was paradoxical. The dynamic of capitalism, to which their names were permanently connected, was seen by nationalist Latin Americans as conducive to the exploration of the peripheral regions by the United States. The U.S. capitalists, with apparent sincerity, offered Brazilians an association to overcome underdevelopment. But many Latin Americans had doubts about whether this was really a path for development.

In February 1942, a Brazilian delegation went to Washington, DC, to negotiate exploration of Brazilian rubber. One of the Brazilian delegates wrote to President Vargas saying that it was a favorable moment for advantageous negotiation of Brazil's participation in the war economy. This time they would try not to commit the same mistake they had made at the end of the nineteenth century, during the so-called rubber cycle. Vargas wrote: "We cannot waste any more time . . . we cannot let ourselves be deluded by parties and demonstrations of good will. We have people ready to fulfill their duty. We only lack the material. This is Brazil's moment."[18]

Brazilian leaders were dubious about businessmen/politicians like

Rockefeller, the "dollar-a-year men." Sometimes they thought that these businessmen were not as sincere as the true New Dealers. Rockefeller's OCIAA proposed, in the case of Amazonian rubber, the formation of the Amazon Valley Corporation (Corporação do Brasil para o Desenvolvimento da Bacia Amazônica). Brazilians would hold the honorary presidency, but American technicians would actually run the company. One of these so-called technicians who were assisting Rockefeller in this case was Col. J. C. King, the vice president of Johnson & Johnson, the giant pharmaceuticals company. Rockefeller had been impressed with a book called *Journey to Manaus* by Earl Parker Hanson, published in 1938. Rockefeller had become fascinated mainly by the idea that "the settling of the South America interior would give another breathing spell to our civilized world. . . . I find myself confronted at every turn by the romantic argument that the conquest of the South American wilderness would do for the Western Hemisphere what the conquest of the West did for the United States at a critical time."[19]

Almost half a century earlier (1893), a young historian from Wisconsin, Frederick Jackson Turner, wrote *The Significance of the Frontier in American History*. In this book, the author proceeds to show that the United States, a modern, rich, dynamic country, existed only thanks to the historical expansion to the West. For the author of *Journey to Manaus*, which had pleased Rockefeller so much, the wealth of the Western Hemisphere would be achieved with the expansion to the sertão, the South American frontier.

There is, however, a difference between Turner and Hanson. Turner understood that his country's wealth came with the conquest of the West, which integrated that prosperous world with the rest of the United States. Hanson excluded Latin America when referring to the Western Hemisphere. Hanson's subtext made it clear to the attentive reader that Brazilians would be excluded from "another breathing spell" for the civilized world, to be obtained through the exploration of the Brazilian frontier, the sertão.

When *Journey to Manaus* was published in 1938, the United States was still in crisis, despite Roosevelt's efforts. Unemployment and poverty were part of the American scenario. The "new life" of the civilized world meant overcoming the United States' crisis. Bouças had good reason to distrust U.S. politicians in 1944, and in 1945 there were even more reasons for this mistrust.

Oswaldo Aranha, Brazil's Americanist minister, believed Berent Friele, head of the OCIAA in Brazil and Rockefeller's subordinate and a trusted confidant. According to Friele, Brazilians could relax, because their place in the United Nations Security Council was practically secured.[20]

The new American secretary of state, Stettinius, stopped in Brazil on his return from the Yalta Conference. Roosevelt, the disabled president who had fascinated Vargas in 1936, was in the final days of his life. Stettinius did not promise, nor did he guarantee, Brazil's distinguished place in the new world order.

Roosevelt died. The war ended. Days and months passed. Vargas was deposed. Brazil did not receive its promised seat on the Security Council. Thanks to American pressure, the post was occupied by France.

Aside from Europe, the attention of the Americans moved quickly from the American subcontinent to Asia. The cold war made China, Korea, and even India crucial areas for U.S. foreign relations. Over there, communism and nationalism were more dangerous than in Latin America. There was no imminent "Communist enemy" in Latin America.

The agency created in 1940 as the Office for the Coordination of Commerce and Cultural Relations between the American Republics, which in 1941 changed its name to Office of the Coordinator of Inter-American Affairs and in 1944 was simply called Office of Inter-American Affairs, was finally closed down by an act signed by President Truman in May 1946. The "ideology factory" was closed. There was no use for it anymore.

The Americanization of Brazil, obviously, did not happen passively. There was an interaction between U.S. and Brazilian culture. The "culture shock" created by the strong presence of the U.S. communications media did not destroy Brazil's culture, but most certainly it produced new cultural manifestations. It is useful, but not enough, to draw on the notion of cultural resistance to understand this process. Throughout this book, I have used this concept as a variation of a more far-reaching approach, drawing it closer to the idea of cultural anthropophagy so dear to modernists like Oswald de Andrade. Even so, it is not sufficient to comprehend this complexity. Maybe the fusion of these ideas can explain Brazil's unique Americanization.

A symbolic explicit manifestation of resistance happened, in my opinion, in Tarquinia, Italy, where Brazilian forces prepared to fight the Germans who were entrenched in the mountains. Brazilian soldiers camped there were visited by U.S. general Mark Clark for a review of the troops. According to the statement of a Brazilian sergeant: "[T]he soldiers received a slip of paper on which 'God Bless America' was typed in Portuguese . . . the infantry general, fat, stuffed [into his uniform], took his position facing the troops. Next to the platform stood a musician sergeant, holding the baton. The general commanded: 'Sixth Regiment!' The sergeant raised the baton, but no voices were heard. The soldiers refused to sing that song honoring America, obviously North America and not South America."[21]

In the 1942 U.S. Office of War Information's promotional film *Sing with the Stars*, Carmen Miranda interprets an American soldiers' song, "K . . . K . . . K . . . Katy:

K . . . K . . . K . . . Katy	K . . . K . . . K . . . Katy
Pegando a cuíca	Playing a cuica [Brazilian musical instrument]
Eu sou brasileira	I am Brazilian
Morena faceira	A cheerful girl
Não posso negar . . .	I cannot deny . . .

She sang a verse in Portuguese and immediately afterward, the master of ceremonies requested that she sing in English. But in English the song changed to pure irreverence as she sang and interpreted it, in a certain resistance to Americanization. Even the emblematic Americanization of Carmen Miranda happened in an anthropophagic way.

It can be said that the Americanization of Brazil in the 1940s occurred under certain conditions. Thirteen years after the war, a Brazilian folk-song composer, Gordurinha, seems to have better understood this condition:

Só boto be-bop no meu samba	I put bebop in my samba only
Se o Tio Sam pegar no tamborim	If Uncle Sam plays the tambourine

Oliveira Vianna had already suggested that the Anglo-Saxon culture would be "welcome" as long as it "was expurgated of Americanism, of individual-istic values and the utilitarian mold."[22]

Peoples of one nation incorporate a specific cultural value from another nation if it makes sense in the general collectivity of the culture. This means that cultural assimilation does not occur by imitation, but, rather, by a complicated process of re-creation. Cultural assimilation never occurs in blocks. A nation would not accept all the cultural elements of another, only a part, and even so, only if it conveyed a new meaning. This assimilation involves, therefore, a choice and a re-creation.

Resistance, anthropophagy, conditioning, and syncretism occur simul-taneously; that is, cultural assimilation is not simple imitation, as stated by some Marxist critics. Americanization "is neither a reproduction nor a repetition."[23] It forms a unity but maintains a distinction: "Unified but dif-ferentiated, like soldiers in a platoon."[24]

Notes

*Antonio Pedro Tota's notes appear with arabic numerals, and
Daniel J. Greenberg's notes appear with roman numerals.*

Foreword Notes by Daniel J. Greenberg

i. See, e.g., Edward O. Guerrant, *Roosevelt's Good Neighbor Policy*; Bryce Wood, *The Making of the Good Neighbor Policy*; Samuel F. Bemis, *The Latin American Policy of the United States*. For further discussion, see D.G. note iv, in "Introduction" here.

ii. The best study of Wilson's intervention in Mexico is Robert Quirk, *An Affair of Honor: Woodrow Wilson and the Occupation of Veracruz*.

iii. Alexander De Conde, *Herbert Hoover's Latin American Policy*.

iv. The Nicaraguan intervention is analyzed in Neill Macaulay, *The Sandino Affair*.

v. The case of U.S. intervention against the short-lived Gráu San Martín government is studied in Jules R. Benjamin, *The United States and the Origins of the Cuban Revolution*, 87–102; Irwin F. Gellman, *Roosevelt and Batista: Good Neighbor Diplomacy in Cuba, 1933–1945*, chaps. 3–4; Robert Freeman Smith, *The United States and Cuba: Business and Diplomacy*, chap. 10.

vi. The best study of Rio Branco's diplomacy is Bradford E. Burns, *The Unwritten Alliance: Rio-Branco and Brazilian-American Relations*.

vii. Frank D. McCann, Jr., *Soldiers of the Patria: A History of the Brazilian Army, 1889–1937*; see chap. 7 on tenentismo.

viii. See, e.g., John W. F. Dulles, *Vargas of Brazil: A Political Biography*, pp. 19–39; 59–62, 83–94; Robert J. Alexander, "Brazilian Tenentismo," *Hispanic American Historical Review* 36, no. 1, May 1956, pp. 229–242.

ix. The complex negotiations that culminated in the accord are thoroughly studied in Frank D. McCann, Jr., *The Brazilian-American Alliance, 1937–1945*; also see Dulles, *Vargas of Brazil*, chaps. 7–8; and John Wirth, *The Politics of Brazilian Development, 1930–1954*.

x. The story of Brazil's FEB in World War II is best told by Frank McCann, *The Brazilian-American Alliance*, chap. 14.

xi. See Bryan McCann's original and illuminating *Hello, Hello Brazil: Popular Music in the Making of Modern Brazil*, esp. chap. 4. Part of the value of McCann's study is his grasp of ethnomusicology, which enables him to trace the multiethnic roots of Brazilian popular music.

xii. For a beautifully written account of this contradictory friendship, see Louis Pérez, Jr., *On Becoming Cuban: Identity, Nationality, and Culture*.

xiii. The postwar pro-U.S. stance of the Brazilian armed forces is analyzed in Alfred

Stepan, *The Military in Politics: Changing Patterns in Brazil*; and John W. F. Dulles, *Unrest in Brazil: Political-Military Crises, 1955–1964*.

Introduction Notes by Antonio Pedro Tota

1. "When agreeing to excellent things, my wife instinctively presses the lobe of the ear. My grandsons raise their thumbs. This gesture became popular in Brazil after 1942, introduced by North American aviators. The mechanics raised their thumbs, thumbs up, signaling to the pilots that the engines were functioning well after repairs. From the airports the sign spread . . . . In the Rome of the emperors, as well as during the time of the Republic, when the Romans made the *dextram pollice*, the sign meant to grant life to the defeated gladiator in the stadium. When inverting the thumb, *pollice verso*, the loser would be sacrificed by the winner. It has been a classic gesture for at least 2,000 years" (Luís da Câmara Cascudo, *História dos nossos gestos*, p. 154).

2. Monteiro Lobato, *América*, pp. 66–67.

3. José Ramos Tinhorão, *Música popular: Um tema em debate*, p. 58.

4. Ciro Marcondes Filho, "Imperialismo cultural, o grande vilão da destruição da 'nossa' cultura," pp. 79–84.

5. Carlos Drummond de Andrade, *Obras completas*, pp. 553–556, as cited by José Carlos Sebe Bom Meihy, *A colônia brasilianista: História oral de vida acadêmica*, p. 50.

6. Sérgio Buarque de Holanda, "Considerações sobre o americanismo," pp. 23–24.

7. Luís da Câmara Cascudo, *Locuções tradicionais no Brasil*, p. 204. See also Peter Fry, *Para inglês ver* (an idiomatic expression that means something is impressive or its appearance is great), pp. 17–18.

8. Juó Bananére was the nickname of Alexandre Ribeiro Marcondes Machado (1892–1933), satirist and poet from São Paulo who mixed Portuguese and Italian in his work.

9. *Malandro*, a swindler-trickster, a typical Brazilian character "of European origin (pícaro, Schelm), [which] underwent a change in Brazil: local socioeconomic conditions forced him to create survival tactics and assume a lifestyle described by Roberto Mata as the 'ponto certo do equilibrio entre a ordem e a desordem' (the point of equilibrium between order and disorder' in *Brecht's Reception in Brazil* by Lorena Ellis (Roberto da Matta, *Carnavais, malandro e herois*, as quoted by Leopoldo M. Bernucci, "O prazer da influência," 30.

10. "Americanization demands a certain atmosphere, a specific social structure (or the strong desire to create it) and a certain type of state. The state is the liberal state" (Antonio Gramsci, *Maquiavel*, "A política e o estado moderno," p. 388).

11. Vianna Moog, *Bandeirantes e pioneiros: Paralelo entre duas culturas*, pp. 123–124ff.

12. Ibid., p. 124.

13. These reflections are based on proposals contained in Gary Gerstle, *Working-class Americanism: The Politics of Labor in a Textile City, 1914–1960*; Luiz W. Vianna, *A revolução passiva: Iberismo e americanismo no Brasil*; and James Oliver Robertson, *American Myth, American Reality*.

14. Charles Maland, *Dr. Strangelove*, pp. 290–303.

15. Gumercindo Saraiva, *Câmara Cascudo, musicólogo desconhecido*, pp. 83–86.

16. Conversations with Richard Morse in Washington, D.C., spring 1992.

17. See Tocqueville, *Democracy in America*, p. 445.

18. Dunshee de Abranches, *A illusão brasileira (justificação histórica de uma atitude)*, p. 353.

19. See Jean-Paul Sartre, *La mort dans l'âme* (1949), quoted by Susan Sontag, "Fascinating Fascism," pp. 73–105.

20. Sontag, "Fascinating Fascism."

21. Joseph McBride, *Frank Capra: The Catastrophe of Success*, p. 446.

22. An *integralista* was a member of the AIB (Ação Integralista Brasileira), created in 1932 by Plínio Salgado and inspired by Italian fascism. "The AIB has a strong nationalistic and anti-communist character and is supported by the middle class, small businesses, *latifundiários* (big landowners), the military, the police and the Church" (Ellis, *Brecht's Reception in Brazil*, p. 136).

23. To the reactionary modernists—using the typical concept of the ideal created by Jeffrey Herf—a project for Germany would have to be based on the principle of inwardness (*Innerlichkeit*) added to modern technology. The big German paradox was the result of the combination of *Volkische Kultur* and *Zivilisation*, that is, the traditional culture of the race and rationalism. See Jeffrey Herf, *O modernismo reacionário*, p. 15.

24. Ibid.

25. Frank McCann, *The Brazilian-American Alliance*, p. 153.

26. American newspapers from the beginning of the century published various caricatures in which Latin America was always represented as a woman and the United States by the traditional Uncle Sam. See John J. Johnson, *Latin America in Caricature*.

27. Edgard Carone, *A Terceira República (1937–1945)*, p. 60.

28. Getúlio Vargas, *Diário*, vol. 2: *1937–1942*, pp. 319–320.

29. Ibid., p. 320.

30. "I come to pay a call of friendship . . . I would wish to symbolize the friendly visit of one good neighbor to another. In our daily life good neighbors call upon each other as the evidence of solicitude for common welfare and to learn of circumstances and point of view of each, so that there may come both understanding and respect which are cementing forces of all enduring society" (de Conde, *Herbert Hoover's Latin American Policy*, p. 18).

31. The Brazilians had prepared "a welcome such as few men ever received in Brazil . . . or in any other South American nation" (*New York Times*, December 22, 1928; also see ibid., p. 23).

32. This reflection is based on the interesting work by Fredrick B. Pike, "Latin-America and the Inversion of United States Stereotypes in the 1920's and 1930's: The Case of Culture and Nature," pp. 131–162.

33. Lobato, *América*, pp. 126, 128.

34. Warren I. Susman, *Culture as History: The Transformation of American Society in the Twentieth Century*, p. 105.

35. Nathan Irvin Huggins (ed.), *Voices from the Harlem Renaissance*, p. 85.

36. Ibid., p. 137.

37. Ibid., p. 148.

38. Johnson, *Latin America in Caricature*.

39. Marionilde Dias Brepohl de Magalhães, "Alemanha: Mãe-pátria distante; utopia pangeranista no sul do Brasil," p. 110.

40. "In 1942, Wallace phoned Waldo Frank on the eve of the latter's departure on a Latin American lecture tour. The phone conversation convinced the Jewish seer that Wallace was another true believer in the vision of creating a new American hemisphere" (Pike, "Latin-America and the Inversion of United States Stereotypes," p. 155).

41. Fireside chats were radio addresses, many times transmitted directly from the room in which the main fireplace was located in Roosevelt's house in Hyde Park, New York. See Betty Houchin Winfield, *FDR and the News Media*.

42. Marshall W. Stearns, *The Story of Jazz*, p. 142.

43. Gary Gerstle, "Inventing Liberal Traditions in America, 1900–1945," p. 2.

44. Quotation from *Ariel* by José Enrique Rodó, p. 69. See also http://www.utexas.edu/utpress/excerpts/exrodari.html. Carpentier quotation from *O recurso do método*, p. 37.

45. See Ricardo Antônio Silva Seitenfus, *O Brasil de Getúlio Vargas e a formação dos blocos: 1930–1942—O processo do envolvimento brasileiro na II Guerra Mundial*, pp. 205–206.

46. Fredrick B. Pike, *FDR's Good Neighbor Policy: Sixty Years of Generally Gentle Chaos*, p. 253.

47. Lilly Library, Bloomington, Indiana University, Manuscript Department, Orson Welles Manuscripts, box 9, folder 37, tape 47/1.

Introduction Notes by Daniel J. Greenberg

i. Parnamirim Field, near Natal in the Brazilian state of Rio Grande do Norte, was the first of several American air bases built to ferry troops to West Africa and thence to the European theater of World War II. The "Brazil-America agreement," negotiated by the governments of Franklin D. Roosevelt and Getúlio Vargas, provided for the leasing of this and three other air bases and a naval base in the Brazilian Northeast. In return, Washington agreed to reequip the Brazilian armed forces and to construct an integrated steel plant in Brazil, financed by Export-Import Bank loans and with U.S. technical support. The United States pledged to bear primary responsibility for protecting Brazil's long coastline and to include Brazil in an expanded version of Lend-Lease. For its part, Brazil offered its abundant strategic raw materials to supply Allied war needs. Rio also sent the FEB, an expeditionary force, to join in the liberation of Europe. The complex negotiations that culminated in the accord are thoroughly studied in Frank McCann, *The Brazilian-American Alliance*; also see Dulles, *Vargas of Brazil*, chaps. 7–8; Wirth, *The Politics of Brazilian Development*.

ii. In late 1807, Napoleon invaded Portugal. With the retreat of Portugal's army, João VI, then prince regent and later king, boarded a British warship and fled with his court to Brazil. Thus, from 1808 until 1821, the Portuguese monarchy led a government-in-exile from Brazil, with Rio de Janeiro as its capital. Also see note vii in Chap. 2 here.

iii. Tupi-Guarani is the indigenous lingua franca of the native peoples of Brazil and Paraguay. In using a Tupi-Guarani word, Lamartine was emphasizing his Brazilian identity and contraposing it to what he considered the foreign corruptions of Brazilian culture.

iv. In his 1933 inaugural address, Franklin Roosevelt announced the policy. It was a straightforward disavowal of the use of armed intervention in dealing with Latin America, a frequent U.S. practice in preceding decades, which had generated deep resentment. While FDR professed liberal internationalism, in reality, the policy served U.S. interests during the Depression and World War II. The Depression forced Washington to turn its attention toward the solution of domestic economic and social problems. Meanwhile, it needed Latin American cooperation to protect its extensive economic interests in the region. With the coming of World War II, FDR shifted the policy's emphasis to pressing for enhanced regional strategic cooperation. His objective was the creation of a U.S.-led hemispheric pact against the expansion of European fascism to South America. A large literature exists on the policy. See, e.g., Samuel F. Bemis, *The Latin American Policy of the United States*; Edward O. Guerrant, *Roosevelt's Good Neighbor Policy*; Bryce Wood, *The Making of the Good Neighbor Policy*.

v. Vargas's June 11, 1940, speech is also discussed in Chap. 2 here, and in note i in that chapter.

vi. The history of Germans in Brazil is a subject still little explored by U.S. Latin Americanists. An exception is Frederick Luebke's monograph, which focuses on the period ending in 1930. See *Germans in Brazil: A Comparative History of Cultural Conflict during World War II*.

vii. Ambassador Ritter's haughty arrogance toward Foreign Minister Aranha was occasioned by the Vargas government's crackdown on Nazi Party meetings, German press organs, cultural institutions, and imprisonment of German nationals. Vargas took those steps in response to the failed Integralist coup of May 1938, and Rio's discovery of plans for a revolt by Germans and German-Brazilians in the southern states. The fascist Integralist movement under Plínio Salgado attempted to seize power by infiltrating the armed forces and attacking Vargas's Rio Guanabara Palace. Friction between Rio and Berlin over these issues led to Ritter's expulsion in September; relations were not renewed until June 1939. See Dulles, *Vargas of Brazil*, pp. 175–197 and note i in Chap. 2 here.

Chapter 1 Notes by Antonio Pedro Tota

1. Pike, *FDR's Good Neighbor Policy*, p. 253.

2. Lobato, *América*, p. 221.

3. Gerard Colby and Charlotte Dennett, *Thy Will Be Done: The Conquest of the Amazon: Nelson Rockefeller and Evangelism in the Age of Oil*, pp. 37–39.

4. Donald W. Rowland, *History of the Office of the Coordinator of Inter-American Affairs: Historical Report on War Administration*.

5. Colby and Dennett, *Thy Will Be Done*, p. 79.

6. In Chap. 2, I show how Drew Pearson and Bob Allen disseminated this point of view via radio.

7. Colby and Dennett, *Thy Will Be Done*, p. 93.

8. "Appendix," in Rowland, *History of the Office of the Coordinator of Inter-American Affairs*, p. 279.

9. Colby and Dennett, *Thy Will Be Done*, p. 96.

10. Ibid., p. 133.

11. Elizabeth Cobbs Hoffman, *The Rich Neighbor Policy: Rockefeller and Kaiser in Brazil*, p. 9.

12. Rowland, *History of the Office of the Coordinator of Inter-American Affairs*, p. 12.

13. Cary Reich, *The Life of Nelson A. Rockefeller: Worlds to Conquer, 1908–1958*, p. 211.

14. Ibid., p. 21.

15. As cited by Vicente A. Aquino de Figueiredo, "As artimanhas na busca de um consenso: O DIP, o DEIP-SP e a II Guerra Mundial."

16. Rowland, *History of the Office of the Coordinator of Inter-American Affairs*, p. 20.

17. "Other American republics in films—a list of 16 mm motion picture films on South and Central America and where they can be secured—Released by Coordinator of Inter-American Affairs," Columbia University Library, School of Library Services, Government Papers.

18. See Martha Gil-Montero, *Brazilian Bombshell: The Biography of Carmen Miranda*, p. 97. Also see http://www.youtube.com/watch?v=eDwQN4UeF8E; accessed December 15, 2008.

19. Report of John Hay Whitney from Rio de Janeiro, August 29, 1941, Rockefeller Archive Center (hereafter RAC), record group 4, series O, box 7, folder 56.

20. Douglas Fairbanks, Jr., interview with the author, April 1, 1989. See also Douglas Fairbanks, Jr., *The Salad Days: An Autobiography*, pp. 380ff.

21. Ibid.

22. See Clayton R. Koppes and Gregory D. Black, *Hollywood Goes to War: How Politics, Profits, and Propaganda Shaped World War II Movies*, chaps. 2 and 3.

23. Gil-Montero, *Brazilian Bombshell*, pp. 102–103.

24. Steven Watts, "Walt Disney: Art and Politics in the American Century," pp. 84–110.

25. Rowland, *History of the Office of the Coordinator of Inter-American Affairs*, p. 72.

26. *Brazilian Quartz Goes to War*, National Archives (hereafter NA), Washington, D.C., Motion Picture Division (hereafter MPD), section M 1495, reel EF 119.

27. United News newsreel, in ibid., reels 208 UN 23–UN 59.

28. Walt Disney/OCIAA, in ibid., section M 1515, reels 306.241–252.

29. Catherine Benamou, *It's All True*, documentary about Orson Welles's unfinished three-part film about South America. Directed by Bill Krohn and Myron Meisel in 1993. See http://www.imdb.com/title/tt0107233.

30. "To the Coordinator, from Brazilian Division, Rio de Janeiro, August 15, 1942," NA, MPD, memorandum CO, no. 1692.

31. Ella Shohat and Robert Stam, *Unthinking Eurocentrism: Multiculturalism and the Media*, p. 232.

32. *Brazil*, NA, MPD, section M 1492, 226 D 6221.

33. RAC, record group 4, series 4, box 9, folder 73. In this document, Don Fran-

cisco also explains that "we are dealing not with one area, but with twenty different Nations, each varying according to political and psychological background. Programs suitable for us may not be suitable for any part of Latin America, and programs suitable for Mexico may not be appropriate for Argentina. Likewise, the question of Brazil, where programs must be written in Portuguese, is a problem itself."

34. "Südamerika—Programm des Deutschen Kurzwellensenders," Fundação Getúlio Vargas/Centro de Pesquisa e Documentação Contemporânea do Brasil (CPDOC), 7238/83.

35. Fred Fejes, *Imperialism, Media, and Good Neighbor: New Deal Foreign Policy and United States Shortwave Broadcasting to Latin America*, p. 126.

36. CBS News, Library Special Projects, Latin American Section, New York, June, 5 1940.

37. *Vida doméstica*, September 1943, p. 11.

38. "Data and rates of radio stations in the other American republics and Puerto Rico, prepared by the Office of Inter-American Affairs" (Washington, D.C., 1945), Columbia University Library, Government Papers.

39. Rowland, *History of the Office of the Coordinator of Inter-American Affairs*, p. 66.

40. RAC, record group 4, box 0, 12, folder 92, "Program during his visit in Brazil—September, 1 to 12, 1942."

41. "Sentimental Bulletin of the War in Recife," http://www.revista.agulha.nom. br/mmota1.html#boletim; accessed December 15, 2008.

42. At the end of the 1930s, VARIG was already using the powerful Junker 52/3m, and Pan American–Panair do Brasil had Catalina and Consolidate-Comodoro hydroplanes. The competition was intense and was related to strategic issues of air security. Therefore, a special U.S. effort was necessary to defeat the Germans. See Ronald Edward George Davies, *A History of the World's Airlines*, pp. 152–153; Frank McCann, *The Brazilian-American Alliance*, pp. 213ff; Moniz Bandeira, *Presença dos Estados Unidos no Brasil (Dois séculos de história)*, p. 282.

43. RAC, record group 4, series 0, box 9, folder 70, memo from the Office for Emergency Management of OCIAA.

44. Ibid., box 5, folder 40, memo "Funds for vocational training."

45. Pedro Martinello, *A "Batalha da Borracha" na Segunda Guerra Mundial e suas conseqüências para o vale amazônico*, p. 87.

46. See Thomas G. Paterson, J. Garry Clifford, and Kenneth J. Hagan, *American Foreign Policy: A History since 1900*, p. 309.

47. Report of John Hay Whitney from Rio de Janeiro, August 29, 1941, RAC, record group 4, series 0, box 7, folder 56.

48. Philip F. Dur, *Jefferson Caffery of Louisiana: Ambassador of Revolutions—An Outline of His Career*.

49. Reich, *The Life of Nelson A. Rockefeller*, p. 232.

50. RAC, record group 4, series 0, box 5, folder 37, letter from F. D. Roosevelt to Way Coy, from the Office for Emergency Management, dated July 14, 1941.

51. Cited by Seitenfus, *O Brasil de Getúlio Vargas*, pp. 71–72. Also see Magalhães, "Alemanha."

52. Cited by Frank McCann, *The Brazilian-American Alliance*, p. 80.

53. Biblioteca Central da Faculdade de Ciências e Letras, UNESP-Araraquara,

microfilm, reel VI, OSS/State Department, Intelligence and Research Report XIV, Latin American, 1941–1961, p. 6.

54. Ibid.

55. Ibid.

56. See *The Triumph of the Will*, a classic and polemical movie made by Leni Riefenstahl in 1934.

57. Bradley F. Smith, *The Shadow Warriors: OSS and the Origins of the CIA*, p. 70. The agent said: "We want to take off the gloves and emulate Goebbels."

58. RAC, record group 4, series 0, box 5, folder 37.

59. Richard Dunlop, *Donovan, America's Master Spy*, pp. 304–305.

60. Rowland, *History of the Office of the Coordinator of Inter-American Affairs*, p. 197.

61. RAC, record group 4, series 0, box 9, folder 10.

Chapter 2 Notes by Antonio Pedro Tota

1. NBC had the privilege of making the first televised transmission. NBC was part of the RCA group and was known as "the world's greatest broadcasting system." See *Broadcasting*, May 15, 1939, pp. 16–17.

2. Both Costa and Niemeyer yet to be known, by the late 1950s, for planning Brasília, a city built from the ground up to be Brazil's new capital.

3. Library of Congress, Motion Picture, Broadcasting, Record & Sound Division (hereafter MPBRSD), RWA 4792.

4. Armando Vidal, "O Brasil na Feira Mundial de New York," *Relatório geral*, 2 vols. (Rio de Janeiro: Imprensa Nacional, 1942), photo in vol. 1.

5. Ibid., p. 283.

6. Ibid.

7. Ibid.

8. Ibid.

9. Library of Congress, MPBRSD, RWA 2361.

10. Vidal, "O Brasil," p. 286.

11. *Daily Worker*, New York, October 17, 1940, in ibid.

12. NA, Associated Recorded Program Service, record group 229, "Let us visit our Americas in story and in song."

13. Ibid.

14. Telegram from Berent Friele, NA, record group 229, 05.4 (2), "Telegram to New York," Rio de Janeiro, May 26, 1943.

15. See Sérgio Cabral, *No tempo de Ary Barroso*, pp. 207ff.

16. RAC, record group 4, series 0, box 9, folder 70, "Brazilian composer arrives to visit United States Music Centers," February 5, 1942.

17. OCIAA, NA, record group 229, 05.4 (2), "Coordinator of Inter-American Affairs of the United States—São Paulo, inter-organization letter only, Rio/644."

18. Library of Congress, MPBRSD, RWA 57-63, box 43-108.

19. *Pan-American Radio* 1, no. 3, April 1942, p. 5.

20. Library of Congress, MPBRSD, 5554, record group 15.

21. See Vasco Mariz, *Heitor Villa-Lobos, compositor brasileiro*, p. 72.

22. *O Estado de São Paulo*, January 1941.

23. Three of Portinari's murals can be seen in the section of the Library of the Congress misleadingly called the Hispanic Division.

24. *O Estado de São Paulo*, March 7, 1940.

25. See Carlos Guilherme Mota, "Cultura e política da Boa Vizinhança: Dois artistas norte-americanos no Brasil," p. 491.

26. Jim Crow laws were related to the concept of separate but equal.

27. The news program sponsored by Brazil was aired until March 1941. There were six programs altogether by these two journalists: Library of Congress, MPBRSD, *News of the World*, RWA 574; *Evening News World*, RWA 5694-R674 B1; *News of the World*, RWA 5678-R658 B1; *The Good Neighbor Program*, RWA 5682 R662 AL; *Good Neighbors*, 16659-96 A disc 18395A 95 A box 41-38; *United States of Brazil World News*, RWA 570.

28. *New York Times*, review and financial review sections, January 3, 1943, p. 3.

29. Biblioteca Central da Faculdade de Ciências e Letras, UNESP-Araraquara, microfilm, reel VI, OSS/State Department, Intelligence and Research Report XIV, Latin America, 1941–1961, p. 6.

30. Ibid.

31. Recording available in Special Features, *Believe It or Not!*, Radio Yesteryear, 1991.

32. Martha Gil-Montero, *Carmen Miranda*, p. 74.

33. Ibid., p. 76.

34. See Max Wyllie, *Best Broadcasts of 1940–41*, p. 49.

35. Library of Congress, MPBRSD. Four of Rudy Vallee's programs were heard: RWA 3602, RWA 3813, LWO 12736, and RWA 3811.

36. *Chess Review*, October 1945, p. 27.

37. Gil-Montero, *Carmen Miranda*, p. 88.

38. Ibid., p. 110.

39. Vinícius de Moraes came to be known in America in conjunction with Antônio Carlos Jobim. They also contributed to the creation of bossa nova.

40. Vinícius de Moraes, *O cinema de meus olhos*, p. 86.

41. See Sérgio Augusto, *Este mundo é um pandeiro: A chanchada de Getúlio a JK*, p. 40.

42. Lilly Library, Bloomington, Indiana University, Manuscript Department, Orson Welles manuscripts, box 9, folder 37, "President Vargas birthday." The program was broadcast in English with the exception of some songs performed by Brazilian artists and some words in Portuguese spoken by Welles.

43. See Cordell Hull, *The Memoirs of Cordell Hull*, vol. 2, p. 1149.

44. Orson Welles and Peter Bogdanovich, *This Is Orson Welles*, p. 112.

45. In reality, Brazil is larger than the forty-eight North American states in 1942. With the admission of Alaska and Hawaii, the United States became larger.

46. See Dur, *Jefferson Caffery of Louisiana*, p. 36.

47. For information concerning the Estado Novo, see note i in this chapter.

48. See Irwin F. Gellman, *Good Neighbor Diplomacy: United States Policies in Latin America, 1933–1945*, p. 211.

49. Arquivo Nacional, Rio de Janeiro, Acervo Sonoro da Agência Nacional, Divisão

de Documentação Audiovisual, CBS, New York, tape LB 318-427, 10 min., I English Commentary on Pres. Getúlio Vargas's speech at the celebration of Brazilian Independence Day, DIP, 1945.

50. Allen L. Woll, *The Latin Image in American Film*, p. 66.

Chapter 2 Notes by Daniel J. Greenberg

i. On November 10, 1937, President Vargas, who had risen to power in the coup of 1930 but had been serving as constitutional president since enactment of the Constitution of 1934, seized dictatorial power in a "self-coup." Decreeing the Constitution annulled, Vargas announced the creation of the Estado Novo, an authoritarian regime that eliminated elections, annulled democratic rights, and provided him with sweeping powers to rule as he saw fit. In seizing power, Vargas cited dangers to Brazil's sovereignty and independence, which he claimed came from foreign subversives and ideologies. Vargas used the failed Communist uprising of November 1935 to justify the rightist coup. In 1938, he employed tremendously expanded police power to crush the Ação Integralista Brasileira (the Nazi Fascist Integralist movement) after those rightists, under Plínio Salgado, made their own, violent, attempt to seize power. See, for example, Dulles, *Vargas of Brazil*; Robert M. Levine, *The Vargas Regime: The Critical Years, 1934–1938*; Thomas F. Skidmore, *Politics in Brazil, 1930–1964: An Experiment in Democracy*, chaps. 1–2.

ii. Since the late nineteenth century, Brazil's economy had depended on one product—coffee. From the 1870s, Brazil was the world's dominant producer; at century's end, it produced nearly 80 percent of the world's supply. The Great Depression brought a sharp drop in coffee exports, most of which went to the United States. Thus, maintaining dominance in that market was crucial for the nation's economic well-being. See, e.g., E. Bradford Burns, *A History of Brazil*, pp. 133–150, 217–261, 288–292.

iii. Rio de Janeiro was Brazil's national capital from independence in 1822 until 1960. In that year, Pres. Juscelino Kubitschek (1955–1961) completed construction of the new capital in Brasília, located in the interior state of Goiás.

iv. Brazilians' assertion that their society is a "racial democracy" has long been cherished in their national consciousness. They contend that, unlike North Americans, they have never felt or acted in a discriminatory manner toward people of different racial backgrounds. In particular, partisans of this concept cite Brazilians' tendency to form social associations and sexual and marital unions with those of a different race. In literature this was perhaps first popularized and revealed to the outside world by sociologist Gilberto Freyre. Significantly, all of Freyre's books were translated and read by a broad public in the United States and Europe. Generations of U.S. academics took the concept at face value. More recently, many have begun to sharply question the validity of the hypothesis. See Freyre, *The Masters and the Slaves*; idem, *The Mansions and the Shanties: The Making of Modern Brazil*; and, especially, idem, *New World in the Tropics: The Culture of Modern Brazil*. For the contrary view, see Carl Degler, *Neither Black nor White: Race Relations in Brazil and the United States*; George Reid Andrews, *Blacks and Whites in São Paulo, Brazil, 1888–1988*; and Edward E. Telles, *Race in Another America: The Significance of Skin Color in Brazil*.

v. Tiradentes ("Tooth puller," real name, Joaquim José da Silva Xavier) was a prominent leader of the Inconfidência Mineira, a 1788–1789 Minas Gerais movement for Brazilian independence. Executed for treason by the Portuguese in 1792, today he is revered as an independence hero/martyr. See John A. Crow, *The Epic of Latin America*, pp. 514–518.

vi. The sertão refers to the arid and semiarid hinterland located west of the country's densely populated Atlantic coastal strip and extending inland for several hundred miles. For centuries after the arrival of the Portuguese, this vast area remained virtually empty. Racked by drought, appalling rural poverty, and exploitation of the rural poor by large landowners, the sertão has long been a seedbed of social and political unrest. In the colonial era (1500–1822), escaped African slaves created the *quilombo* (slave republic) of Palmares deep in Alagoa's sertão; it lasted for over half a century. In the Republican era (post-1889), the region became a center of opposition to the central government and a focus for millenarian messianic movements. In the 1890s, the followers of religious mystic Antônio Conselheiro created the commune of Canudos; in 1912, the Contestado rebellion erupted. In the 1920s, notorious bandit and popular hero Lampião terrorized Bahia's backlands and made fools of the federal and state police who pursued him. In the 1920s, Lt. Luiz Carlos Prestes led a column of military rebels and their poor rural followers on a multiyear trek from São Paulo in the South to Piauí in the North. Pursuing federal troops were unable to defeat or catch Prestes; he escaped with his troop and entered Bolivia. In common with the North American West, the sertão's sparse population, arid and semiarid climate, and remoteness from centers of power created a culture of lawlessness, rebellion, and unrest. Many studies have revealed the backlands' colorful history. See, e.g., Richard M. Morse, ed., *The Bandeirantes: The Historical Role of the Brazilian Pathfinders*; Robert M. Levine, *Vale of Tears: Revisiting the Canudos Massacre in Northeastern Brazil, 1893–1897*; Todd A. Diacon, *Millenarian Vision, Capitalist Reality: Brazil's Contestado Rebellion, 1912–1916*; Ralph Della Cava, *Miracle at Joaseiro*; Billy Jaynes Chandler, *The Bandit King: Lampião of Brazil*; Josué de Castro, *Death in the Northeast*.

vii. Dom Pedro I, a member of the Portuguese House of Orléans e Bragança, remained in Brazil as prince regent after his father, King João VI, returned to the home country in April 1821. The following year, the Portuguese Cortes (parliament) ordered Pedro to rejoin the court in Lisbon. Instead, the prince declared Brazil's independence on September 7, 1822. Between that year and 1889, Brazil was unique among newly independent Latin American nations in possessing a constitutional monarchy. The Empire of Brazil was governed by Pedro I (1822–1831), a regency council (1831–1841), and Pedro II (1841–1889). See, e.g., Clarence H. Haring, *Empire in Brazil: A New World Experiment with Monarchy*; Emília Viotti da Costa, *The Brazilian Empire: Myths and Histories*.

viii. FDR's comment refers both to Brazil's close trading relationship and Vargas's role as one of Washington's closest regional allies. In the series of Pan-American conferences called after 1937, the United States attempted to confront the rise of fascism by forging a hemispheric alliance against its expansion. While Vargas maintained official neutrality until breaking relations with the Axis in early 1942, his government offered reliable support for U.S. initiatives at the foreign ministers' meetings. Among the opponents were Argentina and Chile. Both saw the maintenance of neutrality as synonymous with following their economic interests and maintaining foreign policy independence from Yankee hegemony. Moreover, Argentina's Castillo government (1938–1943) evinced frank sympathy for the Axis. Brazil and Argentina's contrasting stance is brilliantly studied in Frank McCann, *The Brazilian-American Alliance*; also see Stanley Hilton, *Brazil and the Great Powers, 1930–1939: The Politics of Trade Rivalry*; Daniel J. Greenberg, "From Confrontation to Alliance: The United States and Peronist Argentina, 1946–52."

ix. In fact, the State Department and the Pentagon already had advanced this analysis and used it to justify extending Lend-Lease provisions to Brazil. The debate within U.S. government circles had to remain secret, as isolationists in Congress still blocked such a step. So the United States worked privately to assist Brazil; FDR used his executive power wherever possible, ordering preferential trade treatment and military cooperation with Rio de Janeiro. This is superbly documented by Frank McCann, who had access to both U.S. and Brazilian military archives and officers. See *The Brazilian-American Alliance*, chaps. 4–6; also see Wirth, T*he Politics of Brazilian Development*.

x. While Brazil and the United States were both federal republics, the radio program overstated this aspect. The U.S. Constitution's federalism is sharply "tilted" toward a powerful central government, while Brazil's Constitution of 1891 placed most power in the hands of the states. The Constitution of 1934, promulgated by Vargas while he was attempting to rule as a democrat, shifted the locus of power to the national government and stripped the states of power. But this was the organic law that Vargas overthrew in his Estado Novo coup of November 1937. In fact, by late 1940, the concept of Brazilian federalism had already become a legal fiction: the Estado Novo placed nearly all power in Vargas's hands. See, for example, Ronald M. Schneider, *A Political History of Brazil*, chap. 4; Frank McCann, *The Brazilian-American Alliance*, p. 26.

xi. See note vii. A biography of Pedro II is found in Lilia Moritz Schwarcz, *The Emperor's Beard: Dom Pedro II and the Tropical Monarchy of Brazil.*

xii. In August 1942, Brazil declared war on Germany and followed with similar declarations against the remaining Axis countries. The step had been provoked by German U-boats sinking Brazilian ships, leading to hundreds of deaths and significantly harming the nation's ability to meet its commercial shipping needs. Two years later, Brazil became the first and only Latin American ally to send troops to fight in Europe. During their time in Italy, fighting alongside U.S. and other Allied troops and discovering that their countries, unlike Brazil, were governed democratically, Brazilian officers began to turn against Vargas and his dictatorship. In 1945, when the gaúcho leader seemed determined to resist the call for democratic reform and orchestrate his reelection, the officers deposed him and held the first popular direct elections since 1930. Ironically, the first president elected was Gen. Eurico Dutra, one of the top officers who had approved Vargas's ouster. See, e.g., Skidmore, *Politics in Brazil*, chap. 2; Dulles, *Vargas of Brazil*, pp. 249–287; Stepan, *The Military in Politics*, chaps. 1–2.

Chapter 3 Notes by Antonio Pedro Tota

1. The Catete Palace is an urban mansion in Rio de Janeiro's Flamengo neighborhood. The property (several buildings and a large garden) stretches from Rua

do Catete to Praia de Flamengo. From 1894 to 1960, it was Brazil's presidential palace and the site of Getúlio Vargas's suicide. It now houses a museum and theater. The Catete subway stop is adjacent; see http://en.wikipedia.org/wiki/Catete_Palace (accessed December 15, 2008).

2. Franklin Delano Roosevelt Library, Hyde Park, New York, PPF-6697, letter from Errol Flynn to Franklin D. Roosevelt, June 15, 1940.

3. Vargas, *Diário*, vol. 2, p. 323.

4. *O Diário de São Paulo*, February 10, 1940.

5. Ibid.

6. Ibid., March 1, 1940.

7. Ibid., October 22, 1940.

8. Ibid., July 26, 1940.

9. Augusto, *Este mundo é um pandeiro*, p. 43.

10. *O Diário de São Paulo*, August 22, 1940.

11. Ibid., August 7, 1940.

12. Ibid., October 27, 1940.

13. *O Globo Juvenil*, January 24, 1942.

14. *Newsreel brasileiro*, vol. 2, no. 106, March 12, 1942, Cinemateca Brasileira-IPHAN.

15. The mil-réis was the Brazilian currency at that time. Back then, 20$000 (twenty mil-réis) bought one dollar.

16. *A Noite*, Rio de Janeiro, April 4, 1942.

17. NA, MPD, record group 229, memorandum CO no. 1810, September 4, 1942.

18. Roberto da Matta, "On Animals in Popular Culture: Brazil and the United States."

19. NA, MPD, record group 229, memorandum CO no. 1810, September 4, 1942.

20. See Dorfman and Mattelart, *How to Read Donald Duck*.

21. I would speculate that Disney's omission of nonwhites reflected Hollywood's more general refusal to include black characters (except as servants and other inferiors) in the making of films in the United States. By treating blacks as "invisible" except in inferior roles, Hollywood reinforced racist stereotypes. Other studios—e.g., Warner Brothers—did the same thing in cartoons of the same era, such as "Bugs Bunny."

22. *O Estado de São Paulo*, September 10, 1943.

23. See Alfredo Óscar Salun, "Zé Carioca vai à guerra," pp. 104–105.

24. NA, MPD, United News Reels, 1942, 208 UN 23.

25. NA, MPD, 05.4 (2), record group 229, letter from Frank E. Natier, OCIAA in Rio, to Col. José Bina Machado, Ministry of War, May 19, 1944.

26. NA, MPD, 05.4 (2), record group 229, Brazilian Military Effort, c. February 2, 1943, "Motion picture budget number 4—'Production of non-theatrical motion picture.'"

27. NA, MPD, "Translator Summary of Communication," 832.406 1, Motion Picture/266. Carlos Ferraro wanted

to make a great film [for] 20th Century Fox . . . about Brazilian life, from its discovery to the inauguration of his highness the honorable Dr. Getúlio Vargas and his government. The excellent Brazilian work and progress, as well as greatness of the North American nation should also be shown in this film.

The film is written by me, based on feelings that affect the Brazilian and the American people. Since here in Brazil I cannot film because we do not have the necessary basics, I need a lot of support, but guarantee that once this film is completed, it will provide great profit to the company or this nation because the American people will accept it with great pleasure and enthusiasm.

This film produced in that nation and shown in Brazil would be the biggest gift that Your Excellency could give to my great president, because being an American film it also entails much of Brazil. This project would show the Brazilian people how good our leader is, how much he works, and how much courage he shows in the defense of your government, which came to ensure stability and progress in Brazil. . . . I have already contacted the studio, where I have more works to be filmed. And being there if necessary I could be a soldier in the great American Army. . . .

I thank you in advance.

Your highnesses' faithful soldier, Carlos Ferraro.

28. In Meihy, *A colônia brasilianista*, p. 119.

29. Jordan Young, interview with the author, Princeton, New Jersey, April 1992.

30. *O Diário de São Paulo*, June 12, 1940.

31. *Fortune*, April 1941, p. 77.

32. NA, MPD, Sound Division, record group 229, telegram, May 23, 1941.

33. Arquivo Nacional, Rio de Janeiro (hereafter ANRJ), Acervo Sonoro da Agência Nacional, Divisão de Documentação Audiovisual, 1943, cassette LA 255-430, 15 min., program no. 13, FC 51.

34. "(Peggy Terry) The first work I had after the Depression was at a shell-loading plant in Viola, Kentucky. . . . We were just moving around, working wherever we could find work. I was eighteen. My husband was nineteen. We were living day to day. When you are involved in staying alive, you don't think about big things like war. It didn't occur to us we were making these shells to kill people. It never entered my head" (Studs Terkel, *The Good War: An Oral History of World War II*, p. 108).

35. ANRJ, Acervo Sonoro da Agência Nacional, Divisão de Documentação Audiovisual, 1943, cassette LA 255-430, 15 min., program no. 13, FC 51.

36. ANRJ, General Sound Corporation, New York, 1943, cassette LA 260-435, 15 min., program no. 6, FC 50.

37. See Cobbs Hoffman, *The Rich Neighbor Policy*, pp. 209–211.

38. ANRJ, Acervo Sonoro da Agência Nacional, Divisão de Documentação Audiovisual, New York, 1943, cassette LA 256-432, 15 min., program no. 6, FC 49. There seems to be a mistake in the date of this document: the B-29 was not deployed until June 1944.

39. Ibid.

40. ANRJ, New York, 1943, cassette LB 221-301, 6 min., FC 26, Columbia Broadcasting System, International News, broadcast from New York and Washington via DIP, October 31, 1944.

41. *A história em ação: A guerra chega em Red Oak*, ANRJ, General Sound

Corporation, New York, May 20, 1943, cassette LA 00-431, 30 min., program no. 53, FC 68.

42. See James P. Woodard. *Marketing Modernity: The J. Walter Thompson Company and North American Advertising in Brazil, 1929–1939.*

43. University of the Air: Portuguese Program for Brazil, Library of Congress, MPBRSD, LWO 16 798 R 79 B3, disk 2001-2b, box E 41-15.

44. ANRJ, General Sound Corporation, New York, 1943, cassettes LB 00-245, 18, 00-250, 101ff, Columbia Broadcasting System, Noticiário Internacional, transmitted from New York and Washington via DIP.

45. ANRJ, Acervo Sonoro da Agência Nacional, Divisão de Documentação Audiovisual, July 30, 1945.

46. See Chap. 2.

47. IBOPE is the most famous polling organization in Brazil.

48. IBOPE archive/E. Leuenroth, Universidade Estadual de Campinas, July 1944.

49. See Pike, "Latin America and the Inversion of U.S. Stereotypes," p. 133.

50. Valter Krausche, *Música popular brasileira: Da cultura de roda à música de massa*, p. 39.

51. Frank, *South American Journey*, pp. 8–9.

52. Luís da Câmara Cascudo, *História da alimentação no Brasil*, vol. 1, p. 103.

53. Frank, *South American Journey*, p. 13.

54. Richard M. Morse, *O espelho de Próspero: Cultura e idéias nas Américas*, p. 86.

55. Lobato, *América*, pp. 230–231.

56. See Edson Luís Nars, "Um olhar sobre o Brasil pelas lentes de Jean Manson: De JK a Costa e Silva," p. 79.

57. Frank, *South American Journey*, pp. 54–57.

58. Eduardo Prado, *A illusão americana*, pp. 31–32.

59. Frank, *South American Journey*, p. 24.

60. Ibid.

61. Ibid., p. 27.

62. Ibid., p. 41.

63. See José Castello, *Vinícius de Moraes: O poeta da paixão—Uma biografia*, p. 125.

64. Moraes, *O cinema de meus olhos*, p. 97.

65. Frank, *South American Journey*, p. 43.

66. T. W. Adorno, "O fetichismo da música e a regressão da audição," p. 193.

67. Jairo Severiano and Zuza Homem de Mello, *A canção no tempo: 85 anos de músicas brasileiras*, vol. 1, pp. 231–232.

68. This term is a reference to the Anthropophagy modernist movement created by Oswald de Andrade in the 1920s. This will be discussed in more detail in the Conclusion.

Chapter 3 Notes by Daniel J. Greenberg

i. Vargas's June 11 speech and the U.S.-Brazilian diplomatic maneuvering it elicited is analyzed in Dulles, *Vargas of Brazil*, pp. 210–211; and Frank McCann, *The*

Brazilian-American Alliance, pp. 185–190. More likely, ambiguous references like those in the June 11 speech were part of Vargas's calculated strategy of playing off the United States against Germany, both of which sought his alliance and from which he sought advantages for Brazil. See, e.g., Wirth, *The Politics of Brazilian Development*, passim.

ii. A *boleadera* is a Brazilian lariat formed by a V-shaped rope whose ends are attached to stones wrapped in leather (*boleadora* in Argentina and Uruguay). The cowboy flings the lariat at a running animal, trapping the hind legs at the ankles.

iii. The FEB's famous insignia was created, allegedly, as a Brazilian riposte to Hitler's scoff that Brazil would no more send troops to fight Germans in Europe than a snake would smoke a pipe. This is one of the many significant details revealed by Frank McCann in *The Brazilian-American Alliance*, p. 375.

iv. This arrangement, begun even before Brazil had broken relations with Germany and Italy in early 1942, was concluded by private agreement between the United States and Brazil, which the respective armed forces then implemented (ibid., pp. 276–277). Interestingly, neither this nor the eventual military alliance between the countries was ever ratified by formal treaty.

v. Stein and Young were members of a postwar generation of U.S. Latin Americanists who made important contributions to Brazilian historiography. See, e.g., Stein's *Vassouras: A Brazilian Coffee County, 1850–1900*; idem, *The Brazilian Cotton Manufacture: Textile Enterprise in an Underdeveloped Area, 1850–1950*; idem and Barbara Stein, *The Colonial Heritage of Latin America: Essays on Economic Dependence in Perspective*; Young, *The Revolution of 1930 and the Aftermath*.

vi. For Vargas's authoritarianism, see note i in Chap. 2 here.

vii. For information on the 1780s Inconfidência and its leader, Tiradentes, see note v in Chap. 2 here. In fact (Monroe Doctrine professions to the contrary), the United States did not support independence movements in most of Latin America in the late eighteenth and early nineteenth centuries. Instead, the newly independent nation attempted to avoid alienating its former ally, imperial Spain, and adopted the same posture with Portugal. Madrid had provided the American rebels assistance against England in the War of Independence. This is thoroughly studied in the classic by Arthur Preston Whitaker, *The United States and the Independence of Latin America, 1800–1830*.

viii. Samuel Wainer, a Paulista journalist, was a former Vargas critic who became a supporter and crony. During the 1950s, he reported for the Getulista *Diário de São Paulo*. Later, at Vargas's suggestion, he founded and became editor of the oficialista Rio daily, *Última Hora* (Dulles, *Vargas of Brazil*, pp. 289, 305–306).

ix. In July 1932, São Paulo opponents of Vargas organized an armed uprising. While they called their movement the "constitutionalist revolution" (declaring their objective to be the restoration of the old federal Constitution of 1891), the Paulistas' real goal was the reversal of Vargas's ending the regime of "café com leite" (coffee with milk), which between 1889 and 1930 granted special preference to populous, wealthy states like São Paulo in utilizing federal budget revenues and making other vital national decisions. Under that regime, São Paulo, Minas Gerais, and, to a lesser extent, Rio Grande do Sul had alternated in choosing the president and benefited from favored treatment and access to national revenues. Vargas's suppression of the 1932 movement was bloody and decisive, but he followed by treating the Paulista leaders with leniency and decreeing a constitutional reform that would create the democratic Constitution of 1934. These events are studied in Dulles, *Vargas of Brazil*, pp. 87–116. For the emergence of the University of São Paulo as a center of anti-Vargas resistance, see idem, *The São Paulo Law School and the Anti-Vargas Resistance (1938–1945)*.

x. Luís Carlos Prestes was a young military engineer who led the "Tenentes'" rebellion of 1924. Following the rebellion's failure, he was able to avoid capture and led a group of survivors and their civilian supporters on a two-year "long march" through the Brazilian interior. The federal army steadily pursued Prestes's ragtag group, but the leader's ability to defeat or elude the much larger national force led admirers to christen him the "knight of hope." The famed Prestes Column became a beacon of opposition to the Republican elite and a rallying cry for those who sought social and political reform. After his escape to Bolivia, Prestes was approached by representatives of the Comintern, who succeeded in converting him to Marxism-Leninism and later brought him to the Soviet Union for indoctrination and training. In 1935, he returned and founded the Alliance for National Liberation (ANL). Vargas prohibited and suppressed the ANL after only one year, but Prestes and others went underground and planned a mass Communist insurrection. The November 1935 uprising, begun in Natal and then spreading to Recife and Rio de Janeiro, failed utterly and was easily suppressed by Vargas. Prestes and Olga Benario, his German Jewish comrade and common-law wife, were both apprehended. While Benario was deported to Germany and ultimately died at Auschwitz, Prestes received a long prison term and was not released until 1945. While imprisoned, Prestes remained the proscribed Communist Party's chairman, a post he held until his ouster in the 1980s. During the 1980s and 1990s, the opening of Soviet and East German secret police archives produced several Brazilian studies of high quality and originality, founded on superb documentary research. See, e.g., William Waack, *Camaradas: Nos arquivos de Moscou, a história secreta da revolução brasileira de 1935*; Fernando Morais, *Olga: Revolutionary and Martyr*; also see Ronald H. Chilcote, *The Brazilian Communist Party: Conflict and Integration, 1922–1972*; and John W. F. Dulles, *Brazilian Communism, 1935–1945: Repression during World Upheaval*. For Prestes's early career and the epochal long march, see Neill Macaulay, *The Prestes Column: Revolution in Brazil*.

Conclusion Notes by Antonio Pedro Tota

1. See Paterson, Clifford, and Hagan, *American Foreign Policy*, p. 349.

2. Ibid., p. 365.

3. *O Estado de São Paulo*, November 28, 1936. Also see *New York Times*, November 28, 1936.

4. *New York Times*, November 28, 1936.

5. *O Estado de São Paulo*, November 29, 1936.

6. Vargas, *Diário*, vol. 1, p. 563.

7. See Michael Gannon, "Invade Brazil," pp. 58–65.

8. Biblioteca Central da Faculdade de Ciências e Letras, UNESP-Araraquara, microfilm, reel VI, OSS/State Department, Intelligence and Research Report XIV, Latin American, 1941–1961.

9. See Rowland, *History of the Office of the Coordinator of Inter-American Affairs*, p. 98.

10. NA, MPD, record group 229, memo CO, no. 1098, May 19, 1942.

11. NA, MPD, record group 229, memo CO, no. 1110, May 20, 1942.

12. NA, MPD, record group 229, memo CO, no. 229, January 9, 1943.

13. See Stanley Hilton, *Oswaldo Aranha, uma biografia*, p. 418.

14. Cobbs Hoffman, *The Rich Neighbor Policy*, p. 3.

15. James B. Reston, "Our Second Line of Defense," p. 7; see also Fejes, *Imperialism, Media, and Good Neighbor*, p. 134.

16. See Gellman, *Good Neighbor Diplomacy*, p. 198.

17. Ibid., p. 199.

18. Letter from Valentim Bouças to Getúlio Vargas, Fundação Getúlio Vargas, CPDOC, Arquivo Getúlio Vargas, 41.01.30, cited in Martinello, *A "Batalha da borracha,"* p. 92.

19. See Colby and Dennett, *Thy Will Be Done*, p. 138.

20. Brazil still has not been allowed to participate as a permanent member of the U.N. Security Council.

21. Boris Schnaiderman, *Guerra em surdina: Histórias do Brasil na Segunda Grande Guerra*, p. 79.

22. See Luiz W. Vianna, "Americanistas e iberistas: A polêmica de Oliveira Vianna com Tavares Bastos," p. 176.

23. Luís da Câmara Cascudo, *Sociologia do açúcar (Pesquisa e dedução)*, p. 393.

24. Ibid.

Bibliography

Books and Articles

Abranches, Dunshee de. *A illusão brazileira (justificação histórica de uma attitude)*. 3rd ed. Rio de Janeiro: Imprensa Nacional, 1917.

Adorno, T. W. "O fetichismo da música e a regressão da audição." In Walter Benjamin et al., *Textos escolhidos*. Coleção Os Pensadores. São Paulo, April 1975.

Alexander, Robert J. "Brazilian Tenentismo." *Hispanic American Historical Review* 36, no. 1 (May 1956).

———. *Latin American Politics and Government*. New York: Harper & Row, 1965.

Andrews, George Reid. *Blacks and Whites in São Paulo, Brazil, 1888–1988*. Madison: University of Wisconsin Press, 1991.

Aquino de Figueiredo, Vicente A. "As artimanhas na busca de um consenso: O DIP, O DEIP-SP e a II Guerra Mundial." Mimeo. São Paulo: Pontifícia Universidade Católica de São Paulo, 1997.

Augusto, Sérgio. *Este mundo é um pandeiro: A chanchada de Getúlio a JK*. São Paulo: Companhia das Letras, 1989.

Bandeira, Moniz. *Presença dos Estados Unidos no Brasil (Dois séculos de história)*. Rio de Janeiro: Civilização Brasileira, 1973.

Barnouw, Erik. *A Tower in Babel: A History of Broadcasting in the United States to 1933*. New York: Oxford University Press, 1966.

Barreto, Lima. "O nossa 'ianquismo.'" *Revista Contemporânea* (March 22, 1919).

Baxter, John. *Hollywood in the Thirties*. London & New York: Tantivy Press; A. S. Barnes, 1975.

Bell-Metereau, Rebecca Louise. *Hollywood Androgyny*. New York: Columbia University Press, 1985.

Bemis, Samuel Flagg. *The Latin American Policy of the United States: An Historical Interpretation*. New York: Harcourt, Brace, 1943.

Benamou, Catherine. "It's All True." In *Orson Welles: Theater-Radio-Film*. Exhibition catalog, New York University, April 25–May 15, 1988.

Benjamin, Jules R. *The United States and the Origins of the Cuban Revolution*. Princeton, N.J.: Princeton University Press, 1990.

Benjamin, Walter. *Magia e técnica, arte e política: Ensaios sobre literatura e história da cultura*. In Walter Benjamin, *Obras escolhidas*. Vol. 1. São Paulo: Brasiliense, 1985.

Berlowitz, Leslie, Denis Donoghue, and Louis Menard. *A América em teoria*. Rio de Janeiro: Forense Universitária, 1993.

Bernstein, Barton J. "The New Deal: The Conservative Achievements of Liberal Reform." In *Towards a New Past: Dissenting Essays in American History*. New York: Vintage, 1960.

Bernucci, Leopoldo M. "O prazer da influência: John Gay, Bertolt Brecht e Chico Buarque de Hollanda." *Latin American Translation Review* 27, no. 2 (Spring 1994).

Bilby, Kenneth W. *The General: David Sarnoff and the Rise of the Communications Industry*. New York: Harper and Row, 1986.

Black, Jan Knippers. *United States Penetration of Brazil*. Philadelphia: University of Pennsylvania Press, 1977.

Blum, John M., et al. *The National Experience: A History of the United States*. Parts 1 & 2. New York: Harcourt Brace & World, 1963.

Bogdanovich, Peter. *John Ford*. Berkeley & Los Angeles: University of California Press, 1978.

Braisted, Paul J. *Cultural Affairs and Foreign Relations*. Washington, D.C.: Columbia Book Publishers, 1968.

Buarque de Holanda, Sérgio. "Considerações sobre o americanismo." In Sérgio Buarque de Holanda, *Cobra de vidro*. São Paulo: Perspectiva, 1978.

Burligame, Roger. *A sexta coluna*. Rio de Janeiro: Civilização Brasileira, 1964.

Burns, E. Bradford. *A History of Brazil*. New York: Columbia University Press, 1970.

———. *The Unwritten Alliance: Rio-Branco and Brazilian-American Relations*. New York: Columbia University Press, 1966.

Cabral, Sérgio. *No tempo de Ary Barroso*. Rio de Janeiro: Francisco Alves, n.d.

Cândido, Antônio. *A dialética da malandragem*. São Paulo: Revista do Instituto de Estudos Brasileiros, 1970.

Cardoso Júnior, Abel. *Carmen Miranda: A cantora do Brasil*. Sorocaba: Published by the author, 1978.

Carone, Edgard. *A Terceira República (1937–1945)*. Coleção Corpo e Alma do Brasil. São Paulo & Rio de Janeiro: Difel, 1976.

Carpentier, Alejo. *El recurso del metodo*. Mexico City: Siglo Veintiuno Editores, 1975.

Cascudo, Luís da Câmara. *História da alimentação no Brasil*. Vol. 1. Belo Horizonte & São Paulo: Itatiaia/Editora da Universidade de São Paulo, 1979.

———. *História de nossos gestos*. Belo Horizonte & São Paulo: Itatiaia/Editora da Universidade de São Paulo, 1987; São Paulo, Editora 34, 2000.

———. *Locuções tradicionais no Brasil*. Recife: Universidade Federal de Pernambuco, 1970.

———. *Sociologia do açúcar (Pesquisa e dedução)*. Coleção Canavieira, no. 5. Rio de Janeiro: Divulgação do mic, Instituto do Açúcar e do Álcool—Divisão Administrativa, Serviço de Documentação, 1971.

Castello, José. *Vinícius de Moraes: O poeta da paixão: Uma biografia*. São Paulo: Companhia das Letras, 1994.

Castro, Josué de. *Death in the Northeast*. New York: Random House, 1966.

Chandler, Billy Jaynes. *The Bandit King: Lampião of Brazil*. College Station: Texas A&M University Press, 1978.

Chase, Francis, Jr. *Sound and Fury*. New York: Harper and Brothers, 1942.

Chilcote, Ronald H. *The Brazilian Communist Party: Conflict and Integration, 1922–1972*. Oxford: Oxford University Press, 1973.

Childs, Harwood, and John B. Whitton. *Propaganda by Shortwave*. Princeton, N.J.: Princeton University Press, 1942.

Cobbs Hoffman, Elizabeth. *The Rich Neighbor Policy: Rockefeller and Kaiser in Brazil*. New Haven, Conn.: Yale University Press, 1992.

Colby, Gerard, with Charlotte Dennett. *Thy Will Be Done: The Conquest of the Amazon: Nelson Rockefeller and Evangelism in the Age of Oil*. New York: HarperCollins, 1995.

Considine, Bob. *Ripley, the Modern Marco Polo*. Garden City, N.Y.: Doubleday, 1961.

Costa, Emília Viotti da. *The Brazilian Empire: Myths and Histories*. Dorsey Press, 1985.

Cowie, Peter. *Hollywood 1920–1970*. New York: A. S. Barnes, 1977.

Crow, John A. *The Epic of Latin America*. 4th ed. Berkeley & Los Angeles: University of California Press, 1992.

Culbert, David Holbrook. *News for Everyman: Radio and Foreign Affairs in Thirties America*. Westport, Conn.: Greenwood Press, 1976.

———, and Richard E. Wood. *Film and Propaganda in America: A Documentary History*. 4 vols. New York: Greenwood Press, 1990.

Dallek, Robert. *Franklin D. Roosevelt and American Foreign Policy, 1932–1945*. New York: Oxford University Press, 1979.

Dalton, W. M. *The History of Radio*. 3 vols. London: A. Hilger, 1975.

Da Matta, Roberto. *Carnavais, malandro e herois*. Rio de Janeiro: Zahar Editores, 1979.

———. "On Animals in Popular Culture: Brazil and the United States." Paper presented at the conference "Popular Culture: America and the World," Woodrow Wilson Center, Washington, D.C., October 8–10, 1998.

Davies, Ronald Edward George. *A History of the World's Airlines*. New York: Oxford University Press, 1964.

De Cicco, Cláudio. *Hollywood na cultura brasileira*. São Paulo: Convívio, 1979.

De Conde, Alexander. *Herbert Hoover's Latin American Policy*. Stanford, Calif.: Stanford University Press, 1951.

Degler, Carl. *Neither Black nor White: Race Relations in Brazil and the United States*. New York: Macmillan, 1971.

Della Cava, Ralph. *Miracle at Joaseiro*. New York: Columbia University Press, 1970.

Desmond, James. *Nelson Rockefeller: A Political Biography*. New York: Macmillan, 1964.

Diacon, Todd A. *Millenarian Vision, Capitalist Reality: Brazil's Contestado Rebellion, 1912–1916*. Durham, N.C.: Duke University Press, 1991.

Divine, Robert A., et al. *America: Past and Present*. 2 vols. 2nd ed. Glenview, Ill.: Foresman/L. Brown, 1990.

Dooley, Roger Burke. *From Scarface to Scarlett: American Films in the 1930's*. San Diego: Harcourt Brace Jovanovich, 1984.

Dorfman, Ariel, and Armand Mattelart. *How to Read Donald Duck: Imperialist Ideology in the Disney Comic*. New York: International General, 1975.

Dozer, Donald M. *Are We Good Neighbors?* Gainesville: University of Florida Press, 1959.

Dulles, John W. F. *Brazilian Communism, 1935–1945: Repression during World Upheaval*. Austin: University of Texas Press, 1983.

———. *The São Paulo Law School and the Anti-Vargas Resistance (1938–1945)*. Austin: University of Texas Press, 1986.

———. *Unrest in Brazil: Political-Military Crises, 1955–1964*. Austin: University of Texas Press, 1970.

———. *Vargas of Brazil: A Political Biography*. Austin: University of Texas Press, 1967.

Duner, Bertil. *Cultural Dimensions of Dependency: The Interamerican System*. Uppsala, Sweden: Uppsala University, 1973.

Dunlop, Richard. *Donovan, America's Master Spy*. Chicago: Rand McNally, 1982.

Dur, Philip F. *Jefferson Caffery of Louisiana: Ambassador of Revolutions—An Outline of His Career*. Lafayette: University of Southwestern Louisiana Libraries, 1982.

Ellis, Lorena. *Brecht's Reception in Brazil*. New York: Peter Lang, 1995.

Eisenberg, Peter Louis. *Guerra civil americana*. São Paulo: Brasiliense, 1982.

Elder, Robert Ellsworth. *The Information Machine: The United States Information Agency and American Foreign Policy*. Syracuse, N.Y.: Syracuse University Press, 1968.

Espinosa, J. Manuel. *Inter-American Beginnings of U.S. Cultural Diplomacy 1936–1948*. Rio de Janeiro: Civilização Brasileira, 1973.

Fairbanks, Douglas, Jr. *The Salad Days: An Autobiography*. London: Collins, 1988.

Fejes, Fred. *Imperialism, Media, and Good Neighbor: New Deal Foreign Policy and United States Shortwave Broadcasting to Latin America*. Norwood, N.J.: Ablex, 1986.

Ferro, Marc. *Cinema e história*. Rio de Janeiro: Paz e Terra, 1992.

Fish, Hamilton. *FDR: The Other Side of the Coin: How We Were Tricked into World War II*. New York: Vantage Press, 1979.

Fonseca, Pedro Cezar Dutra. *Vargas: Capitalismo em construção (1906–1954)*. São Paulo: Brasiliense, 1989.

Fontaine, Roger W. *Brazil and the United States: Toward a Maturing Relationship*. Washington, D.C.: American Enterprise Institute for Policy Research, 1974.

Frank, Waldo. *South American Journey*. New York: Durell, Sloan & Pearce, 1943.

Freyre, Gilberto. *The Mansions and the Shanties [Sobrados e mucambos]: The Making of Modern Brazil*. Trans. Harriet de Onís. New York: Knopf, 1963.

———. *The Masters and the Slaves [Casa-grande e senzala]: A Study in the Development of Brazilian Civilization*. Trans. Samuel Putnam. New York: Knopf, 1956.

————. *New World in the Tropics: The Culture of Modern Brazil*. New York: Knopf, 1959.

Fry, Peter. *Para inglês ver*. Rio de Janeiro: Zahar, 1982.

Frye, Alton. *Nazi Germany and the American Hemisphere, 1933–1941*. New Haven, Conn.: Yale University Press, 1967.

Furtado, Celso. *A hegemonia dos Estados Unidos e o subdesenvolvimento da América Latina*. Rio de Janeiro: Civilização Brasileira, 1973.

Galbraith, John Kenneth. *Uma vida em nossos tempos*. 2nd ed. Brasília: Editora da Universidade de Brasília, 1986.

Gandavo, Pero de Magalhães. *História da província de Santa Cruz e tratado da terra do Brasil*. Intro. Capistrano de Abreu. Coleção Cadernos de História. São Paulo: Obelisco, n.d.

Gannon, Michael. "Invade Brazil." *Proceedings—U.S. Naval Institute* 125, no. 10 (October 1999).

Gantenbein, James W. (ed.). *The Evolution of Our Latin American Policy: A Documentary Record*. New York: Octagon Books, 1971.

Gellman, Irwin F. *Good Neighbor Diplomacy: United States Policies in Latin America, 1933–1945*. Baltimore, Md.: Johns Hopkins University Press, 1956.

————. *Roosevelt and Batista: Good Neighbor Diplomacy in Cuba, 1933–1945*. Albuquerque: University of New Mexico Press, 1973.

Gerstle, Gary. "Inventing Liberal Traditions in America, 1900–1945." Paper presented at the Catholic University of America, February 1992.

————. *Working-class Americanism: The Politics of Labor in a Textile City, 1914–1960*. New York: Cambridge University Press, 1989.

Gil, Federico G. *Latin American–United States Relations*. New York: Harcourt Brace Jovanovich, 1971.

Gil-Montero, Martha. *Brazilian Bombshell: The Biography of Carmen Miranda*. New York: D. I. Fine, 1989.

————. *Carmen Miranda: A pequena notável*. Rio de Janeiro: Record, n.d.

Goldman, Eric F. *The Crucial Decade: America, 1945–1955*. New York: Knopf, 1956.

Gramsci, Antonio. *Maquiavel: A política e o estado moderno*. Rio de Janeiro: Civilização Brasileira, 1976.

Green, Fitzhugh. *American Propaganda Abroad*. New York: Hippocrene, 1988.

Greenberg, Daniel J. "From Confrontation to Alliance: The United States and Peronist Argentina, 1946–52." *Canadian Journal of Latin American and Caribbean Studies* (November 1987).

Guerrant, Edward O. *Roosevelt's Good Neighbor Policy*. Albuquerque: University of New Mexico Press, 1950.

Haines, Gerald K. *The Americanization of Brazil: A Study of U.S. Cold War Diplomacy in the Third World, 1945–1954*. Wilmington, Del.: SR Books, 1989.

Hamilton, Alexander, James Madison, and John Jay. *The Federalist Papers*. New York: Mentor, 1961.

Haring, Clarence H. *Empire in Brazil: A New World Experiment with Monarchy*. Cambridge, Mass.: Harvard University Press, 1958.

Hele, Julian Anthony Stuart. *Radio Power: Propaganda and International Broadcasting*. Philadelphia: Temple University Press, 1975.

Henderson, John William. *The United States Information Agency*. New York: Praeger, 1969.

Herf, Jeffrey. *O modernismo reacionário: Tecnologia, cultura e política na República de Weimar e o III Reich*. São Paulo & Campinas: Ensaio/Editora da Universidade Estadual de Campinas, 1993.

Herring, Hubert. *Good Neighbors: Argentina, Brazil, Chile, and Seventeen Other Countries*. New Haven, Conn.: Yale University Press, 1946.

Higham, Charles. *Hollywood in the Forties*. New York: A. S. Barnes, 1968.

Hill, Lawrence. *Diplomatic Relations between the United States and Brazil*. New York: Kraus Reprint Co., 1969.

Hilton, Stanley. *Brazil and the Great Powers, 1930–1939: The Politics of Trade Rivalry*. Austin: University of Texas Press, 1975.

————. *Oswaldo Aranha, uma biografia*. Rio de Janeiro: Objetiva, 1994.

Holt, Robert T. *Strategic Psychological Operations and American Foreign Policy*. Chicago: University of Chicago Press, 1960.

Hoopes, Townsend. *Driven Patriot: The Life and Times of James Forrestal*. New York: Knopf, 1992.

Huggins, Nathan Irvin. *Harlem Renaissance*. New York: Oxford University Press, 1971.

———— (ed.). *Voices from the Harlem Renaissance*. New York: Oxford University Press, 1994.

Hull, Cordell. *The Memoirs of Cordell Hull*. 2 vols. New York: Macmillan, 1948.

Humphrey, R. A. *Latin America and the Second World War*. 2 vols. London: Athlone, 1981.

Jacob, Lewis. *The Rise of the American Film: A Critical History*. New York: Harcourt, Brace, 1939.

Johnson, John J. *Latin America in Caricature*. Austin: University of Texas Press, 1993.

Jones, Ken D. *Hollywood at War: The American Motion Picture and World War II*. New York: Castle, 1973.

Koppes, Clayton R., and Gregory D. Black. *Hollywood Goes to War: How Politics, Profits, and Propaganda Shaped World War II Movies*. Berkeley & Los Angeles: University of California Press, 1990.

Krausche, Valter. *Música popular brasileira: Da cultura de roda à música de massa*. Coleção Tudo É História. São Paulo: Brasiliense, 1983.

Lavine, Harold. *War Propaganda and the United States*. New Haven, Conn.: Yale University Press, 1940.

Lears, T. J. Jackson. *No Place of Grace: Antimodernism and the Transformation of American Culture, 1880–1920*. New York: Pantheon, 1981.

Lessa, Orígenes. *Reportagens*. Coleção Brasil Moço. Rio de Janeiro: MEC/José Olympio, 1973.

Levine, Robert M. *Vale of Tears: Revisiting the Canudos Massacre in Northeastern Brazil, 1893–1897*. Berkeley & Los Angeles: University of California Press, 1995.

————. *The Vargas Regime: The Critical Years, 1934–1938*. New York: Columbia University Press, 1970.

Lichty, Lawrence W., and Malachi C. Topping. *American Broadcasting: A Source Book on the History of Radio and Television*. New York: Communication Arts Books & Hastings House, 1975.

Lobato, Monteiro. *América*. São Paulo: Brasiliense, 1959.

Lopez, Telê Porto Ancona. *Mário de Andrade: Ramais e caminhos*. São Paulo: Duas Cidades, 1972.

Ludden, Howard Rowland. *The International Information Program of the United States: State Department Years, 1945–1953*. New Jersey, 1966.

Luebke, Frederick. *Germans in Brazil: A Comparative History of Cultural Conflict during World War II*. Baton Rouge: Louisiana State University Press, 1987.

Macaulay, Neill. *The Prestes Column: Revolution in Brazil*. New York: New Viewpoints, 1974.

————. *The Sandino Affair*. Durham, N.C.: Duke University Press, 1985.

MacDonald, J. Fred. *Don't Touch That Dial!: Radio Programming in American Life, 1920–1960*. Chicago: Nelson-Hall, 1979.

Macmahon, Arthur Whittier. *Memorandum on the Postwar International Information Program of the United States*. Washington, D.C.: Government Printing Office, 1945.

Magalhães, Marionilde Dias Brepohl de. "Alemanha: Mãe-pátria distante; utopia pangermanista no sul do Brasil." PhD dissertation, Universidade Estadual de Campinas, 1993.

Maland, Charles. "Dr. Strangelove (1964): Nightmare Comedy and the Ideology of Liberal Consensus." In Randy Roberts and James S. Olson (eds.), *American Experiences*. 2nd ed., vol. 2. Glenview, Ill.: Scott, Foresman, 1990.

Marcondes Filho, Ciro. "Imperialismo cultural, o grande vilão da destruição da 'nossa' cultura." *Comunicação e Sociedade*, no. 9 (1983).

Mariz, Vasco. *Heitor Villa-Lobos, compositor brasileiro*. Rio de Janeiro: Ministério da Cultura/Fundação Nacional Pró-Memória/Museu Villa-Lobos, 1977.

Martinello, Pedro. *A "Batalha da borracha" na Segunda Guerra Mundial e suas conseqüências para o vale amazônico*. Serie "C" Estudos e Pesquisas. Rio Branco: Universidade Federal do Acre, 1988.

Martz, John D., and Lars Schoultz (eds.). *Latin America, the United States, and the Inter-American System*. Boulder, Colo.: Westview, 1980.

May, Henry. *The Discontent of the Intellectuals: A Problem of the Twenties*. Chicago: Rand McNally, 1970.

McBride, Joseph. *Frank Capra: The Catastrophe of Success*. New York: Simon & Schuster, 1992.

McCann, Bryan. *Hello, Hello Brazil: Popular Music in the Making of Modern Brazil*. Durham, N.C.: Duke University Press, 2004.

McCann, Frank D., Jr. *The Brazilian-American Alliance, 1937–1945*. Princeton, N.J.: Princeton University Press, 1973.

————. *Soldiers of the Patria: A History of the Brazilian Army, 1889–1937*. Stanford, Calif.: Stanford University Press, 2003.

Meihy, José Carlos Sebe Bom. *A colônia brasilianista: História oral de vida acadêmica.* São Paulo: Nova Stella, 1990.

Melosh, Barbara. *Engendering Culture: Manhood and Womanhood in New Deal Public Art and Theater.* Washington, D.C.: Smithsonian Institution Press, 1991.

Meneguello, Cristina. "Poeira de estrelas: O cinema hollywoodiano na mídia brasileira nas décadas de 40 e 50." Master's thesis, Universidade Estadual de Campinas, 1992.

Moog, Vianna. *Bandeirantes e pioneiros: Paralelo entre duas culturas.* 9th ed. Rio de Janeiro: Civilização Brasileira, 1969.

Moraes, Vinícius de. *O cinema de meus olhos.* São Paulo: Cinemateca Brasileira & Companhia das Letras, 1991.

Morais, Fernando. *Olga: Revolutionary and Martyr.* Trans. Ellen Watson. New York: Grove Press, 1990.

Morgan, Ted. *FDR: A Biography.* New York: Simon & Schuster, 1985.

Morris, Alex Joe. *Nelson Rockefeller: A Biography.* New York: Harper & Brothers, 1960.

Morse, Richard M. *O espelho de Próspero: Cultura e idéias nas Américas.* São Paulo: Companhia das Letras, 1986.

——— (ed). *The Bandeirantes: The Historical Role of the Brazilian Pathfinders.* New York: Knopf, 1965.

Mota, Carlos Guilherme. "Cultura e política da Boa Vizinhança: Dois artistas norte-americanos no Brasil." In O. Coggiola (org.), *Segunda Guerra Mundial: Um balanço histórico.* São Paulo: Faculdade de Filosofia, Letras e Ciências Humanas, Universidade de São Paulo, 1995.

Moura, Gerson. *Sucessos e ilusões: Relações internacionais do Brasil durante e após a Segunda Guerra Mundial.* Rio de Janeiro: Editora da Fundação Getúlio Vargas, 1991.

———. *Tio Sam chega ao Brasil.* São Paulo: Brasiliense, 1984.

Nars, Edson Luís. "Um olhar sobre o Brasil pelas lentes de Jean Manson: De JK a Costa e Silva." Master's thesis, Universidade Estadual Paulista, 1996.

Ostrander, Gilmar M. *American Civilization in the First Machine Age, 1890–1940.* New York: Harper Torchbooks, 1972.

Paterson, Thomas G., J. Garry Clifford, and Kenneth J. Hagan. *American Foreign Policy: A History since 1900.* 3rd ed. Lexington, Mass.: D. C. Heath, 1983.

Pérez, Louis, Jr. *On Becoming Cuban: Identity, Nationality, and Culture.* Durham: University of North Carolina Press, 1999.

Persico, Joseph E. *The Imperial Rockefeller: A Biography of Nelson A. Rockefeller.* New York: Simon & Schuster, 1982.

Pike, Fredrick B. *FDR's Good Neighbor Policy: Sixty Years of Generally Gentle Chaos.* Austin: University of Texas Press, 1995.

———. "Latin America and the Inversion of United States Stereotypes in the 1920's and 1930's: The Case of Culture and Nature." *The Americas* 42, no. 2 (October 1985).

———. *The United States and Latin America: Myths and Stereotypes of Civilization and Nature.* Austin: University of Texas Press, 1992.

Pirsein, Robert William. *The Voice of America: A History of the International Broadcasting Activities of the United States Government, 1940–1962*. New York: Arno Press, 1979.

Prado, Eduardo. *A ilusão americana*. Rio de Janeiro: Civilização Brasileira, 1933.

Pratt, Julius W. *A History of United States Foreign Policy*. 2nd ed. Englewood Cliffs, N.J.: Prentice-Hall, 1965.

Quirk, Robert. *An Affair of Honor: Woodrow Wilson and the Occupation of Veracruz*. Lexington: University of Kentucky Press, 1966.

Radler, Don H. *El Gringo: The Yankee Image in Latin America*. Philadelphia: Chilton, 1962.

Radosh, Ronald, and Murray N. Rothbar. "The Myth of New Deal." In Ronald Radosh and Murray N. Rothbard (eds.), *A New History of Leviathan: Essays on the Rise of the American Corporate State*. New York: E. P. Dutton, 1972.

Rama, Ángel. *A cidade das letras*. São Paulo: Brasiliense, 1985.

Rangel Guevara, Carlos. *The Latin Americans: Their Love-Hate Relationship with the United States*. New York: Harcourt Brace Jovanovich, 1977.

Reich, Cary. *The Life of Nelson A. Rockefeller: Worlds to Conquer, 1908–1958*. New York: Doubleday, 1996.

Renov, Michael. *Hollywood's Wartime Woman: Representation and Ideology*. Ann Arbor, Mich.: UMI Research Press, 1988.

Reston, James B. "Our Second Line of Defense." *New York Times Magazine*, June 29, 1941.

Ribeiro, Darcy. *As Américas e a civilização*. Rio de Janeiro: Civilização Brasileira, 1970.

Robertson, James Oliver. *American Myth, American Reality*. New York: Hill & Wang, 1980.

Robinson, David. *Hollywood in the Twenties*. New York: A. S. Barnes, 1968.

Rodó, José Enrique. *Ariel*. Campinas: Editora da Universidade Estadual de Campinas, 1991.

———. *Ariel*. Trans. Margaret Sayers Peden. Austin: University of Texas Press, 1988.

Rolo, Charles J. *Radio Goes to War*. New York: G. P. Putnam's Sons, 1942.

Rotagno, Irene. "Waldo Frank's Crusade for Latin American Literature." *The Americas* 96, no. 1 (July 1989).

Rowland, Donald W. (dir.). *History of the Office of the Coordinator of Inter-American Affairs: Historical Report on War Administration*. Washington, D.C.: Government Printing Office, 1947.

Ruiz García, Enrique. *América Latina, hoy II*. 2nd ed. Madrid: Guadarrama, 1971.

Salun, Alfredo Óscar. "Zé Carioca vai à guerra." Master's thesis. Pontifícia Universidade Católica de São Paulo, 1996.

Saraiva, Gumercindo. *Câmara Cascudo, musicólogo desconhecido*. Recife: Companhia Editora de Pernambuco, 1969.

Sarris, Andrew. *Politics and Cinema*. New York: Columbia University Press, 1978.

Schiller, Herbert I. *Communication and Cultural Domination*. White Plains, N.Y.: International Arts & Sciences Press, 1976.

————. *Mass Communications and American Empire.* Boston: Beacon Press, 1971.

Schnaiderman, Boris. *Guerra em surdina: Histórias do Brasil na Segunda Grande Guerra.* São Paulo: Brasiliense, 1985.

Schneider, Ronald M. *A Political History of Brazil.* Boulder, Colo.: Westview Press, 1991.

Schulman, Holly Cowan. *The Voice of America Propaganda and Democracy, 1941–1945.* Madison: University of Wisconsin Press, 1990.

Schwarcz, Lilia Moritz. *The Emperor's Beard: Dom Pedro II and the Tropical Monarchy of Brazil.* Trans. John Gledson. New York: Hill & Wang, 2004.

Seitenfus, Ricardo Antônio Silva. *O Brasil de Getúlio Vargas e a formação dos blocos: 1930–1942—O processo do envolvimento brasileiro na II Guerra Mundial.* São Paulo: Companhia Editora Nacional, 1985.

Settel, Irving. *A Pictorial History of Radio.* New York: Grosset & Dunlap, 1967.

Severiano, Jairo, and Zuza Mello Homem de. *A canção no tempo: 85 anos de músicas brasileiras.* 2 vols. São Paulo: Editora 34, 1997.

Sheina, Robert L. *Latin America: A Naval History, 1810–1987.* Annapolis, Md.: Naval Institute, 1987.

Sherwood, Robert E. *Roosevelt e Hopkins: Uma história da Segunda Guerra Mundial.* Brasília: Editora da Universidade de Brasília, Nova Fronteira, Faculdade da Cidade Editora, 1998.

Shindler, Colin. *Latin America: A Naval History, 1810–1987.* Boston: Routledge & Kegan Paul, 1979.

Shohat, Ella, and Robert Stam. *Unthinking Eurocentrism: Multiculturalism and the Media.* New York: Routledge, 1994.

Shuster, George N. "The Nature and Development of the United States Culture Relations." In Paul J. Braisted (ed.), *Cultural Affairs and Foreign Relations.* Washington, D.C.: Columbia Books, 1968.

Skidmore, Thomas F. *Politics in Brazil, 1930–1964: An Experiment in Democracy.* New York: Oxford University Press, 1967.

Sklar, Robert. *Movie-made America: A Social History of American Movies.* New York: Vintage Books, 1976.

Smith, Bradley F. *The Shadow Warriors: OSS and the Origins of the CIA.* New York: Basic Books, 1983.

Smith, Joseph. *Unequal Giants: Diplomatic Relations between the United States and Brazil, 1889–1930.* Pittsburgh, Pa.: University of Pittsburgh Press, 1991.

Smith, Robert Freeman. *The United States and Cuba: Business and Diplomacy, 1917–1960.* New York: Bookman, 1961.

Soley, Lawrence C. *Radio Warfare: OSS and CIA Subversive Propaganda.* New York: Praeger, 1989.

Sontag, Susan. "Fascinating Fascism." In Susan Sontag, *Under the Sign of Saturn.* New York: Farrar, Strauss & Giroux, 1980.

Sorensen, Thomas C. *The Word War: The Story of American Propaganda.* New York: Harper & Row, 1968.

Spears, Jack. *Hollywood: The Golden Era.* South Brunswick, N.J.: A. S. Barnes, 1971.

Stearns, Marshall W. *The Story of Jazz*. New York: Mentor Books/New American Library, 1968.

Stein, Stanley. *Vassouras: A Brazilian Coffee County, 1850–1900*. Cambridge, Mass.: Cambridge University Press, 1957.

———, and Barbara Stein. *The Colonial Heritage of Latin America: Essays on Economic Dependence in Perspective*. Oxford: Oxford University Press, 1970.

Stepan, Alfred. *The Military in Politics: Changing Patterns in Brazil*. Princeton, N.J.: Princeton University Press, 1971.

Summers, Harrison Boyd. *A Thirty-year History of Programs Carried on National Radio Networks in the United States, 1926–1956*. New York: Arno Press, 1971.

Susman, Warren I. *Culture as History: The Transformation of American Society in the Twentieth Century*. New York: Pantheon, 1973.

Syrett, Harold C. *Documentos históricos dos Estados Unidos*. São Paulo: Cultrix, 1960.

Telles, Edward E. *Race in Another America: The Significance of Skin Color in Brazil*. Palgrave Macmillan, 2002.

Terkel, Studs. *The Good War: An Oral History of World War II*. New York: Pantheon Books, 1984.

Thomson, Charles Alexander, and H. C. Laves. *Cultural Relations and U.S. Foreign Policy*. Bloomington: Indiana University Press, 1963.

Tinhorão, José Ramos. *Música popular: Um tema em debate*. São Paulo: Editora 34, 1997.

Tocqueville, Alexis de. *Democracy in America*. Vol. 1. New York: Vintage Books, 1945.

———. *Democracy in America*. New York: Modern Library, 1981.

Townsend, Joyce Carol. *Bureaucratic Politics in American Decision Making: Impact on Brazil*. Washington, D.C.: University Press of America, 1982.

Trask, David F., and Michael C. Meyer (eds.). *A Bibliography of United States–Latin American Relations since 1810: A Selected List of Eleven Thousand Published References*. Lincoln: University of Nebraska Press, 1979.

Tyson, James L. *U.S. International Broadcasting and National Security*. New York: Ramapo Press/National Security Information Center, 1983.

Vargas, Getúlio. *Diário*. Vol. 2: *1937–1942*. Rio de Janeiro & São Paulo: Fundação Getúlio Vargas–Siciliano, 1995.

Vasconcellos, Gilberto Felisberto. *O príncipe da moeda*. Rio de Janeiro: Espaço e Tempo, 1997.

———. *Trinta anos depois*. Juiz de Fora, Brazil: Universidade Federal de Juiz de Fora, 1994.

Veríssimo, Érico. *Gato preto em campo de neve*. Porto Alegre: Globo, 1984.

Vianna, Luiz W. "Americanistas e iberistas: A polêmica de Oliveira Vianna com Tavares Bastos." *Dados* 34, no. 2 (1991).

———. *O problema do americanismo em Tocqueville*.

———. *A revolução passiva: Iberismo e americanismo no Brasil*. Rio de Janeiro: Revan/Instituto Universitário de Pesquisas do Rio de Janeiro, 1997.

Vianna, Oliveira. "O melting pot e seus métodos de análise matemática." In *Raça e assimilação*. 4th ed. Rio de Janeiro: José Olympio, 1959.

Vidal, Armando. "O Brasil na Feira Mundial de New York." *Relatório geral*. 2 vols. Rio de Janeiro: Imprensa Nacional, 1942.

Virillo, Paul. *Guerra e cinema*. São Paulo: Scritta, 1993.

Waack, William. *Camaradas: Nos arquivos de Moscou, a história secreta da revolução brasileira de 1935*. São Paulo: Companhia das Letras, 1993.

Watts, Steven. "Walt Disney: Art and Politics in the American Century." *Journal of American History* 82, no. 1 (June 1995).

Webb, Michael. *Hollywood, Legend and Reality*. Boston: Little, Brown/Smithsonian Institution Traveling Exhibition Service, 1986.

Wechsler, James Arthur. *Institute for Propaganda Analysis*. New Haven, Conn.: Yale University Press, 1940.

Welles, Benjamin. *Sumner Welles: FDR's Global Strategist*. New York: St. Martin's Press, 1997.

Welles, Orson, and Peter Bogdanovich. *This Is Orson Welles*. Ed. Jonathan Rosenbaum. New York: HarperCollins, 1992.

Wesson, Robert G. *The United States and Brazil*. New York: Praeger, 1981.

———. *The United States and Brazil: Limits of Influence*. New York: Praeger, 1981.

Whitaker, Arthur Preston. *The United States and the Independence of Latin America, 1800–1830*. Baltimore, Md.: Johns Hopkins University Press, 1941.

Whitton, John B., and John Herz. "The Radio in International Politics." In Harwood Childs and John B. Whitton, *Propaganda by Shortwave*. Princeton, N.J.: Princeton University Press, 1942.

Winfield, Betty Houchin. *FDR and the News Media*. Urbana: University of Illinois Press, 1990.

Winkler, Allan M. *Home Front USA: America during World War II*. Arlington Heights, Ill.: H. Davidson, 1986.

———. *The Politics of Propaganda: The Office of War Information, 1942–1945*. New Haven, Conn.: Yale University Press, 1978.

Wirth, John. *The Politics of Brazilian Development, 1930–1954*. Stanford, Calif.: Stanford University Press, 1970.

Woll, Allen L. *The Latin Image in American Film*. Los Angeles: Latin American Center Publications, University of California, 1980.

Wood, Bryce. *The Making of the Good Neighbor Policy*. New York: Columbia University Press, 1961.

Woodard, James P. *Marketing Modernity: The J. Walter Thompson Company and North American Advertising in Brazil, 1929–1939*.

Woods, Randall Bennett. *The Roosevelt Foreign-Policy Establishment and the "Good Neighbor": The United States and Argentina, 1941–1945*. Lawrence: Regents Press of Kansas, 1979.

Wyllie, Max (ed.). *Best Broadcasts of 1940–41*. New York: Whittlesey House, 1942.

Young, Jordan. *The Revolution of 1930 and the Aftermath*. New Brunswick, N.J.: Rutgers University Press, 1967.

Archives

Acervo Sonoro da Agência Nacional. Divisão de Documentação Audiovisual Arquivo Nacional. Rio de Janeiro.

Arquivo Multimeios do Centro Cultural São Paulo. Secretaria Municipal de Cultura de São Paulo. São Paulo.

Biblioteca Central da Faculdade de Ciências e Letras, UNESP-Araraqura. São Paulo.

Biblioteca Nacional. Rio de Janeiro.

Centro de Pesquisa e Documentação de História Contemporânea do Brasil/Fundação Getúlio Vargas. Rio de Janeiro.

Cinemateca Brasileira/IPHAN. São Paulo.

Columbia Broadcasting System. News Division Library of Special Projects. Latin American Section. New York.

Columbia University Library. School of Library Services. Government Papers. New York.

Franklin Delano Roosevelt Presidential Library. Hyde Park, N.Y.

Indiana University. Lilly Library. Manuscript Department. Bloomington.

Instituto Brasileiro de Opinião Pública e Estatística Archive. São Paulo.

New York Public Library. New York. Rockefeller Archive Center. Tarrytown, N.Y.

United States. Library of Congress. Motion Picture, Broadcasting and Recorded Sound Division. Washington, D.C.

United States. National Archives. Motion Picture Division. Washington, D.C.

Newspapers and Journals

Broadcasting, 1939–1940.
Business Review and Financial Review.
Chess Review, 1945.
Diário de São Paulo, 1940–1944.
Em Guarda: Para a Defesa das Américas, 1941–1945.
O Estado de São Paulo, 1936–1943.
Folha de São Paulo, 1939–1945.
Fortune, 1941.
O Globo Juvenil, 1942.
Harper's, 1941.
New York Times, 1940–1945.
A Noite, 1942.
Pan American Radio, 1942.
Revista do Rádio. August 1961.
Seleções do Reader's Digest, 1942–1945.
Vida Doméstica, 1943.

Illustration Credits

1. FGV/CPDOC, Arquivo Getulio Vargas.

2. Cohen, Barbara, et al. *Trylon and Perisphere: The 1939 New York World's Fair.* New York: Harry N. Abrams, 1989, pp. 18, 45.

3. Cohen, Barbara, et al. *Trylon and Perisphere: The 1939 New York World's Fair.* New York: Harry N. Abrams, 1989, pp. 18, 45.

4. Cohen, Barbara, et al. *Trylon and Perisphere: The 1939 New York World's Fair.* New York: Harry N. Abrams, 1989, pp. 18, 45.

5. Wurts, Richard, et al. *The New York World's Fair, 1939–1940.* New York: Dover Publications, 1977, p. 122.

6. Franklin D. Roosevelt Library.

7. Arquivo Nacional, Fundo Agenda Nacional, p. 65.

8. Arquivo Nacional, Fundo Agenda Nacional, p. 836.

9. Arquivo Nacional, fotos do Correio da Martha, 26/8/41.

10. Copyright © The Disney Publishing Group.

11. Arquivo Nacional, fotos do Correio da Martha, 26/8/41.

12. Reich, Cary. *The Life of Nelson Rockefeller: Worlds to Conquer, 1908–1958.* New York: Doubleday, 1996. Photo provided by Rockefeller Archives Center.

13. FGV/CPDOC, Arquivo Oswaldo Aranha.

14. Arquivo Nacional, Fundo Agenda Nacional, p. 1603.

15. Arquivo Nacional, Fundo Agenda Nacional, p. 239.

16. *Fortune*, Vol. XXII, No. 4, April 1941, p. 77.

17. *Vida Doméstica*, ano XXIV, No. 306, September 1943, p. 41.

18. Arquivo Nacional, Fundo Agenda Nacional, p. 1108.

19. Author's personal archive.

20. Jordan Young's personal archive.

21. *O Estado de S. Paulo*, Year XI, No. 174, p. 11, mid-January 1941, supplemento em Rotogravura.

22. *Em Guarda*, Year IV, No. 12, cover.

23. *Em Guarda*, Year IV, No. 11, cover.

24. *Em Guarda*, Year II, No. 2, cover,

25. *Pan American Radio*, New York, 1942, p. 11

26. *Em Guarda*, Year I, No. 12, p. 25.

27. Genevieve Naylor, *Faces and Places in Brazil*, seção Copacabana, foto 2.

28. "Programas de ondas curtas em portugues dos ee. uu. para o Brasil," advertisement. *Vida Domestica*, Year XXIV, No. 306, September 1943, p. 11.

29. Raymond Neilson, *Second Visit of Roosevelt to Brazil*. Oil on canvas. Image provided by Franklin D. Roosevelt Library, Hyde Park, New York.

30. *Em Guarda*, Year III, No. 12, p. 29.

31. *Em Guarda*, Year III, No. 8, p. 38.

32. Associação dos Ex-Combatentes do Brasil, seção São Paulo, via Cesar Campiani Maximiano.

33. Arquivo Nacional, Fundo Agenda Nacional, p. 1285.

34. "Agora! Beba os vegetais: 8 de uma vez!" Advertisement. *Seleçöes do Reader's Digest*, t. x, No. 57, October 1946.

35. Tierney, Tom. *Carmen Miranda: Paper Dolls in Full Color*. New York: Dover Publications, 1982, pp. 1–2.

36. Author's personal archive.

Name Index

Abbott, Bud, 114
Abranches, Dunshee de, 9–10
Abreu, Zequinha de, 86
Adorno, Theodor W., 106–107
Allen, Robert (Bob), 67–69, 125n6
Alves, Ataulfo, 77
Andrade, Oswald de, 14–15, 105, 119, 135n68
Aquino de Figueiredo, Vicente, 126n
Aranha, Oswaldo, 13, 20, 44, 52, 59, 93, 103, 115, 118
Armando, Carlos (composer), 107
Assis Chateaubriand, Francisco de, 103, 108
Assis Valente, José de, 107, 109
Astaire, Fred, 82, 114
Augusto, Sérgio, 129n41
Austin, Mary, 17

Babo, Lamartine, 4–5, 100, 109
Baker, Josephine, 62
Bananére, Juó, 4, 122n8
Bandeira, Manuel, 61
Bandeira, Moniz, 127n42
Barata, Júlio, 47, 90
Barbosa, Quartin, 93
Barro, João de, 107
Barroso, Ary, 64, 86
Batista, Fulgencio, xi, 109, 111
Batista, Linda, 77–78
Batista, Wilson, 107
Bell, Alexander Graham, 71
Berle, Adolf, 27, 56, 78, 115
Berlin, Irving, 98

Bernucci, Leopoldo M., 122n9
Berrien, William, 3
Bikel, Karl August, 57
Bittencourt, Paulo, 103
Boas, Franz, 17
Bogart, Humphrey, 90
Bogdanovich, Peter, 76
Bolívar, Simón, 102
Borba, Emilinha, 77
Bouças, Valentin, 118
Bow, Clara, 16
Brean, Denis, 107, 109
Buarque de Holanda, Sérgio, 3
Burke, Billie, 83
Burle Marx, Walter, 62–63

Caetano, Pedro, 107
Caffery, Jefferson, 13, 20, 44, 52–53, 75, 78, 115
Caldwell, Robert, 49
Câmara Cascudo, Luís da, 1, 100, 122nn1, 7
Camargo Guarnieri, Mozart, 65
Camões, Luís Vaz de, 103
Campanella, Tomaso, 102
Capra, Frank, 10–11, 42
Caracciolo, Aline, 81
Cárdenas, Lázaro, xi, 115
Carmichael, Hoagy, 99
Carpentier, Alejo, 20, 124n44
Carvalho, Marcelino de, 33
Casino, Margarita Carmen. See Hayworth, Rita, 66
Cavalcante, Carlos, 33

Chan, Charlie, 37, 74
Churchill, Winston, 24
Clark, John M., 32
Clark, Mark, 119
Coelho, Olga, 65–66
Collier, John, 17
Conde, Alexander de, 123n30
Conselheiro, Antônio, 131n vi
Coolidge, Calvin, x, 15–16
Corry, Andrew V., 57
Costa, Lúcio, 60
Costa, Miguel, xii
Costello, Lou, 114
Coward, Nöel, 79
Crosby, Bing, 2–3, 83, 98–99
Cummings, Irving, 74

Daniel, Josephus, 116
Darío, Rubén, x
Davies, Ronald Edward George, 127n42
Davis, Bette, 37, 74
Davis, Jimmy, 73
Day, Loraine, 83
Dietrich, Marlene, 83
Disney, Walt, 2, 36, 38, 41, 84–85, 87, 114
Donovan, William (Bill), 52–56, 113
Doolittle, Jimmy, 105
Dorfman, Ariel, 2, 86
Drummond de Andrade, Carlos, 3–4
Dubin, Al, 5
Dutra, Farnésio. *See* Farney, Dick

Eco, Umberto, 3
Ellington, Duke, 42, 66
Ellis, Lorena, 122n9
Estrella, Arnaldo, 65

Fairbanks Jr., Douglas, 38, 126n20
Falcão, Waldemar, 60–61
Farney, Dick, 2–3
Ferraro, Carlos, 88–89, 133n27
Fitzgerald, F. Scott, 19
Flanagan (Father), 83
Flynn, Errol, 81–82, 90
Fonda, Henry, 82
Fontes, Lourival, 42, 90, 104

Ford, Henry, 15, 93
Ford, John, 39, 88, 89
Fosdick, Raymond, 25
Francisco, Don, 45, 57, 126n33
Frank, Waldo, 17–18, 21, 35, 67, 99–109, 117, 124n40
Franklin, Benjamin, 102
Frazão (composer), 77
Freyre, Gilberto, 17, 61, 100, 130n iv
Friele, Berent, 51–52, 85, 118
Frischauer, P., 77
Fry, Peter, 122n7

Gable, Clark, 87
Galhardo, Carlos, 99
Gallup, George, 36, 51
Garza, Eva, 65–66
Gellman, Irwin F., 121n
Gershwin, George, 7, 17, 64
Gerstle, Gary, 122n13
Gillespie, Dizzy, 73
Goebbels, Joseph, 55
Góis Monteiro, Pedro Aurélio de, 12, 79
Gomes, Carlos, 45, 66
Goodman, Benny, 66
Gordurinha (Waldeck Artur de Macedo), 76
Graça Aranha, José Pereira da, 103
Gramsci, Antonio, 122n10
Grant, Ulysses S., 8
Gunther, John, 34

Hanson, Earl Parker, 118
Haya de la Torre, Víctor Raúl, x
Hayworth, Rita, 66, 114
Hemingway, Ernest, 100
Henreid, Paul, 74
Herf, Jeffrey, 123n23
Herrick, Robert, 17
Hilton, Stanley, 138n.
Hitler, Adolf, 23, 68
Holly, Vera, 98
Hoover, Herbert, x, 14–15, 24, 56, 111, 123n30
Hoover, J. Edgar, 32
Hopkins, Harry, 27, 29

Houston, Elsie, 62, 63, 65, 99
Hull, Cordell, 32, 51, 111, 115

Jacaré, 43
James, Harry, 47
Jamieson, Francis A., 32
Jararaca e Ratinho, 76
Jatobá, Luís, 47
Jean, Gloria, 83
Jefferson, Thomas, 102–103
João VI, Dom, 4, 124nii
Johnson, John J., 123n26

Kaiser, Henry, 93, 117
King, J. C., 118
Kleist, Paul Edvald von (field marshall
    of German army), 105
Kraushe, Valter, 100
Kubitschek, Juscelino, 101, 130n

Lago, Mário, 77
Lanfield, Sidney, 114
Leão Veloso, Hildegardo, 61
Lessa, Orígenes, 33
Lima, Jorge de, 104
Lima Barreto, Alfonso Enriques, 1
Lindbergh, Charles, 24
Linhares, José, 79
Lins do Rego, José, 106
Litvak, Anatole, 11–12
Lobo, Haroldo, 107
Louis, Joe, 98
Louis, Washington, xii

Machado, Geraldo, xi
McCann, Bryan, 121n xi
McCann Jr., Frank D., 121nn vii, ix, x,
    124n i, 127n42, 135n i, 136n iii
Machado de Assis, Joaquim Maria, 61
Machado, Carlos, 76–77
McHugh, Jimmy, 5
Magalhães Jr., R., 77
Magalhães, Raimundo, 33, 47
Maia, Lauro, 107
Manstein, Erich von (field marshall of
    German army), 105

Mariátegui, José Carlos, x
Maristany, Christina, 45
Marques Júnior, Arlindo, 77
Martins, Roberto, 107
Matta, Roberto da, 122n9
Mattelart, Armand, 2, 86
Mello Franco, Afrânio de, 103
Melville, Hermann, 106
Menuhin, Yehudi, 66
Meyer, Ewaldo, 87
Mignone, Francisco, 45. 64
Miller, Glenn, 7
Miranda, Carmen, xii, xv, 5–6, 36–39,
    44, 48, 59, 63, 71–74, 86, 98, 107–109,
    114, 120
Mistral, Gabriela, 103
Monteiro Lobato, José Bento, 2, 14, 25, 101
Monteiro, Ciro, 109
Moraes, Vinicius de, 104–105, 129n39
Morgenthau, Henry, 39
Morse, Richard M., 123n
Mosconi, Enrique, x
Moses, Herbert, 103
Mota, Mauro, 49
Mumford, Lewis, 17

Násara, Frzáo (composer), 77
Naylor, Genevieve, 67
Nazareth, Ernesto, 62
Nepomuceno, Alberto, 45, 66
Niemeyer, Oscar, 60
Nin, Anaïs, 100

O'Brien, George, 82
Olgilvie, J. W. G., 57
Oliveira Vianna, Francisco José de, 100,
    120
Oliveira, Aloysio de, 86
Oliveira, José de (Zezinho), 86
Ormandi, Eugene, 66

Paiva, Vicente, 6, 76
Paley, William (Bill), 46, 90
Parker Hanson, Earl, 118
Parker, Charlie "Bird," 73
Patton, General, 87

Pearson, Drew, 67–69, 125n6
Pedro I, Dom, 66, 131n vii
Pedro II, Dom, 9, 70, 112, 131n vii, 132n xi
Peixoto, Afrânio, 35
Peixoto, Luís, 6
Pessoa, Alfredo, 95
Pike, Frederick B., 17, 102, 123n32,
    124n40
Pinto, Mariana, 77
Porter, Cole, 66, 71, 79
Portinari, Cândido, 61, 67
Pound, Ezra, 100
Powell, Eleanor, 82
Prado, Eduardo, 9, 103
Prestes, Luís Carlos, xii, 105
Pringle, Henry F., 73
Proust, Marcel, 104

Queirós, Eça de, 6

Ramirez, Roger "Ram", 73
Ramos Tinhorão, José, 2
Ratinho and Jararaca, 76
Rauschning, Hermann, 53, 55, 112
Raynaud, Paul, 24
Rebouças, André, 9
Redondo, Carmen, 65
Ribeiro, Alberto, 77, 107
Riefenstahl, Leni, 10, 128n56
Rio, Dolores Del, 66
Ripley, Bob, 47, 70, 92
Ritter, Karl, 20, 125n vii
Robertson, James Olivier, 122n13
Rocha Pombo, José Francisco da, 61
Rockfeller, Nelson Aldrich, xii, 23–33,
    36, 38–39, 42, 44, 46–49, 51–57, 59–
    60, 66–70, 78, 81, 85, 108, 113, 115–117
Rockfeller Jr., John D., 24
Rodó, José Enrique, x, 124n44
Rommel, Erwin, 1
Roosevelt, Eleanor, 61
Roosevelt, Franklin Delano, ix, 13–14,
    19, 21, 23–24, 26–27, 30, 38–39, 41,
    51, 53, 56, 61, 68, 75, 78, 82, 104,
    108, 111–112, 115, 119, 124n41, 125n iv,
    127n50, 131n, 133n viii

Rosa, Noel, 4–5, 44, 105
Rosemberg, Anna, 56
Rossi, Spartaco, 45
Rovensky, Joseph, 24–25, 57
Rubinstein, Arthur, 62–63
Ruml, Beardesley, 27
Russel, Bertrand, 34

Salgado, Plínio, 123n22
Salles Oliveira, Armando de, 93
Sampaio, Paulo, 49
San Martin, Ramón Grau, xi
Sandino, Augusto César, x
Sarmiento, Domingo Faustino, 86
Sarnoff, David, 46
Sartre, Jean–Paul, 10
Sayão, Bidu, 64
Segall, Lasar, 67
Shakespeare, William, 43, 76
Sherman, William Tecumseh, 8
Sherman, James, 73
Shohat, Ella, 44
Shore, Dinah, 98
Siqueira Campos, Antônio de, xii
Silva, Ifigênia, 101–102
Silva, Romeu, 62, 109
Silva, Walfrido, 107
Silva Paranhos, José Maria da, xi
Sklar, Robert, 8
Souza, Ciro de, 107
Souza, Octavio Tarquínio de, 106
Souza Costa, Artur da, 12
Stam, Robert, 44
Stein, Stanley, 89
Stettinius Jr., Edward R., 115, 117–118
Stokowsky, Leopold, 66
Susman, Warren I., 15

Tannember, Otto R., 53
Taylor, Edmund, 55
Taylor, Frederick W., 15, 93
Taylor, Robert, 102
Terkel, Studs, 134n34
Tiradentes, Joaquim José da Silva
    Xavier, 64, 130n v
Tocqueville, Alexis de, 8

Toland, Greg, 88
Toscanini, Arturo, 66
Truman, Harry, 78, 119
Turner, Frederick Jackson, 117

Valentino, Rodolfo, 16
Vallee, Rudy, 48, 71–72, 129n35
Vargas, Getúlio, ix, xi, xii, 5–6, 13–15,
    21, 27, 37–38, 41–42, 48, 61, 75–76,
    78, 82–83, 85, 88, 98, 101–104, 111–112,
    119, 124n i, 130n i, 131n viii
Vaughan, Sarah, 72
Ventura, Ray, 76
Veríssimo, Érico, 83
Vianna, Luiz W., 122n13
Vianna Moog, Clodomir, 5
Vic and Joe (acrobats), 76
Vidal, Armando, 61, 63, 67
Villa–Lobos, Heitor, 61, 63, 65
Volúsia, Eros, 114

Wagley, Charles, 50
Wagner, Richard, 108

Wainer, Samuel, 104, 136n viii
Wallace, Henry, 23, 29, 31, 52, 115–117,
    124n40
Walter, Bruno, 65
Wanger, Walter, 39
Washington, Georges, 103
Welles, Orson, 21, 42–44, 67, 75–78, 84,
    99, 106
Welles, Sumner, xii, 13, 27, 29, 38, 49,
    51, 112, 115
Whalen, Groven, 60
Whitney, John Hay (Jock), 36–39, 42,
    51–53, 67, 90
Wills, Hellen, 14
Wilson, Woodrow, x, 121n ii
Winfield, Betty Houchin, 124n41

Young, James W., 57
Young, Jordan, 134n29

Zanuck, Darryl, 38–39
Zukor, Adolfo, 82